W9-CKS-308

COLBY JUNIOR COLLEGE FOR WOMEN
PARATI SERVIRE
MENS ANIMUS
CORPUS
1837

THE YAZOO RIVER

RIVERS OF AMERICA BOOKS

(already published are:)

THE ALLEGHENY by Frederick Way, Jr.
THE ARKANSAS by Clyde Brion Davis
THE BRANDYWINE by Henry Seidel Canby
THE CHAGRES by John Easter Minter
THE CHARLES by Arthur Bernon Tourtellot
THE CHICAGO by Harry Hansen
THE COLORADO by Frank Waters
THE CONNECTICUT by Walter Hard
THE DELAWARE by Harry Emerson Wildes
THE EVERGLADES by Marjory Stoneman Douglas
THE FRASER by Bruce Hutchison
THE GILA by Edwin Corle
THE HOUSATONIC by Chard Powers Smith
THE HUDSON by Carl Carmer
THE HUMBOLDT by Dale L. Morgan
THE ILLINOIS by James Gray
THE JAMES (New Revised Edition, 1945)
by Blair Niles
THE KAW by Floyd Benjamin Streeter
KENNEBEC by Robert P. Tristram Coffin
THE KENTUCKY by T. D. Clark

LOWER MISSISSIPPI by Hodding Carter
THE MACKENZIE by Leslie Roberts
THE MISSOURI by Stanley Vestal
THE MOHAWK by Codman Hislop
THE MONONGAHELA by Richard Bissell
THE OHIO by R. E. Banta
THE POTOMAC by Frederick Gutheim
POWDER RIVER by Struthers Burt
RIVERS OF THE EASTERN SHORE by Hulbert Footner
THE SACRAMENTO by Julian Dana
THE ST. JOHNS by Branch Cabell and A. J. Hanna
THE ST. LAWRENCE by Henry Beston
THE SALINAS by Anne B. Fisher
SALT RIVERS OF THE MASSACHUSETTS SHORE by Henry F. Howe
THE SANGAMON by Edgar Lee Masters
THE SASKATCHEWAN by Marjorie Wilkins Campbell
THE SAVANNAH by Thomas L. Stokes
THE SHENANDOAH by Julia Davis
SUWANNEE RIVER by Cecile Hulse Matschat
THE TENNESSEE: THE NEW RIVER, Civil War to TVA
by Donald Davidson
THE TENNESSEE: THE OLD RIVER, Frontier to Secession
by Donald Davidson
TWIN RIVERS: The Raritan and the Passaic
by Harry Emerson Wildes
UPPER MISSISSIPPI (New Revised Edition, 1944)
by Walter Havighurst
THE WABASH by William E. Wilson
THE WINOOSKI by Ralph Nading Hill
THE WISCONSIN by August Derleth
THE YAZOO RIVER by Frank E. Smith

SONGS OF THE RIVERS OF AMERICA edited by Carl Carmer

Rivers of America

edited by

CARL CARMER

as planned and started by

CONSTANCE LINDSAY SKINNER

The YAZOO RIVER

by Frank E. Smith

Rinehart & Company, Inc. New York Toronto

Jean Crawford, ASSOCIATE EDITOR

Philip Fiorello, ART EDITOR

illustrated by Janet E. Turner

Grateful thanks are extended to the following for permission to reprint material from their copyrighted works:

W. C. HANDY and HANDY BROTHERS MUSIC COMPANY, INC., New York, New York, for permission to reprint the lyrics from "Yellow Dog Blues" on pages 208-209. Copyright, 1914, by W. C. Handy; Copyright Renewed, 1942, by W. C. Handy.

RANDOM HOUSE, INC., New York, for permission to reprint the several excerpts from the works of William Faulkner in the Chapter on Yoknapatawpha County, *and for permission to use quotations from "The Bear," Copyright, 1942, by William Faulkner, in the chapter entitled* Go Down, Moses.

PUBLISHED SIMULTANEOUSLY IN CANADA
BY CLARKE, IRWIN & COMPANY, LTD., TORONTO

PRINTED IN THE UNITED STATES OF AMERICA

LIBRARY OF CONGRESS CATALOG CARD NUMBER: 53–9242

In Memory of My Brother
Fred Cecil Smith
Who loved the Yazoo country
and died defending it,
at Guadalcanal,
November 13, 1942

CONTENTS

INTRODUCTION

The first tributaries of the Yazoo rise where the Tennessee hills meet the Delta of Mississippi, and eventually they drain all of the western half of the state down to Vicksburg. The actual Yazoo watershed includes a few miles in Tennessee, southeast of Memphis, but the river and its basin belong only to Mississippi. The Yazoo carries the waters of the Coldwater, the Tallahatchie, the Yalobusha, the Yocona, the Skuna, the Sunflower, the Quiver, and other sizable streams like Steele's Bayou, Bogue Phalia, and Deer Creek, which somehow missed the dignity of being called a river. In late summer, before rains, they are clear, pale-green ribbons among the willows. In the winters and springs they are ever-widening seas of yellow mud, taking to the Gulf the wealth of the land they drain.

With its satellite streams, the Yazoo is one of the major tributaries of the Mississippi, outranked only by the Ohio among the streams which flow from the east into the Father of Waters. With the extreme limit of its watershed barely touching Tennessee, the Yazoo is entirely within the state of Mississippi, not even forming part of a state boundary line. Although confined to the northwest quarter of one state, the story of the Yazoo is, more than anything else, the story of the Deep South, a region that was an American frontier for one hundred and fifty years. The story of the Yazoo country is the story of the role of cotton and high water and their influence on American life.

Memphis, on the Mississippi, is the metropolis of the

Yazoo country today and a likely starting point for any traveler who wants to go south to visit the area, but the Yazoo wilderness had a world-wide fame long before Memphis was even a flatboat landing. Today the Yazoo is still an agricultural region, with no towns of any size. Vicksburg, on the Mississippi at the mouth of the Yazoo, is the largest and best known. But the Yazoo-Mississippi Delta, richest and broadest of all the Mississippi Valley bottom lands, is America's most fabled fertile farmland, the last stronghold of King Cotton and the Southern plantation.

The river's basic stream begins with the Coldwater, which becomes a respectable river long before it meets the Tallahatchie 220 miles down in the Delta. The Tallahatchie has already curved 190 miles through the hills as the "Little Tallahatchie" and is big enough to dominate at the merger and give its name to the new stream. The Tallahatchie moves south 111 miles through Delta land before it is joined by the Yalobusha, fresh from 165 miles in the upland hills. Together they become the official Yazoo, with 189 more miles to go before joining the mother Mississippi at Vicksburg. The 520 miles of the Coldwater-Tallahatchie-Yazoo make it one of the major tributaries of the Mississippi. For the purposes of this book, I have included all the streams of the Yazoo system, for they are all part of the same story of the cotton country of Mississippi.

The most accepted geological theory is that the Yazoo was once the Ohio. The wide, sweeping scars which have been left on the Delta land in the form of crescent lakes and bayous are too broad and big to have been cut by the Yazoo itself. The Mississippi is known to have been still in place to the west at the time these scars were in the making, and so geologists are convinced that once the Ohio came down the path of the Yazoo, before erupting earth changed its route from south to west and established the Tennessee River as another part of its old channel.

Our story will not be of that geological mystery, but of the people whose lives were influenced and fashioned by the Yazoo and those who today are attempting to better their way of life by refashioning the Yazoo itself. Of necessity the story has to be about cotton, for the fleecy staple has dominated all the history of the white man on the Yazoo, who so often has come to believe it a kind of white gold.

The bluffs and rolling hills of the upper Yazoo country were the great prizes to be wrested from the Choctaws and Chickasaws in the years immediately after Mississippi became a state. This was the frontier of cotton during the famous flush times of the Southwest. The planters of the region where cotton was so vigorously ruling were chief among the Secessionists in 1860, eager to preserve the system which had opened up new land for them, and which annually brought forth a heavy harvest from the fertile acres.

Postponement of the conflict for a few years might have greatly dampened their enthusiasm for the plantation system and slavery. The topsoil was thin throughout the upper Yazoo basin, and it began to wash away into poverty just as soon as farming returned to its peak after the failure of the War for Southern Independence. The evils of the cash-crop economy which the tyrant of the new plantation credit system soon shackled on the land were a major contributing factor to the rapid erosion of the land, but the decline in fertility was inevitable from the start.

Only the Delta land, the major portion of the Yazoo basin, was rich enough to sustain the new cotton system for a long period of time. Before the war the flat Delta country, which had fed to a richness surpassing the Nile Valley on the regularly overflowing rivers, was known as the Wilderness. Bold men willing to push out from the steamboat landings found it a morass of forest and swamp and cypress brake, seemingly all of it under water half the time. Pioneer settlement of both planters and squatters began even before the land was ceded by the Indians, but the Delta was still a frontier for years after the Civil War. This was the time for a new type of pioneer, one who could get the most results from the black laborers who were now free men and thus establish the last stronghold of the feudal plantation system, which did not change materially until it felt the impact of the economic revolution which got underway in the 1930's.

The people of the Delta define their region as the Yazoo Delta, to differentiate it from the technical delta of the Mississippi south of New Orleans, and they have made the story of the Delta the principal part of the story of the Yazoo. Rich land makes the Delta richer, if the richness has only been by comparison with the poverty-stricken hill cotton country of Mississippi. The symbol of the richness has been Delta cotton, which traditionally commands a premium of at least two cents per pound because of its long staple quality. The Delta pattern of life for all of its people, black and white, has been richer in the same comparison, both for those who lived it and those who watched it.

Even though one or two small factories are now found in nearly all the towns of the basin with as much as two or three thousand population, cotton is still the dominant factor in the economy. There is an oil refinery on the banks of the river south of Yazoo City, near the site of the Confederate shipyard, but petroleum development has touched only a portion of the Yazoo country largely outside of the Yazoo watershed. Traditional Southern cotton production is shifting to California and the Southwest, but the Yazoo Delta will likely stay with cotton for a long time still to come.

The Delta is all sky and level lands that never fall beyond the horizon in any direction, for the high riding clouds are tumbled down behind the bayou cypress. No trees are in the cotton that shimmers white through the brown foliage in the September sun, but every field is broken by the lines of willows and cypress that follow a bayou. Delta sunsets bring the whole land into a blaze that gives the brownish light of fire to every object until the grayness of dusk moves in.

There are no theatrical Southern "mammies" here, dressed in store-bought bandannas and gingham for the benefit of tourists. The Delta has not attempted to sell the romance of cotton and the plantation instead of the staple itself. By the same token, the Delta has never known much of the provincialism of other portions of the rural South; the hard lessons of experience have taught Deltans never to let the struggle for livelihood interfere with the enjoyment of life.

In common with most of the rest of the South, the Delta makes a food specialty of barbecue and Brunswick stew, but nowhere else does every segment of the population share in the common institution of the fish fry. Game fish of considerable variety inhabit more than one hundred lakes left like scars on the land by the meandering rivers of other days, but the big cats from the Yazoo itself are standard fare for the best fish fry. True Delta catfish in its most delectable form is prepared by rolling large slices of the fish in meal and salt and frying it in hot pork grease. The very ease of preparation is deceptive, for only a true fish artist can know just the right sizzle for the grease and just the right golden tone that announces the finely done fish.

In the midst of the mechanized farms and the new commerce and industry of the towns, there is still enough left of the hurried combination of frontier and plantation eras to provide a distinctive flavor of both. Little more than a hundred years ago the Delta was a deep forest, with water oak, cypress, sweet gum, and pecan trees blending with walnut, maple, and cottonwood to hide the sun from the virtually impenetrable cane and brush. The Yazoo rose every year to spread a lake over the land, with a new film of rich topsoil left behind for the reservoir of fertility. In the summer and fall it had all the beauty of a placid lake. In 1821, while painting a great-footed hawk which he killed on the river, Audubon described "a beautiful stream of transparent water, covered by thousands of geese and ducks and filled with fish."

With all the wealth and the lost beauty, the name in Choctaw means "River of Death." The Indians supposedly gave it the name when they died by thousands from the unknown maladies probably left behind by the soldiers of Hernando De Soto. The death struggle of the Indians was continued by the white settlers who faced the same deadly scourges. The disease of malaria was eventually conquered, but not until the river itself, in combination with the cotton culture, was on the verge of destroying the new civilization in its basin through flood and erosion of both land and people. The people have fought back, however, and they are confident now that the Yazoo will never be death to them.

THE YAZOO RIVER

The Yazoo River
GEORGE ANNAND
MEMPHIS
TENNESSEE
MISSISSIPPI
ARKANSAS
LOUISIANA
DE SOTO
MARSHALL
BENTON
TIPPAH
TATE
TUNICA
PANOLA
UNION
LAFAYETTE
PONTOTOC
QUITMAN
COAHOMA
YALOBUSHA
CALHOUN
CHICKASAW
TALLAHATCHIE
BOLIVAR
GRENADA
LEFLORE
SUNFLOWER
MONTGOMERY
WEBSTER
CARROLL
CHOCTAW
WASHINGTON
HUMPHREYS
ATTALA
HOLMES
WINSTON
SHARKEY
LEAKE
NESHOBA
ISSAQUENA
MADISON
WARREN
HINDS
ARK.
MISS.
LA.
Hernando
Ashland
Holly Springs
Arkabutla Reservoir
Tunica
Coldwater
Ripley
Senatobia
Helena
Yazoo or Moon L.
Yazoo Pass
Sardis
Sardis Reservoir
New Albany
Batesville
Oxford
Clarksdale
Water Valley
Tutwiler
Charleston
Coffeeville
Parchman
Pittsboro
Barrows L.
Glendora
Grenada
Philipp
Schlater
Whaley
Shaw
Sunflower
Itta Bena
GREENWOOD
Carrollton
Winona
Indianola
Rising Sun
Leland
Moorhead
Sidon
Chester
Greenville
Sheppardtown
Cruger
Isola
Belzoni
Louisville
Percy
Murphy
Lexington
Midnight
Kosciusko
Eden
Mayersville
Rolling Fork
Benton
YAZOO CITY
Satartia
Canton
Redwood
VICKSBURG
JACKSON
Mississippi R.
Mississippi River
Arkansas R.
Coldwater R.
Pigeonroost Cr.
Tallahatchie R.
Yocona R.
Otuckalofa Cr.
Skuna R.
Yalobusha R.
Tippo Bu.
Sunflower R.
Dougherty Bayou
Quiver R.
Clear Cr.
Bogue Phalia
Indian Bu.
Deer Cr.
Black Bayou
Sandy Cr.
Millstone Bu.
Chicopa Cr.
Fannegusha Cr.
Black Cr.
Tchula L.
Silver Cr.
Panther Cr.
Tesheva Cr.
Piney Cr.
Big Black R.
Alligator Cr.
Steele Bayou
YAZOO R.
Yazoo R.
N
E
S
W

1

Name on a Map

An English traveler passing along the mouth of the Yazoo in 1796 noted that he was in the vicinity of the Yazoo country, "the land of speculation."

Years later a Georgia political veteran, in his memoirs of the first years of Georgia statehood, wrote:

> The wonderment and perplexity and curiosity which the very word Yazoo used to excite in juvenile minds in Georgia fifty and sixty years ago I have never been able to forget. Its strange exotic sound to the ear and look in print was the first and not a very small thing. . . .
>
> Most frequently it was of the Yazoo fresh they spoke . . . and yet where was Yazoo and what was it?

The Yazoo speculative fever was to last from the time of John Law in France until the great cotton crash of 1920. During the first years of the American republic, however, it was largely speculation upon the romantic opportunities stemming from a name on a map.

John Law, the Scotch adventurer who attempted to resuscitate the ailing finances of Louis XIV with his "Mississippi Bubble," actually achieved more results with his Yazoo grants than any of the other speculative enterprises which followed. In 1718 the Mississippi Company made grants for settlement along the Yazoo to the "Compagnie des Indes Occidentales," headed by M. Le Blanc, the Minister of War, and several other members of the court. In ten years the company had fourteen tobacco farms in operation, yielding a return, however meager, to the proprietors back in Paris. The Indian revolt and massacre of 1729 intervened to bring the colonization scheme to an abrupt end.

For fifty years after the Revolution land speculation was a principal form of investment for some of the biggest names among the Revolutionary leaders. Washington, Franklin, Patrick Henry, Robert Morris, James Wilson, and James Gallatin were some of those who followed the practice, with varying degrees of ethicality.

The state of Georgia claimed all the territory westward to the Mississippi from the thirty-first parallel to the extension of its northern boundary. The Yazoo basin covered most of the western portion of this area, and no part of the Georgia territory was to receive more attention from speculators.

The Bourbon Company, composed largely of South Carolinians and Georgians, was founded in 1785 for the purpose of settling the western country. It was authorized by the Georgia legislature to develop the land bounded by the Yazoo, the Mississippi, the thirty-first parallel, and "the northern limit of territory relinquished by the Indians." The company engaged John Holder, a captain of the Revolution, to take four hundred families to the vicinity of Walnut Hills at the mouth of the Yazoo in 1789, but Captain Holder's mission did not get underway before the Bourbon Company failed.

A reorganization was made during the same year, and the Bourbon Company became the South Carolina Yazoo Company, the new owners of which included Alexander

Moultrie, William Clay Snipes, Isaac Huger, Alexander McGillivray, and Major Thomas Washington. McGillivray was the half-breed Creek chieftain, and Washington was to gain later renown when he was hanged at Charleston in 1791 for counterfeiting South Carolina bonds.

The South Carolina Yazoo Company petitioned the Georgia legislature for confirmation of the interest in the land previously granted the Bourbon Company. The petition announced that settlement of the Yazoo region had begun and affirmed that the company acted "as well from a motive of general good to mankind and a happiness and prosperity of this State and the Union; as their own."

The new company announced already established connections in Europe and said that as soon as the application was granted "an Affrican trade and European commerce" would "take place at the Yazoo to an immense and vast amount."

Despite this ambitious program of the South Carolina Company, another new combination, the Virginia Yazoo Company, succeeded in getting a grant of approximately half of the Yazoo country. The South Carolina Company agreed to pay Georgia $66,964 and the Virginia Company would pay $93,741. The big real estate transaction was noted by President Washington's cabinet, and the President dispatched a warning that the Indian treaties must be observed.

The South Carolina Yazoo Company was most aggressive in its efforts to exploit its grant, which included a considerable amount of territory also claimed by Spain. Dr. James O'Fallon was employed as resident agent. The records give us little information about Dr. O'Fallon, but he must have been one of those individuals worthy of the best traditions of the southwestern frontier freebooter.

Dr. O'Fallon quickly brought the Tennessee political leader, John Sevier, into the Yazoo organization with the grant of a share. With a friend to the north, he next enlisted the co-operation of General James Wilkinson, commander of American troops in the South. O'Fallon must have known of Wilkinson's already established affinity with Miro, the Spanish governor of New Orleans. Wilkinson offered to intercede for the Yazoo Company with the Spanish authorities. President Washington's field commander also assured O'Fallon that the Choctaw deed, which the Yazoo company had been warned to observe, was not worth a "pinch of snuff."

Despite the assurances from General Wilkinson, O'Fallon's relations with the Spaniards were not satisfactory. He moved north to Kentucky as his base of operations and talked of military operations down the Mississippi to gain title to the Yazoo territory. The hero of Vincennes, George Rogers Clark, agreed to head the expedition.

The diary of John Hally, a traveler of the period, includes this entry for April 29, 1791:

> On 29th passed Yazoo River nine miles below new town started by the Spaniards. Sentinels with taps. Called on Governor and he asked me what was the news from Kentucky, and what had become of Dr. O'Fallon and company, and if the men were coming down to settle at that place. I told him not that season. The commandant walked with me and showed me his artillery among which was a 24 pounder. He pointed to it and said it was bone for Dr. O'Fallon. There were 9 or 10 twelve pounders.

The authorities in Washington eventually decided O'Fallon's ambitious plans threatened peaceful relations with Spain. The United States District Attorney was in-

structed to proceed against him. The Carolina Yazoo Company severed its connection and the charges were dropped. The good doctor settled down in Kentucky, marrying the sister of General George Rogers Clark.

Neither the Carolina nor the Virginia Yazoo Company was successful in any settlements in the Yazoo area. Small payments were made on the debt owed to the state of Georgia, principally with the depreciated state currency of the Articles of Confederation period. When the legislature agreed to accept further payments only in specie, nothing more was forthcoming.

Georgia now acted to declare the claims of both land companies to the Yazoo territory fraudulent and void, marking the beginning of a long political fight for restitution in both the state legislature and the national Congress.

Patrick Henry was one of the principal owners of the Virginia Yazoo Company. Let Thomas Jefferson describe how his interest in the company converted Henry from strong states' rights to Federalist bent:

> . . . About the close of the war he (Henry) engaged in the Yazoo speculation, & bought up a great deal of depreciated paper at 2/ and 2/6 on the pound to pay for it . . . from being the most violent of all anti-Federalists, however, he was brought over to the new Constitution by his Yazoo speculation, before mentioned. The Georgia legislature having declared that transaction fraudulent and void, the depreciated paper which he had bought up to pay for the Yazoo purchase was likely to remain on his hands worth nothing, but Hamilton's funding system [whereby the Federal government assumed all outstanding state currency obligations] came most opportunely to his relief, and suddenly raised his paper from 2/6 to 27/6 the pound. Hamilton became his new idol.

Jefferson wrote Washington later that an "enemy of P. Henry" had told him the Virginia Company people had made more from the assumption of state debts sponsored by Hamilton than they ever hoped to make from the regular development of land on the Yazoo, and they were consequently going to drop future claims against Georgia.

With the default in payments from the two Yazoo companies, the Georgia legislature now was persuaded to sell the Yazoo lands again. In 1795 virtually all Georgia lands beyond the state boundaries were sold to four groups of land companies for an average of one and a half cents an acre. Again it is interesting to note some of the stockholders in the venture—Albert Gallatin, Robert Morris, James Wilson, John Sevier, A. J. Dallas, Wade Hampton, William Blount, Jared Ingersoll, and Senator James Gunn of Georgia.

The smell of this transaction reached throughout the state of Georgia. The air was filled with charges against the corruption of the "Yazoo Legislature," and most of its members were swept from office at the next election by the "Anti-Yazoos." The leader of this group was William H. Crawford, launching the career which led him to the Senate, to the Monroe cabinet, and almost to the Presidency.

The Anti-Yazoo group did everything possible to purge Georgia of the fraud. The Purchase Act of 1795 was repealed, then publicly and solemnly burned by "fire from heaven," induced with the aid of a sunglass. Next year the revocation was made permanent as part of the new state constitution.

The Yazoo land fraud fight was still not over. It merely shifted to Washington. When all state territorial lands were ceded to the Federal government, an organization called the New England Mississippi Company purchased the repudiated paper from 1795 purchasers and entered claim against the United States.

The Yazoo claims came to Congress and were fought out there for fifteen years. John Randolph of Roanoke became the chief Anti-Yazoo man. Gideon Granger, who had worked as a lobbyist for the New England Mississippi Company, was made Postmaster General, and Randolph denounced Jefferson's whole menage as "a Yazoo Cabinet."

A Supreme Court decision denied the Yazoo claim, but in 1814, after Randolph had been defeated for re-election, Congress voted five million dollars to compromise the claim. Most of the money is said to have gone to Boston banks, spiritual heirs to John Law.

One hundred years after the first ambitious real estate development by Law, the last Yazoo land fraud case disappeared from the national scene, but there were still no settlers on the Yazoo. It was still a name on a map.

Yazoo was also an attractive name on a map for a Pittsburgh minstrel-song writer named Stephen Collins Foster, who never traveled further south than Kentucky. While Foster was writing the words to "Old Folks at Home," he consulted an atlas to find a smooth-sounding river name somewhere in the South, and Yazoo was his first choice. While the song was being played and sung for the first time, however, Foster's brother raised the objection that the word Yazoo was not soft and melodious enough for the effect of the song. It was finally published reading "Way down upon the Swanee river."

2

Red Men

Mound builders were the earliest humans who have left their traces along the Yazoo. Many of the mounds they erected are still unexplored with the pick and shovel, but enough of them have yielded their prehistoric clues to indicate a relatively prosaic existence some thirty-five centuries ago. Excavations made near Belzoni show that the mound builders came to the area around 1500 B.C., when the Yazoo was part of the Ohio River. They were short men, but thin, with long heads.

They cooked in wooden and skin containers. These could not be placed over a fire, so the heat was supplied by dropping small heated stones into the stew. The "stones" were actually brick—lumps of clay which the mound men baked to use in the stoneless Delta. They hunted with weapons which archaeologists describe as the atlatl and bolas. The atlatl was a device for launching a spear with a sweeping overhand motion. The bolas made use of cords tied together at one end, with egg-shaped bricks tied to the other. Throwing it after gaining momentum, the huntsman could gain some of the effect of buckshot from a shotgun or capture the game in the mesh of the cords.

Around 600 A.D., the mound builders first began to farm the Delta land. As they grew more sedentary, both their bodies and their heads became thicker. They began to carry on extensive trade with other Indians over the heartland of North America—the mounds show remains of copper from Lake Superior and galena from the Missouri River Valley. By 1000 A.D. an organized religion was beginning to emerge from the burial-mound customs of the preceding few centuries. The bow and arrow had been introduced, and agriculture was at an advanced state. In another two centuries a cultural pattern which archaeologists call the "Mississippian" had been established. Small towns grew up around the temple mounds, and the rulers were now performing both a civil and religious function. Their culture dominated the entire Mississippi Valley. As with all American Indians, the pipe was of great ceremonial importance. A clay stone pipe, remarkable for both the skill of the design and craftsmanship, has been taken from one of the mounds; still distinctly outlined is a carving on its base of a naked savage seated with hands resting on knees and legs folded under the body.

Both the archaeological remains and the accounts left from De Soto's expedition of 1541 indicate that the Delta area of Mississippi and other portions of the river valley were thickly populated. By the time of the French exploration toward the end of the seventeenth century, the population had fallen off drastically. There is no evidence that the Indians migrated, or any indication that tribal wars could have accounted for the major part of the decline. Very likely they fell victim to the diseases introduced into the valley by De Soto's army—malaria, smallpox and syphilis. The diseases could easily have run riot through the thickly populated towns and made those who survived easy prey for other Indians on the warpath.

When active white settlement of the Yazoo country began around 1800, the principal Indian tribes in the area were the Choctaw and Chickasaw, two of the major clans of the Muskhogean family. The other Southern Muskhogean tribes were the Cherokees and the Creeks, neither of which penetrated into Mississippi. The Choctaws and Chickasaws themselves did not move into the Yazoo basin in any number until the various minor tribes along the river had been eliminated or reduced to fragmentary size.

French exploration has given us a record of the tribes in the Yazoo country around 1700. They are evidently remnants of the old Mississippi culture which had been flourishing to the south when De Soto first crossed the north Delta to reach the Mississippi.

Scattered throughout the state were many lesser tribes, three of which were in the Upper Yazoo basin. The Ibitoupa had villages in what are now Holmes and lower Carroll Counties. Black Hawk, a Carroll County village, is believed to have been an original Ibitoupa village and is consequently perhaps the oldest town in Mississippi—perhaps in the country.

The Chakchiuma tribe, sometimes called Chocchuma, inhabited the area which is now Leflore County and a part of western Carroll County, while the Taposa were settled farther north in what are now parts of Quitman and Coahoma Counties. These three tribes had the unfortunate lot to settle in an area between the Chickasaws and Choctaws, and often suffered heavy casualties when drawn into the conflicts between these two traditional enemies.

Five more tribes were settled on the lower Yazoo—the Tiou, Tunica, Koroa, Griga, and Yazoo. Farthest north of these were the Tiou, in Sunflower and Humphreys Counties. The Yazoo were well down the river, just a few miles north of Vicksburg, while the Tunica were in the same general area.

In the southern part of the state were the Pascagoula and Acolapissa, on the Pascagoula and Pearl Rivers, respectively. These two tribes and the Indians on the upper Yazoo are believed to have been not-too-far-removed cousins of the Muskhogean family.

The lower Yazoo tribes are considered by ethnologists to have been part of the Chitimacha strain. The famed Sioux family, from which came most of the tribes that fought settlement in the West, was represented in Mississippi by the Biloxi, on the coast, and the Ofo (called Dog People by the French), who lived between the Yazoo and Mississippi rivers in what is now Issaquena County.

Life among the Yazoo Indians was basically the same even if their tribal customs and traditions had many outward variations. They were all hunters, but they lived close to the rivers and streams that could supply fish the year round.

Regular winter hunting trips were part of the tradition of each brave—some of these trips carrying the hunters as far as Ohio and the Carolinas. The hunting lasted until springtime, with the women left in the village to eke out the existence for the children. From planting time until early corn was ripe, fish and small game, supplemented with berries and roots, made the diet ample. When the late corn came in in August, life was comparatively easy for a few months, and most of the traditional ceremonies took place in the early fall.

The smaller tribes had to erect all of their villages as forts, for they had no frontier to offer initial protection from enemies. All of the huts in this type village would face a central square.

In the squares of the Chakchiuma, tall poles were

placed on which to hang scalps, beads, bones, skins and other prized articles. The trophies hanging from the poles often made a queer whistling noise in the wind. This whistling sound, the prophets said, was a voice telling them a Choctaw or Chickasaw was killing a Chakchiuma. Accordingly, a war party would be formed to go on the warpath for a brief encounter. Their mission was to kill the first Choctaw or Chickasaw they met and bring back his scalp to hang upon the pole that had whistled.

During the windy season, life was never dull for the Chakchiumas, and perhaps that is why the tribe remained small and eventually all but disintegrated. The few Chakchiumas who were left in 1836 merged with the Chickasaw Nation to leave Mississippi for reservations in Oklahoma.

The Catholic missionaries from Canada who lived among the Tunica and the Yazoo in the early 1700's have left the best description of these tribes in their letters and reports. They found the Tunicas gathered in a series of villages, all within four miles of each other, some two thousand persons living in about 260 dirt and timber houses.

> Their houses are made of palisades and earth, and are very large; they make fire in them only twice a day, and do their cooking outside in earthen pots.
>
> The married women are covered from the waist to the knees. The girls are naked up to the age of twelve years and sometimes until they are married, and they wear clothes which scarcely cover them, being made after the fashion of fringes, which they simply place in front.
>
> As for the men, they are dressed in their skins and are very peaceable people, well disposed, much attached to the French, living entirely on Indian corn, they are employed solely on their fields; they do not hunt like other Indians.
>
> The Indian corn of this country grows 15 to 20 feet high; they gather it only as they need it. . . .
>
> The Natchez, who are twelve leagues down, put men to death on the death of their chief.
>
> It must be avowed that they are very foolish to allow themselves to be killed in this way; yet, it is a thing they esteem as great honour and noble-heartedness.
>
> They have a pretty large temple, with three columns well made, serpents and other like superstitions.
>
> The temple is encircled by an enclosure made like a wall; it is almost covered with skulls.

They would not let us enter, saying that those who entered died. We entered half by force, half by consent.

By this time the total population of the minor tribes along the Yazoo was probably no more than five thousand, with the number being reduced each year by smallpox and other diseases contracted from the white man.

The friendly missionaries assumed all the Indians held no malice toward the French, but the Yazoo tribes were too close to the savage Natchez to escape their influence. The Natchez chieftains were determined to send the white men out of the Mississippi Valley, and they massacred the entire French garrison of soldiers and settlers at Fort Rosalie. The Yazoo and the neighbor tribes struck at the same time, on December 31, 1729, killing the resident missionaries and the French soldiers who had established Fort St. Peter as a garrison on the Yazoo.

Retribution from the French was swift. The Indians who were not destroyed by French soldiers from New Orleans, or by their Choctaw allies, managed to escape across the Mississippi or disappear into obscure Choctaw and Chickasaw villages. The Yazoo basin was invitingly open for new Indian settlers, and the Choctaws and Chickasaws began to move in. The white man was to allow them possession for less than a hundred years.

THE CHOCTAWS

The Choctaws were the largest and most powerful of the tribes which inhabited Mississippi. Their domain spread across most of what is now the central part of the state and into parts of Alabama.

Although the Choctaws were powerful when aroused to war, they were generally a peaceful people and managed to gain friendship with the white settlers who began to move into their territory in the eighteenth century. The friendship with the whites was gained on terms of mutual respect, for the French and English and later the Americans had a healthy knowledge of the fighting ability of the "flatheads."

A Captain Bossu, who served in Mississippi with the French marines, had this to say about the Choctaws:

> The Choctaws love war and are acquainted with stratagems. They never fight in order, or stand their ground. They only harass and tease their enemies much, without being cowards, for when they come to close engagement they fight very cooly. Some of their women are so fond of their husbands as to go into the war with them. They stand by their sides in the battle with a quiver full of arrows, and encourage them continually by telling them they ought not to fear their enemies, but to die like true men.

The Choctaws were called flatheads because of the early custom of trying to shape the heads of the males in that fashion. The English traveler, William Bartram, who toured America and wrote an elaborate travel diary, wrote of the Choctaws after a visit in 1777:

> The Choctaws are called by the traders, Flats or flatheads, all of the males having the fore and hind part of their skulls artifically flattened, or compressed; which is effected after the following manner: As soon as the child is born, the nurse provides a cradle or wooden case, hollowed and fashioned to receive the infant lying prostrate on his back, that part of the case where the head reposes being fashioned like a brick mold. In this portable machine the little boy is fixed,

a bag of sand being laid on his forehead, which by continual gentle compression gives the head somewhat the form of a brick from the temples upwards; and by these means they have high and lofty foreheads sloping off backwards.

The early Choctaws were not the cleanest of Mississippi Indians, for one of their traditions was fear of water, and their children were not given daily initiations to bathing at the age of three, as was the practice of the neighboring Chickasaws.

The education of both male and female children was the responsibility of the mother until they reached the age of twelve, but at that age the boys were turned over to an individual tutor, whom he called his "Ancient," for education in the manly arts of hunting, fighting and farming. This education by "Ancients" was a common practice among the Indians, but the Choctaws followed the distinctive pattern of making the elder brother of the mother the tutor of her sons.

The Ancient not only taught his pupil to run and to jump and to use the bow, but also the moral precepts that were to regulate his life. Whippings or blows of any kind were not given the Indian boy as corrective measures. Appeals to his pride or shame were used to accomplish such purposes. The Ancients received implicit obedience from their pupils, and this faith in their judgment usually carried over into maturity on the part of the pupil. The elderly males were as proud of their nephew pupils as of their sons.

Young Choctaws learned to be marksmen with the bow by shooting at tufts of grass tied together to make a lump the size of a fist and later graduated to small game animals. In marksmanship contests within a clan, the boy who passed a certain standard won the title "Young Warrior," while those whose skill was just short of this were termed "Apprentice Warrior."

The matriarchal basis of the tribe was visible in the marriage customs. The Choctaw warrior who sought a bride applied to the maternal uncle of the girl and paid a price to the uncle upon being received as an acceptable suitor.

If accepted, the groom appeared at a designated spot to loiter till noon. At that time, the bride would leave the lodge of her parents, and "eluding" her gathered friends, would run into the adjacent woods. The female friends of the groom, also gathered on the spot, would immediately give chase and always caught the bride easily if she was anxious for the match.

The bride would then be placed among the groom's friends, and wedding gifts presented.

Like most of the other tribes in Mississippi, the Choctaws were divided into clans, with regulations in force for their perpetuation. According to Albert Gallatin, "The regulations by which the clans were perpetuated amongst the nation were, first, that no man could marry into his own clan; second, that every child belongs to his or her mother's clan. Among the Choctaws there are two great divisions, each of which is subdivided into four clans; and no man can marry into any of the four clans belonging to his division."

Although marriages were not contracted without the consent of the elder members of both families (usually both the mothers and the Ancients), young people were not forced into matings against their will. It is interesting to note that in the folklore of Southern Indians, whenever there is a legend of an elopement, the legend always has a tragic ending.

Leadership among the Choctaws was partly hereditary, but the young man blessed by birth also had to exhibit natural traits of leadership abilities before he could become a chieftain of the first rank. The Indians loved oratory as much as their white neighbors, and their chiefs were usually masters of the art. As with American political oratory, self-praise was standard practice.

Pushmataha, greatest of the Choctaw chiefs, showed his skill in his famous declamation on the legend of his birth, which he could present in both Choctaw and English:

> It was a long time ago; at the season when the glorious sun was pouring down his brightest, balmiest, and greatest life-giving influence; when the gay flowers, bedecked in their most gorgeous habiliments, were sweetest, brightest, and most numerous; when the joyous birds in full chorus were chanting their gleeful songs of life and love, and all the earth was full of inspiration; when all nature seemed to quiver in rapturous emotion.
>
> 'Twas noon. The day was calm and fair and very pleasant. There was a beautiful wide spreading plain, with but few trees on it. One there was of a giant size and venerable age. It was a red oak, and its dark waving branches, overshadowing an immense area of the beautiful plain, had bid defiance and braved unscathed the storms of many winters. There it stood, vast in its proportions, calm in its strength, majestic in its attitude. It had witnessed the rise and fall of many generations of animal life. But everything must have its time, fulfill its destiny.
>
> That magnificent red oak, the prominent feature on that far reaching landscape, as it had been for centuries, had not accomplished the object for which the Great Spirit

had planted it. There it was in full foliage, casting its dark, widely spreading shadow upon the sunlit plain. All nature was clad in smiles of joy on that bright day.

Anon a cloud was rising in the west, a black, angry, threatening cloud, looming upwards and rapidly widening its scowling front. Harshly grumbling as it whirled its black folds onward, nearer and nearer, very soon it overspread the whole heavens, veiling the landscape in utter darkness and appalling uproar. It was a sweeping tornado, fringed with forked lightning, thunders rolling and bellowing; the winds fiercely howled and the solid earth trembled.

In the height of this confusion and war of elements a burning flash of fire gleamed through the black obscurity. A shattering crash, followed by a burst of terrific thunder that, heavily rumbling through the surging storm, seemed to shake down the humid contents of the fast rolling cloud in irresistible torrents. Awful sounds assailed the startled senses in all directions as the frightful tornado swiftly swept by in its devastating course. Soon it passed and all was calm again.

The sun poured down his beaming rays in their wonted brilliancy; but the vast, time honored sylvan king, the red oak, had been shivered into fragments; its odd-shapen splinters lay widely scattered on the rain-beaten plain. Not a vestige remained. The object of its creation was accomplished, and in its place there was a new thing under the sun.

Shall I name it? Equipped and ready for battle, holding in his right hand a ponderous club, standing erect on the place of the demolished red oak, was your dauntless chief, Pushmataha.

Although the Choctaws were feared as both crafty and bold warriors, it is probable that the chief reason for their predominance in Mississippi was their adaptation to the ways of economic success. They became successful farmers in the day when most of the other nomadic tribes hardly knew how to raise the staple crop of corn.

When the white man first came into the area they learned to trade with him successfully and were smart enough to form an early alliance with the dominant Americans. Pushmataha organized an Indian regiment which fought with Andrew Jackson in the War of 1812, both against the British and their Creek Indian allies.

Mississippi became a state in 1817, after approximately twenty years as a territory, and the clamor for the opening of the vast Indian lands grew stronger. President Monroe named General Jackson to represent the United States in treaty negotiations with the Choctaws for the cession of some of these lands. Pushmataha and a group of lesser chieftains met with Jackson at Doak's Stand in 1820. Jackson was interested in gaining virtually all of the territory occupied by the Choctaw Nation, but he settled for less than one half after heeding the eloquent pleas of his old colonel, Pushmataha.

Doak's Stand still left most of the Yazoo-Delta country in the hands of the Indians, and the treaty had hardly been ratified before agitation spread for more Indian land. White men began to move in as squatters on isolated farmland, and the Choctaws found no justice in the white man's courts and before his officials. Only intervention from the top could improve the situation, and Pushmataha left for Washington for a direct appeal to Andrew Jackson and to the Congress. Washington weather was not friendly to the old chief, and he died of pneumonia not long after arriving. Today the

Congress still makes an annual appropriation for the maintenance of the grave in the District of Columbia of "Pushmataha, an Indian chief."

The Treaty of Dancing Rabbit Creek, officially removing the Choctaw Nation west of the Mississippi, opened up half of the Yazoo country to white settlement, but the Choctaws were given generous individual grants in the area if they desired to remain. Careless and corrupt Indian agents, abetted by the ignorance of many of their wards, made it possible for most of the land to be virtually stolen from the rightful Indian owners. One hundred or so Indian families followed the example of Chief Greenwood LeFlore, however, and became normal landholding citizens, and today their descendants have been thoroughly intermingled with those of the pioneer white families of the area.

Pureblood Choctaws still remain in Mississippi, however. Some three thousand members of the tribe chose to remain in the state even when they lost their land grants, and today their descendants live on Federal reservations in Neshoba county, not too far advanced from their original status after more than a century as wards of the government.

THE CHICKASAWS

The great Indian tribe of North Mississippi, with some villages in what is now Tennessee, the Chickasaws had a reputation for fierceness and bravery in battle that rivaled that of any Southern tribe.

In the struggle between the French and English for the control of the Mississippi Valley, the tribe was one of the most important allies of the British, decisively stopping the spread of the French northward from Natchez.

The one war in which they did not join the British as an ally was the last—1812, when their tribal council refused the plea of Tecumseh to join in the Indian revolt and decided to remain neutral in the fighting between Americans and British.

Although they were very similar to the Choctaws, many of their customs were entirely different. Descent among the Chickasaws was in the female line, and property as well as chieftainship was hereditary through the mother. Children were not regarded as related to their father, but were closely related to their mother and were given the same house name.

The husband was always of a different clan. If a man married a woman who had several sisters, he was permitted to marry them all and live with them as their husband at the same time, but this was the only form of polygamy practiced in the tribe. The mother of a man who died leaving a widow had the right to choose the widow's next husband.

Cyrus Harris, a half-breed Chickasaw, wrote of the marriage customs of his people in the later days of the tribe in Mississippi:

> When a man found a girl that suited his fancy, he would send his mother or sister, with perhaps calico enough to make one or two dresses tied up in a shawl or handkerchief, with instructions to ask the mother and father of the girl to give their approval of the intention of the sender. If they gave their consent, the bundle was handed to the girl. If she took the bundle, it was considered a bargain made. . . .
>
> The mother or sister brings back news of the errand.

> The man then hunts up his clothes and dresses himself from head to foot, paints his face with vermillion and other paints, and starts for the residence of his intended. On reaching the place he is invited to take a seat on a cowhide, or the hide of any "varmit" generally used for seats in those days. After the general topics of the day are talked over, supper is announced.
>
> The visitor and the intended father-in-law, in the absence of any other visitor, take supper, unaccompanied by the intended wife or her mother. Some time after supper a bed commonly occupied by the girl is prepared for their accommodation, the girl getting in bed first, previous to the man entering the room. The man comes in and occupies the front side of the bed. This makes them man and wife, and if at any time either one of them gets dissatisfied with the other, by jealousy or otherwise, they separate mutually. This, sir, was the ancient marriage ceremony among the Chickasaws.

Ornaments and paint were necessities in the clothing of both men and women of the Chickasaws. Garters, belts, and headbands were made from bison or opossum skin and made colorful with dyes and beads. Various types of ear ornaments were made from bone and shell. It was an annual custom of both the Chickasaws and Choctaws for small parties of braves to make annual raids into the West to bring back bars of silver and copper, already mined and refined, to be fashioned into ornaments.

Infants did not have much contact with modern rules of cleanliness. Their bodies were rubbed with oil each day, instead of being bathed. The oil served a very practical purpose, however, for it kept down the bites of flies and mosquitoes. The situation changed abruptly when the child became three years old. All children of this age and older were taken each morning to a near-by stream and thoroughly washed. This was a daily practice in both summer and winter.

During the coldest part of the winter both the Chickasaw men and women wore robes of bear or bison skin, but throughout the summer they were half naked and barefooted for a maximum of comfort. The clothing was usually made from deer or porcupine skin, and for dress occasions it was elaborately dyed and painted. Moccasins and leggings were not worn as much as has been visualized by Indian legend. They were used largely to protect the feet and legs from briars and bushes while traveling and hunting.

Although the Chickasaw claimed as their home a large portion of North Mississippi and part of Tennessee and Alabama, it is probable that they never numbered much more than five thousand people. Their towns, long settlements of one street, were a series of loosely joined villages —each village the home of a tribal clan.

Not as good at farming as their neighbors, the Choctaws, they had to rely heavily upon hunting as a means of providing food. Deer were stalked by single huntsmen, but a bear hunt was a community affair where the animal was tracked to his cave and smoked out by fire. The best huntsmen left the small game to boys just learning the art, but even the boys disdained to kill easy prey like the beaver. As early practitioners of conservation, the Chickasaws often established closed areas where it was forbidden to hunt bear.

Although they speared fish and also used the hook and line of today, fishing was often a businesslike pursuit of something to eat. Poisonous plants like the buckeye would be used to stupefy the fish in an entire lake or pond while they were gathered up by a turnout of the whole village.

There is no definite record, but it is probable that the Chickasaws first fought with the white man when Hernando De Soto's expedition cut across North Mississippi in 1540. Despite troubles with the Indians, however, De Soto was allowed to move across the country.

The next contact was with British traders who came from the seaboard colonies of the Atlantic Coast, and the contacts with these traders were so favorable that a lasting alliance with the English resulted. Many of these early traders, a majority of whom were Scotsmen, settled among the Indians and intermarried with daughters of important chieftains. As with most of the other Southern Indian tribes, half-breeds were soon to occupy an important role in their leadership.

French empire leaders from Paris directed that the French colonies on the lower Mississippi spread northward to eventually join Frenchmen moving south from Canada. Bienville, in charge of the garrison at Natchez, made the first military move in this direction against the Chickasaws, who refused to deal with French traders and regularly harassed French outposts established in the northern part of the state.

Bienville marched against the Chickasaws in 1736, and met them in battle at Ackia, an Indian fort near the source of the Yacona river. The French were disastrously defeated. (Perhaps one of the reasons for the defeat was the presence of a band of Natchez warriors who had escaped from the massacre of their tribe by the French a few years earlier.)

Bienville's troops retreated to their base and a new expedition was organized, but the Chickasaws again defeated the white men. Bienville's successor as governor, De Vaudreuil, made the third attempt, in 1752. De Vaudreuil used Bienville's old fort as a supply base, and his troops were supplied with the best equipment fresh from European battlefields, but the Frenchmen were again defeated by the Chickasaws fighting to defend their homes.

The three smashing defeats which the Chickasaws handed the French were to have an important bearing on American history, for they prevented unity between French forces in North America at a time when the British were too weak to stop it. Without this unity, the French were defeated a few years later in the French and Indian War, and North America became largely a British domain.

The Chickasaws remained in Mississippi until the Treaty of Pontotoc, signed on October 20, 1832, between their nation and the United States went into effect. Under its terms the nation ceded all of its possessions in Mississippi and anywhere else east of the Mississippi in return for lands in the Oklahoma Indian reservation.

the white men. Bienville's successor as governor, De Vaudreuil, made the third attempt in 1752. De Vaudreuil used Bienville's old fort as a supply base and his troops were supplied with the best equipment fresh from Europe. In the battles that followed the French were again defeated by the Chickasaws fighting to defend their homes.

The three smashing defeats which the Chickasaws handed the French were to have an important bearing on [illegible] for they prevented [illegible] North America [illegible] the French were too weak [illegible] the French were [illegible] a few years later in the French and Indian War and North America became largely a British domain.

The Chickasaws remained in Mississippi until the Treaty of Pontotoc, signed on October 20, 1832. [illegible] the nation and the [illegible] ceded all of its possessions in Mississippi and Alabama east of the Mississippi in return for lands in the Oklahoma Indian reservation.

3

The Word of God

Men of the cloth pioneered the Yazoo to a greater extent, perhaps, than any other similar river basin in the nation. Except for De Soto's band, which fought a battle at the head of the Tallahatchie and crossed the Coldwater en route to the Mississippi, the first white men on the Yazoo were Catholic fathers from Canada, on the same type of missionary journey that first brought Father Marquette to the Father of Waters.

In 1663 Quebec's first bishop, Laval, founded the Seminary of Quebec. Twenty years later, eighteen priests from the Seminary were doing parish work along the St. Lawrence. The Rev. Francis Jolliett de Montigny was born in Paris in 1661, but migrated to Canada as a young man and was ordained at the Quebec Seminary in 1693. In 1698 he headed a party of four priests assigned to establish a mission for the Seminary on the Mississippi. Nearly a year later, in December, they chose to stop with the Tonica (Tunica) Indians on the bank of the Yazoo, "a quite pretty river."

Before the first mission was established, the long voyage of exploration was a harsh task. The journey up the St. Lawrence and through the lakes took months, and when they arrived at "Chicagau," Brother Alexander had to be left behind with most of their provisions because of an impassable stretch between Lake Michigan and the Illinois River. The supplies which could be carried in one canoe were soon gone, and the brothers lived on bear and deer which they killed with swords—their powder and ball had been exhausted long before. Near the mouth of the Arkansas River they were given dried squash by the Indians, and that sustained them until they reached the Tunicas.

They chose to establish their first mission with the Tunicas because they were needed. They arrived in the midst of an epidemic.

> Sickness was among them when we arrived there . . . They were dying in great numbers . . . One of their chiefs being about to die, M. de Montigny asked him through an interpretor whether he wished to be baptized, to which he replied that he desired to be. . . . he was baptized and died the next day.

In 1700 Iberville, the French governor of Louisiana, came up from Biloxi to inspect the area, visiting each of the missions which de Montigny had established. Leaving Father Davion on the Yazoo, de Montigny returned with Iberville to France. From France his next assignment was in China as secretary to Cardinal de Tournon. Eventually he returned to Paris as director of foreign missions, but he never went back to Quebec.

When four Frenchmen were killed by Koroa tribesmen in 1702, Davion left his mission as unsafe, amid wailing from all the Tunica. Before long the Tunicas persuaded the Koroa chiefs to arrest and execute the Indians guilty of the murder. The news was brought down to Davion at Biloxi by a delegation representing all the river villages. He returned to uninterrupted tranquillity until his retirement to Mobile in 1720.

The report in France of Iberville and de Montigny of fertile soil of the Yazoo, and the peaceful atmosphere at Father Davion's mission, brought the first white settlers. Grants of land were made in Paris as part of John Law's "Mississippi Scheme," and eighty-four French settlers arrived at the mission in 1718. The next year Fort St. Peter was established by a French garrison. More than two hundred French settlers and soldiers were probably in the area at the peak of activity. Fourteen separate farms were in operation, principally growing corn and other foods borrowed from the Indians, but making steady progress in developing a crop of tobacco for export to France.

Iberville had been succeeded by his brother Bienville as Governor. Bienville confined his Indian fighting largely to the Chickasaws far to the north, and harmony prevailed with the Indians around Fort St. Peter and Fort Rosalie (Natchez). Then Bienville was recalled to France in 1726, and the new governor soon began to have difficulties with the Natchez tribe at Fort Rosalie. On November 29, 1729, they wiped out Fort Rosalie and sent emissaries to seek help from the Yazoo and Tunica tribes. Fearful stories were told, and Fort St. Peter was attacked on the night of December 31, 1729. Among the victims was the Reverend John Souel, S.J., the last head of the mission. No Frenchman, either priest, soldier, or farmer, ever came back.

France continued to claim the territory at the mouth of the Yazoo, even though they did not establish another garrison north of Natchez. When the British assumed ownership of West Florida, the northern boundary was carefully drawn to include the site of Fort St. Peter.

Catholic priests brought the first white settlers to the Yazoo, but it was a disciple of John Wesley who pioneered the first permanent settlement of the area. Newitt Vick was a farmer and lay preacher who bought a tract of land at the edge of Walnut Hills, four or five miles south of the ruins of Fort St. Peter, in 1814. The opportunity for a town on the river appeared so good that Brother Vick bought another tract fronting on the Mississippi and subdivided it into city blocks. After his death, when the people of Walnut Hills incorporated their town, they named it Vicksburg. The town was to become the Confederate citadel on the Mississippi during the War Between the States, but a shift in the mouth of the Yazoo puts recent-day Vicksburg actually on the Yazoo instead of the Mississippi.

One of the first interdenominational efforts in New England was the Board of Commissioners for Foreign Missions, organized by representatives of the Presbyterian and Congregational Churches of New England and New York in 1810. In 1816 the Board decided to include American Indians in its program and assigned Elias Cornelius to visit areas where mission posts might be established. Cornelius first consulted Secretary of War John C. Calhoun, in charge of the government's relations with Indians, and a champion of humanitarian treatment. Calhoun believed that if the Indians were given educational opportunities they could gradually take their place as self-supporting citizens, merging with the rapidly expanding American western movement. He thought a government expenditure in the education of Indians would be cheaper than financing unending Indian wars. It was not the first losing battle the South Carolinian fought in government, but perhaps there was none in which he was more completely right in the hindsight of history. Yielding to frontier pressure, the government followed the policy of pushing the Indians constantly westward, with the inevitable Indian wars. After the wars the costs have continued to mount, not merely for education, but for all manner of services needed for people unable to support themselves, plus millions in claims paid to the grandchildren of those who were given raw deals by the Great White Father in their cession treaties.

Secretary Calhoun suggested the Cherokees, Chickasaws and Choctaws for the initial mission work, and Cornelius visited all three Nations before returning to the Board headquarters in Salem. In 1818 the Rev. Cyrus Kingsbury was assigned the task of establishing a mission among the Choctaws. Probably on the advice of Choctaw leaders consulted by Cornelius, he picked a site on the Yalobusha seven miles south of what is now Grenada. The mission station was named Elliot, in honor of John Eliot, the clergyman who had translated the Bible for the Indians of eastern Massachusetts 150 years before. (Somewhere along the way the Yalobusha Elliot gained an extra "l.")

By the time of the school opening in 1819, with ten students, a dozen volunteers from New England had joined Kingsbury and his family. Twenty more volunteer teachers and mechanics came the next year, and there were eighty full-time boarding students at Elliot. Two Choctaw chiefs, Puckshanubbee and Mushullatubbe, came to visit the school, and had their impressions written down as an endorsement of Elliot:

> Brother, our hearts are glad to see our children improving so fast. We are pleased to see our boys go into the woods with their axes, and into the fields with their hoes, under the care of the teacher to learn to work, that they may know how to clear and cultivate our land; for we cannot expect to live any longer by hunting—our game is gone; and the missionaries tell us, the Good Spirit points out to us now this new and better way to get our meat, and provide bread and clothes for ourselves, women, and children. And we are very glad to see our daughters learning to cook, and to make and mend clothes, and do all such things as white women do.

The Choctaws, by popular subscription, had already donated eighty-five cows and seven hundred dollars in cash to the mission. After the inspection by Puckshanubbee and Mushullatubbe, the tribal council agreed to make an annual contribution of six thousand dollars to the school, to be paid from the sixteen thousand dollar annuity from the United States which the Nation received for its first cession of lands east of the Tombigbee. During the next twelve years fourteen additional missions were established in various parts of the Choctaw Nation. The Indian mission schools were undoubtedly better than white children were to have in most of these localities for a generation yet to come.

The Treaty of Dancing Rabbit Creek marked the end of the Choctaw mission in Mississippi, but the Choctaws persuaded the Board of Missions to re-establish the schools on the new reservation in Oklahoma. In addition to the schools, eight churches were established by the Choctaws shortly after they reached Oklahoma, and within a few years one fourth of the Nation belonged to a Protestant church.

Cyrus Byington, an Andover graduate and native of Stockbridge, Massachusetts, was the first teacher at Elliot to preach in the Choctaw language. Along with another teacher, Alfred Wright, he began to reduce the Indian language to writing. They published elementary texts used in all the mission schools, but a lifetime of effort failed to complete a Choctaw grammar and dictionary. The grammar was published in 1877, nearly ten years after Byington's death. Wright published a dictionary in 1880, and in 1915 a latter-day scholar brought out Byington's finally completed dictionary.

The Choctaw mission schools were the most successful result of a flourishing experiment in a joint church and state educational program. Thanks to the friendly policy of Calhoun, a Federal subsidy was authorized by Congress in 1819. In addition to the American Board of Missions, Methodists, Baptists and Roman Catholics received assistance in maintaining Indian schools. In 1825 the Board of Missions was operating eleven Choctaw and five Cherokee schools on an annual budget of $202,070.85. Of this total, $25,370 came from the United States Treasury—$13,620.41 by direct appropriation and the remainder from Indian annuities.

A bill to repeal the authorization for assistance was studied by a Senate committee in 1824. Apparently the repeal effort was part of a general campaign to push the Indians further westward, not because of any opposition to the educational tie between church and state. The Senate committee rejected the repeal bill, reporting:

> The Committee are aware that very considerable aids have been given by different Christian denominations, all of whom feel a deep interest in the paternal views of the Government. But the Committee are well persuaded that, had the Government afforded no pecuniary aid, very few, if any, of the benefits which have been conferred, would have been experienced by the Indians. The annual appropriation . . . has encouraged the benevolent and pious . . . to form associations with the view of aiding the humane purposes of the Government. . . .
>
> It requires but little research to convince every candid mind that the prospect of civilizing our Indians was never so promising as at this time. Never were means for accomplishment of this mission so judiciously devised, and so faithfully applied, as provided in the above act, and the auxiliary aids which it has encouraged. . . .
>
> From the various lights in which the Committee have viewed the policy of this law, they are convinced that it is founded in justice, and should not be repealed.

Direct federal appropriations to sectarian schools for Indians continued for many years. Opposition on the ground that it was financial support of a church activity began to appear after the Civil War, but not until 1879 did Congress adopt a rider to an appropriation bill declaring it to be settled policy that no further aid to sectarian schools would be provided from federal funds. Previous commitments made it impossible actually to shut off these funds for another twenty years, and even today contracts are being made through the Indian Bureau for the care and boarding of Indian children at church schools, with payments made from treaty and trust funds belonging to Indian tribes, but in the care of the United States.

Elliot Mission closed in 1832. Most of the missionaries moved on to other fields, but some of them remained in Mississippi. One of these was a Congregationalist named John Smith, originally from Salem, who established a tavern at Elliot in one of the old mission buildings. Smith gained appointment as a Choctaw Indian agent, but was removed by President Jackson on the protest of Chief Greenwood LeFlore after an episode that can best be told in our story of the Choctaw chieftain. He moved up the river to Pittsburg, bought a large farm from Franklin E. Plummer, and closed the Elliot tavern. The second white settlement on the river was gone.

Richard Abbey of Yazoo City was another one of the lay preachers of the South. He left his home in Rochester, New York, at the age of fifteen in 1820. From a clerkship in a Natchez store, with time out for lay preaching for temperance work in the Methodist Church, he forged ahead to partnership in the store and editorship of the *Ariel*, the first official organ of the Whig Party in Mississippi. Abbey moved to Yazoo County in 1840 after buying a large tract of Delta timberland, which he began to develop into an extensive plantation.

The circuit rider William Winans conducted a revival at Yazoo City and persuaded Abbey to enter the active ministry. The Methodist Publishing House at Nashville chose the former editor and publisher as its financial secretary, and Abbey was important in building it into one of the then major publishing establishments in the world, with a property valuation of $700,000.

The planter-preacher remained loyal to the Union when the War Between the States came, spending most of his time in an unsuccessful effort to keep the Methodist publications bipartisan in their treatment of the war. Instead, they became organs of Confederate propaganda, and the Methodist presses were used for official Confederate printing. When Nashville was abandoned by Confederate troops, Abbey stayed behind to try to protect the property from Union soldiers. He was successful for two years, but General Thomas finally commandeered it for an official Army printing plant.

President Johnson returned the property to the Methodist Church in 1866, virtually destroyed. Representing the publishing house, Abbey instituted a claim for damages against the government. His lawyer was Henry S. Foote, ex-Governor and Senator from Mississippi who had deserted the Confederacy while serving as a Tennessee senator. The general conference of the Methodist Church, South, disowned this representation by two men with such blemished loyalty to the Confederacy and removed Abbey as agent.

Abbey returned to Yazoo County in 1880, to join in the lumber boom sweeping over the Delta. His still fervid lectures on temperance restored him to favor in the church, and he was writing a history of the Methodist Publishing House when he died in 1891, at the age of eighty-six. Five years later the Congress voted $280,000 to the publishing house as payment for the war damages, to vindicate the purpose of the history.

4

The Wild Yazoo

White men did not begin to move into the Yazoo country until after Mississippi had become a state. For the first farmers seeking land, there were enough rich hill bottomlands to turn into farms before attempting to clear the Delta swamplands with their annual threat of overflow. By 1820, however, the wild country to the north had become a symbol of fabulous riches to those in the Natchez country who were not a part of the aristocratic wealth established there. Settlers from Virginia and the Carolinas were making the overland trek through Tennessee and down the Natchez Trace. Indian Charlie's Trace was a trail which turned off the more famous road into the Yalobusha country of the upper Yazoo, and some of the settlers followed Charlie's Trace across the highland between the Tallahatchie and the Yazoo, and down into the "wilderness." Until after the Civil War the Delta country was generally referred to as "the Wilderness."

In the Yazoo country, the stories went, a man planting corn had to step lively so that the shoots wouldn't tear his pants. It was filled with swamps so deep that you could fill a jug with boiling water by lowering it into a sump. The rivers and trees were big, but, most important, the cotton bolls were bigger than any others on earth.

The Yazoo was wild with lush vegetable growth and seemingly unlimited game, but without the threat of the Indian which was so much a part of other frontiers. After the massacre at Fort St. Peter, there was never any violence between white man and Indian. An occasional drunken or renegade Choctaw might fall on an isolated traveler, but such an occurrence was far rarer than the depredations of the white outlaws. The Masons and the Harpes, the famous bandits of the Natchez Trace, often fled to the Yazoo country for safety when law and order began to reach out for them.

Most of the people who settled the Yazoo country were born in other states, for Mississippi was a lightly populated territory before statehood in 1817. Most of the settlers were born in the seaboard Southern states. Among families with growing children, the history was usually of parents born in a seaboard state, the older children in Tennessee or Alabama, and the youngest in Mississippi. Few immigrants from Europe came directly to the Yazoo country, and most of the Yankees who came South to join the frontier boom were interested in being merchants or professional men in the already established towns and cities.

Squatters, so-called because they came into the Indian country and began to cultivate small plots of land while the Yazoo basin was still the property of the Choctaws and Chickasaws, made up a fair proportion of the original settlers. It has been estimated that some three or four hundred families moved into the Yazoo basin like this, generally living alone miles away from their nearest neighbor. They had no trouble with the Indians. Their choice of the best spots for farming, hunting and fishing generally resulted in a good living far above the standard of the traditional frontier squatter. The squatters' only troubles came after the land cession. Some of them were able to purchase the tracts on which they were already farming, either directly or from the Indian assignee, while others had to move on to new sites. The Wilderness offered opportunity for men to live without assurance about property titles for quite a few years more.

The adventures and perils of squatters in the wild Yazoo were romanticized fifty years ago in a novel called *The Legend of McNutt*, written by a Methodist preacher who lived in the area one hundred years after the heroic pioneer couple of his novel braved the elements in 1800. The villain of the piece was an Indian called Red Elm, who was overcome after many hardships and tribulations. The peaceful nature of the Choctaws and the Chickasaws of the time make it evident that the squatters probably encountered more trouble from red elm trees, than from Indians by that name. The Delta was a squatters' paradise, if the squatters could live with mosquitoes.

Cotton moved west and the immigrants with it, but the plantation system of the old South could not keep the pace. Many second sons and others further back from inheritance of huge domains on the seaboard and in the Natchez district were among the pioneer Yazoo immigrants, but the very fact of the frontier made the polished pleasantries of older societies more difficult to achieve. If the new landowner was fortunate enough to start with a sufficiently large group of slaves to get his land cleared quickly, he was usually too busy clearing that land "to grow cotton to buy slaves to grow more cotton" to stop to build the luxurious Georgian mansions fashionable at Natchez or the slightly less elaborate Greek revival types of the black prairie belt to the east.

The ante bellum Yazoo settler built a log cabin one or two rooms deep. As he prospered and had more time, a similar wing was erected across a wide and open windswept hall to make a "dogtrot" cabin. This might be as far as the home ever progressed, for such houses are still used today.

Then again, more prosperity and larger families might mean the walling in of the dogtrot and the addition of a long porch across the whole front. Somewhere along the way the logs would usually be sheathed in with clapboard. There were exceptions, of course, but this was a standard house in the plantation country of the Delta in the prewar days, as well as in the hill country. The danger of floods made anything more elaborate a risky business. Some planters used Indian mounds as building sites, and others evolved a style of architecture which built the house on a high pier. It became a distinct Delta style after the first pioneer days had passed.

The McGehee brothers who moved from Georgia to Mississippi were examples of the rich planters who left worn-out acres on the seaboard to establish new plantation domains in the Southwest. The first brothers established themselves in the Natchez region and built sumptuous mansions in the style of the millionaire planters of the day. The last brother moved overland, not to southwest Mississippi, but to the Yazoo country, moving his children, his Negroes, his carriages, wagons and household goods all in one caravan. His wife rode horseback most of the way. The main portion of the family fortune was contained in a keg of gold in the middle of a bare wagon bed at the center of the wagon train. Young McGehee built a log house not too pretentiously advanced above the dogtrot cabins of his neighbors. His grandson, the writer Stark Young, was born at Como on the Tallahatchie after the family fortunes had crashed with those of the other upland planters of the Yazoo basin, but the boy heard enough of the stories of ante bellum glory to inspire the novel *So Red the Rose*.

Col. James R. Creecy, a Virginian, braved the Yazoo wilds in 1834, and wrote a narrative of his adventures.

> Living, to travelers in those regions [Col. Creecy related], was rude indeed. Log cabins afforded almost the only shelter; and perhaps, in a whole day's ride through an open wilderness, you would not meet with more than two of these. The most miserable apologies for beds sufficed the hardy pioneers, and the worst and simplest furniture was only to be seen.

One particular late afternoon, while journeying near the "Yallabusha" swamp, Col. Creecy, still twelve miles away from the nearest town, came upon a log cabin, in front of which was a woman milking a cow. This is how he relates the discussion that followed when he asked permission to stay the night:

> "My dear madam," said I, "could you give me shelter to-night, and furnish me with food for my horse; I am quite fatigued, and my horse more so. I will pay you liberally, and thank you, indeed, most kindly."
>
> "Well, I dunno," said she; "some mighty mean people pass here sometimes; but we haint got much to steal, and you don't look like you had so much badness in you. You can light and rest till Sam gets home; he went out to shoot some meat 'bout an hour ago, for we haint got none in the house, and I heard the crack of his rifle as I was comin' to the cup-pen."

Creecy unsaddled his horse and made himself comfortable until the husband Sam arrived a few minutes later, carrying the "hind quarter of a fine, fat deer, carelessly wrapped up in the skin." The Indian-country pioneer proved quite friendly, making it clear that he never refused "a bite or a part of my cabin to a stranger so long as he is civil."

Creecy's horse was soon enjoying a repast of corn, fodder and pumpkins, and, by the time the animal had been stabled for the night, its owner was called in for a supper of corn-cakes, venison and milk. The variety was not too plentiful, but the quantity was ample, and with the friendliness of a well-filled stomach the traveler from Virginia was calling his host and hostess Sam and Sally before bedtime.

Sam and Sally's cabin was a one-room affair, and the

Colonel was accorded a pallet on the floor. He related that "my worthy entertainers were quickly in bed and snoring, as none but laborers or gourmands can snore. In defiance of the unmusical concert, fatigue weighed down my eyelids, and I, too, slept."

The peaceful repose did not last through the night. At two o'clock in the morning, the noises of slumber were quickly hushed by a "scream, such as I had never heard before, more like a female in the death-struggle from sudden violence than anything else I could imagine, yet loud, shrill, and strong."

For a few minutes the Colonel shivered on his pallet, certain that the Choctaws had gone against their usual nature and had come to the cabin for scalps. Sam grabbed his rifle and paused long enough to explain that it was just a panther in the cup-pen after the calf. After some shouts and shots and general bedlam in the dark, the panther departed without the calf, and Sam and Sally and guest returned for more sleep before the dawn.

Stagecoach lines began to come into the river area around 1840. They made connections with the inland settlements not on the rivers themselves, and they offered connections to the steamboat lines.

All of the stage schedules of the day were subject to the fate of the weather and the roads, but they were in part adapted to the idea that the roads would be in very poor shape. "If the mud does not quite get over your boot tops when you sit in the saddle, they say it is a middling good road."

Because of the prevailing lack of bridges, except in a few thickly settled districts and the immediate neighborhood of cities, any extended journey by coach or wagon necessitated frequent recourse to ferries. Many of these were nothing but rickety scows which would occasionally collapse under a heavy burden, and accordingly nearly every passage of river by ferry was an hour of anxiety for stagecoach passengers.

For the Mississippians of the day, such experiences were apparently too commonplace to provoke comment, but European visitors never failed to include at least one river ferry story in their writings. An Englishman, Captain Basil Hall, wrote how his coach was ferried across a stream:

> The next job was to ferry the baggage across; and this effected, the horse was towed across by the nose, an operation of some delicacy to both the actors and spectators. Lastly came the transportation of the coach, and here all my seamanship served only to show the hazard incurred of losing the whole conveyance. If the rope, old and much worn, had given way, as I fully expected it would, when the wagon was half-channel over and nothing in sight but four or five inches of railing above the water, we must have bivouac'd where we were. . . .
>
> Fortunately, we succeeded in dragging the carriage across, and when the four wheels fairly touched the bank I thought of course all our difficulties were over. But the united strength of all aboard, males and females, young and old combined, could not budge it more than a foot out of the water. I don't know what we should have done had we not spied near the landing place a fathom or two of chain, one end of which our active little commanding officer soon tied to the carriage, and the horse being hitched to the other, we drew it triumphantly to land, with a cheer that made the forest ring.

The roads the stagecoaches followed were usually the routes to the river landings. Joseph Holt Ingraham, the Episcopal rector and dime novelist, traveled one of these roads in 1834 and was not greatly impressed with the farmers moving cotton to market:

> The cotton teams, containing usually ten bales, are drawn by six or eight yoke of oxen, which accomplish about twenty miles a day in good weather. The teamsters camp every night in an enclosure formed by their waggons and cattle, with a bright fire burning; and occasionally their bivouacs present striking groups for the pencil. The majority of these teamsters are slaves; but there are many small farmers who drive their own oxen, often conveying their whole crop on one waggon. These small farmers form a peculiar class, and include the majority of the inhabitants in the east part of this state. With the awkwardness of the Yankee countryman, they are destitute of his morals, education, and reverence for religion. With the rude and bold qualities of the chivalrous Kentuckian, they are destitute of his intelligence, and the humour which tempers and renders amusing his very vices. They are in general uneducated, and their apparel consists of a coarse linsey-woolsey, of a dingy yellow or blue, with broad-brimmed hats; though they usually follow their teams bare-footed and bare-headed, with their locks hanging over their eyes and shoulders, giving them a wild appearance. Accost them as they pass you, one after another, in long lines, cracking their whips, which they use instead of the goad—perhaps the turnout of a whole district, from the old, gray-headed hunter, to the youngest boy that can wield a whip, often fifteen and twenty feet in length, including the staff—and their replies will generally be sullen or insulting. There is in them a total absence of that courtesy which the country

people of New England manifest for strangers. They will seldom allow carriages to pass them, unless attended by gentlemen, who often have to do battle for the high-way. Ladies, in carriages or on horseback, if unattended by gentlemen, are most usually insulted by them. They have a decided aversion to a broad-cloth coat, and this antipathy is transferred to the wearer. There is a species of warfare kept up between them and the citizens of the shipping ports, mutually evinced by the jokes and tricks played upon by the latter when they come into market; and their retaliation, when their hour of advantage comes, by an encounter in the backwoods, which they claim as their domain. At home they live in log-houses on partially cleared land, labour hard in their fields, sometimes owning a few slaves, but more generally with but one or none.— They are good hunters, and experts with the rifle, which is an important article of furniture in their houses. Whiskey is their favorite beverage, which they present to the stranger with one hand, while they give him a chair with the other. They are uneducated, and destitute of the regular administration of the gospel. As there is no common school system of education adopted in this state, their children grow up as rude and ignorant as themselves; some of whom, looking as wild as young Orsons, I have caught in the cotton market at Natchez, and questioned upon the simple principles of religion and education which every child is supposed to know, and have found them wholly uninformed.

The wild Indian had been peaceably removed from the basin, but there was no way to wipe away the primitive frontier so quickly. The farmers and planters and their slaves were moving in, but it would be the wild Yazoo for years to come.

5

Union Man

Among the French-Canadian traders who followed the rivers from Montreal to New Orleans in the first days of prosperity of the lower Mississippi, was a tall bronzed man named Louis, who left many a broken heart along the St. Lawrence when he moved to the new country. What Louis's full name was has been lost in obscurity, but he came to the Choctaw country as Louis LeFleur. The French-Canadian girls had liked his dancing and, when they called him the "Flower of the Fete," the name held.

LeFleur's charm still prevailed in the South, and he wooed and won as his bride the beautiful Rebecca Cravat, renowned in Choctaw stories as a "high-up lady." Marriage to the niece of the eloquent and mighty Pushmataha, greatest of all Choctaw chieftains, was a major success for LeFleur. He built a tavern on an attractive bluff along the Natchez Trace and set up a trading business with both the Indians and the white men who came along the road to the new southwest. LeFleur's Bluff became a landmark along the Trace, and a generation later the Mississippi state capital of Jackson was built within its shadow.

Rebecca bore Louis eleven children, who were given some of the training of Choctaw noblemen, even though only one of their grandparents had been a full-blooded Muskhogean.

Fourth-born of these children was a son named Greenwood, born on June 3, 1800. The training necessitated for him by his highborn mother was enough for the regular patrons of the tavern to distinguish Greenwood from his other copper-colored playmates, and one of these patrons, Major James Donly, came to regard him as a special friend.

Major Donly lived in Nashville and had the government contract to carry the mails between Nashville and Natchez over the Trace, which established him as an important citizen of the Southwest. He had no trouble persuading the parents of the twelve-year-old boy to let him take Greenwood to Nashville and give him the best education that could be obtained in that rapidly growing frontier town.

Greenwood gained something besides an education in the nearly six years he spent in Tennessee as the protégé of Major Donly, for he won the heart of the Major's daughter, Rosa. He was only seventeen and she fifteen, but such early marriages were common among the Choctaws. With characteristic frankness, he went to Donly and asked for the hand of his daughter. The Major promptly refused to give his consent.

Weeks passed, and apparently the young lad had resigned himself to Major Donly's decision, but one day he caught his benefactor off guard:

"If you were in love with a girl and her parents objected to your marrying her, what would you do?"

The Major unthinkingly replied:

"Why, I would marry her first, and then tell her parents."

Within the hour Greenwood had married Rosa and reported back to her father that he had followed his advice to the letter.

Rosa lived only twelve years after her marriage, and Greenwood took as his second wife Elizabeth Cody, a niece of the Cherokee chief, John Ross, who had a cousin who was to become famous as Buffalo Bill Cody. Elizabeth died a year after the marriage, and for his third bride, Greenwood again chose a daughter of his old benefactor, Major Donly. When Priscilla Donly eloped, she was only sixteen, but she was to live until 1910, when she died at the age of ninety-three.

Among the corruptions of Nashville was that of the English language, and Greenwood LeFleur returned to his parents in the newly created state of Mississippi as Greenwood LeFlore, with the latter spelling and pronunciation to remain through his preference.

LeFlore had ideas about fitting the Choctaws to the advancing white civilization, and the vigorous nephew of Pushmataha won election as chief of the tribe at the age of twenty-two. He succeeded in dividing the Nation into districts for better law enforcement, installed the system of trial by jury, and made it illegal to bring alcoholic liquor within the confines of the Choctaw Nation.

The punishment that the tribal council had decreed for smuggling liquor into the Indian country was flogging. The first man to be found guilty of breaking the law was the husband of one of his sisters, but the stern young chieftain personally administered the whipping.

Greenwood LeFlore realized from the beginning that the fate of the Choctaws appeared to be that of falling before the advancing white men, and his solution was to learn the ways of life of the white man. Any improvements in the Choctaws, however, could not thwart the primary aim of the white settlers of Mississippi—to take control of all the rich Indian lands.

The United States government, through Andrew Jackson's secretary of War, John Eaton, informed the Choctaw chiefs that a council was desired to discuss acquisition of lands from the Indians, and the meeting date was set for Dancing Rabbit Creek in September of 1830.

In addition to Eaton, husband of the famous Peggy Eaton, the government was represented by Jackson's close friend, General William Coffee, who had commanded his Tennesseans at the Battle of New Orleans. Representing the Choctaws were all of their chiefs and minor officials, plus more than six thousand of the twenty thousand citizens of the Nation. With so many people present, there were also dozens of Indian traders with whiskey and trinkets and more substantial goods to sell to those not in a holiday mood.

The government's terms were bluntly stated through John Pitchlyn, an old Indian trader interpreter. They called for removal of the Choctaws to new Indian territory in the West, in return for the cession of all their lands in Mississippi. The mood of the Choctaw negotiators was revealed when Killahota, a young half-breed, spoke in favor of accepting the plan. An old squaw leaped to her feet and tried to stab him to death as he spoke.

Hotheads and old Choctaw patriots alike were angered at the treatment as they remembered the Choctaw record of never opposing the United States in combat, of the regiment of Indian troops that Pushmataha had raised in the War of 1812. There were serious and heated discussions of the Nation's resisting by force this new effort of the Great White Father.

Young Chief Greenwood led the arguments against the folly of fighting, and he proposed the compromise that the United States and the Choctaw Nation finally accepted. The Nation itself would cede its lands in Mississippi in return for grants in the new Indian territory, but any Choctaw who wished to remain behind would be given a section of land in Mississippi with additions for each of his children. With great grumbling, the treaty of Dancing Rabbit Creek was signed, and preparations made for the exodus to the Western lands.

LeFlore, hated by the diehards who would have preferred resistance, cast his lot with the planter civilization of Mississippi and chose a plantation site among the rich creek beds and fertile Delta lands at the foothills opposite the point where the Tallahatchie and Yalobusha joined to form the Yazoo.

Life from that time became a regular race to get a cotton crop harvested and moved down the river to the New Orleans market, but there were interludes of feeling the responsibility of having been a chief of the Choctaws.

Rascally agents appointed to handle the granting of lands to the Indians succeeded in getting the sections into the hands of white men more often than Choctaws. One of the worst offenders was a neighbor of LeFlore's in his new home, John Smith, who had first come to the Yazoo country and into our story as one of the Congregational missionaries at the Elliott mission to the Choctaws, described in an earlier chapter. When the removal of the Choctaws eliminated the need for missionaries, at least among the Indians, Smith set up as tavernkeeper and secured an appointment as an Indian agent.

Several protests to Washington by LeFlore went unheeded, and the young chief decided to present them in person to Andrew Jackson, for apparently Smith was entrenched in his job with sound political backing, and only a direct attack could remove him.

LeFlore received an audience with Jackson the day after arriving in Washington and immediately launched into a long recital of the grievances against the agent. The tirade aroused the quick anger of Old Hickory, who rose from his seat in majestic fierceness and said, "I, Andrew Jackson, President of the United States, know this man to be an honest gentleman." The unruffled young Choctaw stiffened and retorted just as fiercely, "I, Greenwood LeFlore, chief of the Choctaw Nation, know him to be a damned rascal." John Smith was no longer agent when LeFlore returned to Mississippi.

The county of Carroll was established shortly after the Choctaw cession, and LeFlore found himself one of its largest landowners and most prominent citizens. Carroll County named him one of its first representatives to the state legislature. The Mississippi legislature knew the eloquence of Seargeant S. Prentiss, but it also knew the pretentiousness of lesser dandies, who exhibited their proud knowledge of the classics with long quotations from Latin interspersed in their floor debates. The habit reached its height when several made entire addresses in Latin. Then one day LeFlore rose before his startled colleagues and delivered an hour-long oration entirely in Choctaw. There was a sudden termination of the Latin speeches.

Williams Landing, just before the Tallahatchie-Yalobusha junction, was the Yazoo shipping point for LeFlore's cotton, and a bustling village where landowners dreamed of expansion into a profitable town. John Williams, who had given the settlement its name, owned the warehouse where cotton was held pending loading onto river boats, and Titus Howard, another large Carroll county landowner, had commercial interests in the town.

One day a large shipment of cotton from Colonel LeFlore arrived at the warehouse, but there was no room to store it inside, and Williams had it dumped out in the open on the muddy riverbank. The anger of the former chief reached a boiling point when he was given a bill for the storage of the cotton at the same rates charged for the bales inside the warehouse. In the argument that developed, LeFlore swore to break Williams and wipe out the town of Williams Landing. Three miles above the Landing he purchased an entire townsite and named it Point LeFlore. The first structure set up was a sawmill, and soon lumber was at hand for a warehouse. Once that was built, a church, stores, and residences followed.

The river landing with an all-weather route to the hills, where the plantations were, had a big jump on all competition, and Colonel LeFlore built a split log turnpike from Point LeFlore to the first foothill at a cost of $75,000. Point LeFlore began to prosper, and the business at Williams Landing began to feel the effects.

Fighting back was a hard matter, but the Williams

Landing people finally found the solution through Titus Howard. They would officially incorporate a town with the Mississippi legislature. Howard ceded half of the lots in the townsite to the town government, in return for a promise from the town to maintain a road to the hills. The town was to be named Greenwood, in honor of LeFlore, and it was so incorporated in 1844.

Despite his heavy investments in Point LeFlore, Colonel LeFlore relented in his warfare when Williams Landing became Greenwood. Point LeFlore prospered for a while, but without the strong backing of its founder, it began to decline and had faded away by the Civil War. Greenwood moved along with the development of the Yazoo-Delta country and today is one of the three principal towns of the region and the seat of government of the county of Leflore.

The name of Greenwood LeFlore gradually became a symbol of planter richness in north Mississippi, and LeFlore appeared to prosper even in cotton's bad years. He owned fifteen thousand acres of the best land in Mississippi, uncharted sections in Texas, and approximately a thousand slaves, and he financed dozens of small commercial enterprises. After his first excursion into politics as a legislator, he did not again take an active part.

In 1854 LeFlore decided to build a home in keeping with his position as a fabled planter. The French-Indian turned to Paris for his inspiration, which came from the Empress Josephine, after whose home he named his own Malmaison.

A young Georgia architect, James G. Harris, accepted the challenge, and the stately mansion which he built upon a plateau in the forest stood for nearly ninety years as a monument to his skill. The timber used was the hard pine and cypress cut from the seemingly endless acres of forest on the LeFlore estate, but not one piece of lumber incompletely seasoned was allowed to go into the structure of the building. Most of the labor was done by slaves under the direction of Harris, but for the plastering and decorations skilled workmen from Paris were imported.

The great doors of the home were more often opened than closed, inviting the stranger into the wide, cool hallways that met at the center. The drawing room was the only one that had been completely furnished before the Civil War brought a halt to imports from France. Silken damask curtains, hung from gilded cornices, draped the windows of the huge room. Tall mirrors reflected the beauty of the glittering chandeliers, and a seamless, handwoven, crimson and rose-colored carpet covered the highly polished floor. The more than thirty pieces of furniture in the room were of gold leaf over French hickory, upholstered with crimson-silk brocaded damask. When the furniture was shown to the Duchesse d'Orleans in a Paris shop, where it was being made by special order, she immediately ordered that a duplicate be made for her own use.

When the ex-chief came to settle with his architect and builder after the home had been finished, Harris asked not for money, but for the hand of his daughter, Rebecca Cravat LeFlore, for in the two years he had been building the mansion he had found time to win the love of his employer's daughter. One of the Colonel's granddaughters, Martha Halsey, was also preparing to become a bride, and a double wedding was arranged. Friends of the family from all over the state witnessed the tying of the nuptial knots and then adjourned to the lawn, where the wedding supper was served from a delicacy-laden table over a hundred feet long. Each bride received, as a wedding gift from the Colonel, a five-hundred-acre plantation and a hundred slaves.

Festivity at Malmaison was not destined to last many years. Secession was approaching, and LeFlore did not favor it. When he had signed the treaty of Dancing Rabbit Creek he had taken an oath of allegiance to the United States and accepted an honorary colonelcy in the United States Army. Dancing Rabbit had brought him the undying hatred of many of his Choctaw compatriots, and now allegiance to the United States began to cut him off from the planter society in which he had prospered during the second thirty years of his life.

LeFlore never recognized the legality of secession by Mississippi, and he sat out the war on the Malmaison veranda. He would allow no Confederate money to be brought into his home and refused to accept it even when it was tendered for the crops and livestock that had been commandeered by Confederate troops. One of his slaves was seized for damages after he failed to pay taxes to the Confederate state government, but a group of old friends quietly paid the taxes and had the slave returned.

Neighbors who were former friends turned against him and became bitter enemies. Scavengers accepted as their rights the looting of the LeFlore estates, and the old chief had to carry a gun to repulse would-be assassins. The slaves barely succeeded in putting out a fire started by vandals in the east wing of Malmaison itself.

Soldiers of both the Union and Confederate armies were welcomed as guests during the war, but never as soldiers, only as friends. Legend has it that the Confederate General Featherstone dispatched his orderly to Colonel LeFlore one stormy night with the request that lodging be provided for him and his staff.

"Tell General Featherstone," said the proud old chief, "that I will entertain him as an old friend and one that I esteem highly, but it must be distinctly understood not as a Confederate soldier."

When the war came to a close in 1865 with the final Union victory, it was no triumph for Greenwood LeFlore, who had remained a true Unionist where it was hardest to be one. His health was broken, most of his lands and holdings were lost to him through confiscation and disuse, and there were few friends left among either the Choctaws or the white Mississippians.

The end came that year, on an afternoon when the sun brightened the Delta lands west to the Yazoo. Seated on the porch of his beloved Malmaison, he had himself wrapped in the flag of the Union that had become sacred to him, and, looking out over the broad fields he had cleared from virgin forests, the stern old Choctaw consigned his soul to the God he had taught his tribesmen and slaves to respect.

6

The Age of Jackson

One of Mississippi's first representatives in the lower House of Congress typified the western agrarian radicalism of the Jackson era in which he served. Franklin E. Plummer's public career was relatively brief, but he managed to typify the émigré political leadership in the early days of Mississippi and to take an active role in the opening up of the Yazoo basin following the Choctaw cession.

Plummer was born in Richmond, Berkshire County, Massachusetts, in 1805. He left home at fourteen and eventually worked his way south to New Orleans as a deck hand on a coastwise freighter. The Crescent City did not hold the attractions of the new frontier, and Plummer made his way on foot to the new capital of Mississippi, Jackson, being constructed in a wilderness at the site of the treaty Pushmataha and Andrew Jackson had negotiated at Doak's Stand. Jackson in 1822 had plenty of job openings for an able-bodied boy of seventeen, and Plummer worked at most of them before he wound up as a bartender at a tavern popular among members of the legislature.

Before long one of his legislator friends secured his appointment as postmaster at the village of Westville, where

View of Hotel Greenwood LeFlore across the Yazoo, Greenwood, Mississippi

HOTEL GREENWOOD LEFLORE

the postal receipts totalled $7.34 in 1825 and Plummer had a constituency of his own to cultivate. There were other jobs for an ambitious youngster, however, and before long he was part-time deputy sheriff, schoolmaster, and lawyer, admitted to the bar after six weeks of reading one volume of Blackstone and the still-thin Mississippi Code.

New counties are ideal for politicians looking for jobs to create, and Plummer was fortunate enough to be located in one. At the age of twenty he was universally acclaimed Simpson County's first citizen, and he managed to win election to the legislature a few months before he had attained the legal age. He won re-election three times, with but one dissenting vote. At Jackson he conducted an informal school to teach some of his colleagues with less educational background how to read and write. At the age of twenty-five he missed election as speaker by a narrow margin. The Natchez historian and politician, J. F. H. Claiborne, wrote that because of his mastery of parliamentary procedure he could "embarrass the House or disentangle it, at his pleasure."

Plummer was one of the first to urge that Mississippi "establish schools in every neighborhood, accessible to the poor as well as to the rich." He led a campaign against the constitutional requirement of annual sessions of the legislature, saying meetings

> answer no other purpose than convulsing and involving the state in innumerable difficulties, organizing factions—creating party spirit and private animosities about senatorial and other questions, ruinous in the extreme, to the good order of society; and expending the public funds in altering, amending, repealing and tearing to pieces wholesome laws; freeing Negroes, establishing election precincts, sanction-

> ing divorces and fobing the hard earnings of the laborer and agriculturalist who obtain their support by the sweat of their brows in the honorable occupation of cultivating the soil.

When General Thomas Hinds, Mississippi's hero of the Battle of New Orleans, retired from the Congress in 1830, Plummer sought the vacancy. His principal opponent was a wealthy commission merchant, a member of the "Natchez Junto," representative of the aristocratic group which dominated the southwest Mississippi plantation country. The cry of "Plummer for the people, and the people for Plummer" echoed over the state, through the back country, as the young orator took the stump in a style that was to permanently establish itself at Mississippi hustings.

At Benton, in Yazoo county, Plummer made his campaign headquarters at the tavern of Monsieur Parisott, a Frenchman fresh to the Yazoo country. After a comfortable night, Plummer made good use of the bar, had a number of friends in to drink and dine with him, then made his campaign speech and ordered his horse. M. Parisott, with Plummer's bill in his pocket, attended him to the door, intending to present it as the hostler brought up the horse. Before he could speak, Plummer called out to the crowd:

"Attention, Gentlemen! Before leaving Benton, I desire publicly to acknowledge the unbounded hospitality of my worthy friend Parisott, who stands here modestly behind me. He is a true Samaritan. He found me weary, thirsty, and hungry, and he comforted me. He has placed his table and bar at my disposal, as you gentlemen can testify. He is the prince of tavern keepers, delights in feeding his guests, and never a word about a bill. God bless you, my dear friend. Plummer will never forget you. Gentlemen, farewell!"

Vaulting on his horse, Plummer rode off, to the hurrahs of the crowd. Parisott continued to carry the bill, and Plummer carried the county.

From another county, a local observer told the story of the election:

> Three weeks before the election Mr. Plummer was hardly spoken of, and I am certain if the election had come on, at that time, he would not of got 50 votes in the countys adjoining Perry, but he came round two or three weeks before the election, making stump speeches, saying he was the people's man, that he had fought the battle, through every difficulty, in our State legislature, in their behalf, that he was opposed in every point by the members from the Mississippi [river counties] . . . and in one week after he was here, there was no person spoken of but Mr. Plummer.

Plummer had won election, but he had won it by bucking both the Jackson and anti-Jackson factions in the state politics. Senator George Poindexter and John Black, conservative opponents of Jackson, were in the process of changing affiliation to the new Whig party. They tentatively sought Plummer's support, but shied away from the idea when he became a strong supporter of President Jackson in his fight with the Bank of the United States. Nicholas Biddle sought to swing Plummer's vote by pressure from home, but he overlooked the fact that this Bank's principal correspondent in Mississippi had been the boy orator's Natchez opponent in 1830.

President Jackson had many personal friends in Mississippi, dating back to the time he had married Rachel Robards at Natchez. Most of them reflected the views of the conservative press on the Bank, but the great mass of the voters supported Old Hickory. With Plummer firmly aligned with Jackson on the issue, his re-election was a foregone conclusion. An increase in population had allotted Mississippi a second representative, with both to be chosen at large. Most of the prospective candidates sought to align themselves with Plummer, who chose to make the canvass with Judge Harry Cage.

The pair drove a buggy together over the state. One day at noon they stopped at a farmhouse for dinner. The astute Judge Cage pleased the mother of the household greatly by kissing her little girl and praising the child's beauty. The farm wife was completely carried away, however, when Plummer picked up her year-old boy, laid him gently across his lap, turned up the baby's pinafore, and began to hunt for red bugs.

"They are powerful bad," said Plummer, "and mighty hard on babies." The tenderhearted Congressman was not forgotten.

A few days later the campaigners stopped for the night with an aged couple who lived alone. Cage cut a turn of wood and brought it in for the old lady to cook supper. In the morning he awoke to find Plummer already up. He located his partner in the cowpen, where the old lady was milking and the Congressman was holding the sucking calf off by its tail. After a series of such incidents the Judge could not stick it out with Plummer. The two parted company, but the voters did not forget the earlier association. Cage finished second to Plummer in voting and joined the Yankee émigré in Washington.

In his second term in the House, the opponent of Mississippi aristocracy took up the cause of the workingmen's parties in some of the seaboard cities. He liked their "radical" doctrine of no property qualifications for office, direct election of officials, complete separation of church and state, the abolition of monopolies, an ad valorem system of taxation, and the discontinuance of imprisonment for debt and of capital punishment. As the champion of the workingman, he carefully defined the term for rural Mississippi. Working men were not

> those who labored with their own hands exclusively, as contradistinguished from those who did not labor; nor did he mean the poor exclusively, as contradistinguished from those in more opulent circumstances. A man might be a workingman in principle, and advocate the doctrines of the party, without being a mechanic or laborer; he might be a lawyer, a physician, a merchant, or a planter. They compose that portion of the population of Mississippi who stand opposed to the aristocracy, whether composed of birth, of wealth, of office, of learning, or of talents. . . .

On May 26, 1834, Plummer delivered a speech that Arthur M. Schlesinger, Jr., has termed "probably the most radical speech delivered by a Westerner in Congress during Jackson's Presidency."

"There are but two interests in society," Plummer told the House, "one subsisting by industry and the other by law." The great mass of the population belonged to the major class. The minor class, however, ruled the country and divided "the honors and emoluments of the Government," while the mass of the people who "pay the fiddler and other expenses of carrying on the operation, have not a solitary chance in the game."

The principal political factions, regardless of label, were dominated by members of the minor class. No issues were involved, Plummer said. "It is a mere question about men . . . a private quarrel between ins and outs."

The New York *Workingman's Advocate* hailed Plum-

mer as "a young Grand Lama, destined to fill the place of the eccentric, talented, and impartial John Randolph—as a man too determined in his course to be harnessed to the administration team, or join in the cry of the mongrel pack that pursue and bark at it."

The *Workingman's Advocate*, unfortunately, was not widely read in Mississippi, as many another yet unborn Southern Congressman was to discover in regard to praise from the liberal journals of the cities. Plummer spent most of his last two years in the House campaigning for George Poindexter's Senate seat. He succeeded in undermining Poindexter sufficiently to deny him the Democratic nomination, but a combination of factors dating back to his first brush with the old line leadership denied him the support of the party of Jackson.

Although the titular leader of the Democratic regulars, Governor Hiram G. Runnels, was a native, Plummer's Massachusetts origin could not be called a political liability. Walker, Prentiss, Quitman, Foote, Thompson, and most of the other political leaders of Mississippi before the War Between the States were all originally from Pennsylvania or further north. As other young men went to the big city, they came to Mississippi as penniless young men seeking their fortunes.

One of the new circumstances in the picture had developed through the activities of the workingman's champion in land speculation in the new Choctaw cession. He headed a company which bought a section of land on the Yalobusha River and sought to develop a townsite on the spot. The adjacent section was purchased by a company headed by Governor Runnels. Both companies founded towns—Plummer's was Pittsburg and Runnels' Tullahoma.

Real estate speculation and town promotion were a major part of political and economic life in Mississippi at the time. The Indian cessions came at the height of the "flush times" of the Southern frontier, and real estate deals in new lands was an American political tradition dating to before the Revolution. The Pittsburg and Tullahoma companies each owned a section of land fronting on the Yalobusha river, with the section line splitting a budding townsite square through the middle.

The two sections had been purchased, not from Indians, but from two natives of Nashville, John Donly and Peggy Donly Trohan. The records do not show how the brother and sister owned land in the Choctaw cession, but the fact that the Choctaw leader who made the treaty of cession, Greenwood LeFlore, was their brother-in-law is undoubtedly more than a coincidence. The land was not too far from LeFlore's own vast holdings at Teoc.

The combined townsite was a natural location where a river landing met an open country trail, but the promoters refused to consider schemes for merger. With plans for political preferment which each hoped to get through Plummer and Runnels, the early goal was whole hog or none.

Tullahoma consisted of seven or eight dwelling houses, a tavern, and seven or eight combination grogshops and general stores. A church was being subscribed to, but there was no demand for a school. Across the line, Pittsburg was slightly larger, with more dwellings and more saloons. It also boasted a newspaper, *The Bowie Knife*, and the legal post office. (There was some advantage in having Congressman Plummer as a citizen.)

Tullahomans were not happy about having to get their mail addressed to Pittsburg. After one heavy grog session a group of them crossed the city limits, hitched the Pittsburg post office building to a team, and pulled and dragged it across into Tullahoma. Before Washington could be called on to make a decision, Pittsburgers gathered sufficient strength to recapture it without bloodshed.

The Pittsburg newspaper had been the crowning glory

of the Plummer company's promotion—an asset to the town in the struggle for commercial success. Not long after Editor Hamilton had begun to print *The Bowie Knife*, however, Tullahomans learned that he had been induced to come to Pittsburg in return for a loan secured by a mortgage on his printing press. Tullahoma staged a quiet civic drive and loaned Hamilton enough to pay off his mortgage. The newspaper moved to Tullahoma.

"To a Tullahoman, a Pittsburger or anything Pittsburgian was loathsome beyond description, and the Pittsburgers believed the Tullahomans and their civic aspirations as an affront to all respectability and orderly civilization," reported a contemporary. Both towns established ferries across to the western side of the Yalobusha, operating within a mile of each other. The Pittsburg promoters began construction of a turnpike into the near-by Delta country, anxious to have priority on this trade when new farmland was opened up across the way.

In the campaign of 1835 the rivalry between the towns reached fever pitch with the personal rivalry between Plummer and Runnels. The Governor had maneuvered Robert J. Walker into the Democratic nomination for Senator over Plummer through the support of the "old regulars." Plummer turned to the Whigs, not for their nomination, but for undercover support as an independent Senate candidate. A loan of five thousand dollars was arranged from the Planters' Bank of Natchez, the Mississippi agent of the Bank of the United States. Charles Lynch, the wealthy Whig gubernatorial candidate, signed the note. Plummer had already pledged his support to Lynch against his hated rival, the incumbent Runnels, whom he blamed for the loss of the

Democratic nomination, as well as the threat to his investment in the Pittsburg land company.

Financed by Whig money, Plummer canvassed the state in a stylish barouche with a uniformed driver. In his attacks on Runnels he could appeal directly to the people, for the Governor was elected by popular vote, but for his own campaign he had to ask for the election of legislators pledged to him over both Walker and Poindexter, favored by the more conservative Whigs. Twice Runnels unwisely tangled with him on the same platform, and both times Plummer left the Governor sputtering and incoherent, as his sallies caught hold with the crowd. The Walker supporters had the advantage of having most of the incumbent legislators already on their side, but as reports from Plummer's campaign began to trickle in they turned in desperation to a letter from President Jackson stating in normal letter-of-recommendation style, "I have uniformly regarded Mr. Walker as among the first in talents, attainments, and political integrity." Soon the newspaper broadsiders were admonishing the voters, "Jackson or Plummer, choose between them. . . ."

At the height of the campaigning, the town fathers of Tullahoma decided to incorporate their city with boundaries which extended far enough west to take in all of Pittsburg. Governor Runnels, chafing under Plummer's attacks, they reasoned, would be happy to approve the charter of the town. A courier was dispatched to Jackson with the application. Unfortunately, the secret was not well kept in the grogshops, and within five hours Pittsburg, too, had a courier on the road with a counterproposal for the charter of incorporation of their town. The Tullahoma horseman dawdled on the way, and the Pittsburg agent arrived at the capitol hours ahead of him, after having passed his rival on the trail without having revealed his mission. The winged messenger arrived at the capitol hoping to pull a coup, but the Governor decided it would be wisest politically not to show any favors to Tullahoma during the campaign, so both petitions were rejected.

The election results proved the power of Plummer's oratory with the voters, and the effectiveness of the "old regulars" in naming members of the legislature. Lynch was elected Governor over Runnels in the popular vote, and a majority of the legislators named were pledged to Walker over Plummer. Walker gained every vote from the ten new counties just created from the Indian territory. Plummer, the champion of the rough, plain people, had failed to capitalize on his advantage in the new frontier of Mississippi, even though he was one of the migrants himself.

With both Runnels and Plummer out of office, conciliation instead of war became the theme of the rivalry between Tullahoma and Pittsburg. Cool heads saw the futility of the runaway booster spirit, and perhaps the fact that Plummer's brother Joseph was one of the partners in the Tullahoma company had something to do with it. Representatives of both companies worked out a plan that measured up to the best publicity standards of any modern real estate promotions.

The commission agreed to combine the towns into one, which would be incorporated under a new name. Some romanticist sold them on Granada, after the Spanish city, but apparently from the first the spelling has always been Grenada. (From the first the pronunciation was also Americanized "Grin-ader.") The unity of the old towns would be symbolized by a wedding performed by the Methodist circuit rider, the Rev. Mr. Lucas. To help draw the crowd, an all-day barbecue was advertised throughout the Yalobusha country.

Editor Hamilton joined in the fresh start by changing the name of his paper to the Grenada *Bulletin*. He reported the wedding of Tullahoma and Pittsburg as follows:

> Awake ye sleepers . . . apart ye cannot carry on the work that ye would do; ye cannot thrive and live to see another day, unless ye fight as one town, not as two. Stand forth ye Runnels of the Tullahoma camp, and ye Franklin of the Pittsburg side, shake hands, and catch the vision of Grenada.
>
> (both men step forward)
>
> From this day forth ye must unite your strength. Forget past conflicts and all selfish gain, and work together for one city and your people.

Grenada came into being in a period of high optimism. Endless thousands of rich acres of new land had just been made available for the people of Mississippi. Money was there for those who would work to get it. The new city would be the shipping point and trading center for the rich agricultural development in the Yalobusha bottoms. Ex-Congressman Plummer, who had charged in the halls of Congress that the bank directors of the country all had a common purpose "to get the money of the neighborhood under their control, and thereby provide some of themselves with a living without labor, as presidents, cashiers, and clerks" became a founder and member of the board of directors of the Bank of Grenada and was elected its president.

Hard on the heels of this crest of optimism, the panic of 1837 struck havoc throughout the Southwestern frontier. It toppled the fabulous Planters Bank of Natchez, and the Bank of Grenada went down before the financial tornado. The town itself weathered the shock by the hardest, but the dream of riches cast up by the land company promoters was blown away. Runnels turned from banking back to practicing law and farming north of the town at a place called "Oakchickamau."

The champion of the workingman was a comparative youth of thirty-two when he left the House of Representatives after two terms, but he never sought public office again. He demonstrated his continuing mastery on the stump in a Fourth of July speech in 1839, when he blasted a newly passed state law prohibiting the sale of liquor in quantities less than a gallon. His one active role in political life came in 1844, when he joined in the successful effort to carry Mississippi for his old friend in the House, James K. Polk.

The debts which fell upon Plummer with the crash of 1837 were a millstone from which he could never free himself. He turned to drink for release, and before long he was being charged with unethical conduct as a lawyer. In 1843 he was ordered to appear before the Carroll County circuit court and show cause why he should not be stricken from the roll of attorneys "for disgraceful, unprofessional, and dishonorable conduct." At the next term of court, however, he appeared in his own defense and the charges were dropped. Still debt-ridden, and in virtual obscurity, he died from the effects of dissipation at Jackson in 1852; he was only forty-seven years old.

Perhaps no other man of his times better illustrates an absorbing era of American history, with high ideals and visionary hopes, crude charm, and transparent trickery, stunning success, and bitter frustration.

7

Before the War

The Yazoo basin was entirely opened to the permanent settler and landowner within a span of twelve years. Few wider opportunities for large-scale speculation and spectacular individual acquisitions were ever presented to the American public and yet so completely failed to materialize. Widespread promotion schemes were planned, and there was considerable cheating of rightful claimants to the land, but never on the broad scale that might have been imagined in a day when standards of public morality were not high. There were millions of acres of rich land to be had cheaply, but few big planters could move in on it in the same scale on which they were already operating. There were simply not enough slaves to clear new ground and still keep production underway in old areas. Cotton was bringing too good a price to take two or three years out to prepare another plantation for cultivation. A few considered the fabulously fertile Delta soil to be worth such a gamble, but most were careful enough not to take the added risk of an annual destructive overflow.

So even in the Delta sections of the Yazoo country, the average farm of the pre-Civil War period was not the storied Southern plantation. With the exception of two or three counties at the headwaters of the Tallahatchie and Yocona, the population of all the counties of the basin was more than half slave in 1860, and the lower counties were two-thirds slave. Less than one farmer in five, however, owned as many as fifty slaves, and only one in four owned from twenty to fifty slaves. In other words, less than half of the farm operators of the region could be classified as "planters," and most of these were small planters.

The children of the small planters chopped and picked cotton in the fields beside the slaves, and quite often their fathers kept the records of their production on the same page in the farm ledger beside the work record of the slaves. The pioneers of the Yazoo often brought along slaves to share the burden of the preparation of new land for cultivation, but the sweat and callouses were both black and white. Many of those who had attained the planter class by 1860 came into the Yazoo country with no slaves, or with four or five that were part of a dowry or inheritance from a larger estate.

The greater proportion of large plantations was in the Delta area, but even here the farms of nonslaveholders and small slaveholders were interspersed throughout the region. The region was too new for planters to be too outwardly pretentious in the manner of their counterparts in the Natchez country. There was more frontier democracy than anything resembling the "big house" type of ante bellum society romanticized from the history of other Southern regions. Only a few of the new Delta planters were far removed in years from the "yeoman farmer" classification, and the occupational hazards incident to farming in this new wilderness might put most of them back to that stage at any time.

A typical Wilderness plantation in the 1850's consisted of nearly one thousand acres, divided into four separate sections of approximately equal size, each with its own slave cabins, stables and barn. A white overseer was in charge of these four "places," each given a name, with the main portion of the work going on separately on each farm. A general farm manager, who had a residence at the plantation headquarters, was the superior for the overseers and actual operator of the plantation. At the landing on the riverbank, the central plantation gin and the warehouse were placed for convenience in loading the boats which took the baled cotton south to Vicksburg. The plantation owner left most of the management of the enterprise to his manager and consequently attempted to build no elaborate residence on the place. He and his family spent most of their time at a smaller place in the hills, closer to the amenities of civilization.

Each overseer lived in a small cottage in the midst of the farm buildings assigned to his charge. Although all married, they were each young men fresh from the rural areas of near-by states, looking for both experience and a stake towards striking out for themselves in a Delta farming enterprise. Their pay began at five hundred dollars, and might go as high as one thousand dollars a year. Their jobs were the most highly prized in the South for men without capital who wanted to reach planter status.

Some of the slaves were housed in the original log huts built with timber used in claiming the plantation from the wilderness, but they were gradually being moved into boarded two-room cabins, each with a loft, and of only a little less quality than the overseer's cottage. Each family lived separately, with an individual garden, chicken coop, and pigpen, varying in quality according to the energy of the owners. During the season for field work, when all the hands were required to be in the fields six days a week from before sunrise to sunset, a weekly ration was distributed by the overseer to the head of each family. Each person of working age got three pounds of pork, one peck of meal and one quart of molasses. Tobacco and salt were distributed on a monthly basis. Old men and women and otherwise infirm members of the slave community were assigned to work in the "loom-house" where they made clothing, including shoes, for the Negroes.

During some of the winter months when there was no regular field work, the size of the weekly ration was cut down, and the slaves were expected to supplement it from their own produce. They were allowed to sell any part of this limited supply. Usually each family bought a barrel of flour per year with some of the money thus earned from their back yard. On occasion the overseers would help sell the produce by allowing the more sophisticated Negroes to take it to the closest town, but more often trades were consummated with near-by white families, steamboat crews and the like. Liquor, never distributed as part of the ration, was a prize object of trade.

Each overseer had close to one hundred slaves on his farm. The size of the field crews, made up of both men and women, would depend upon the particular day's job, and the size of the clearing in which they happened to be working. The individual crews were bossed by Negro "drivers," who carried whips as the symbol of their authority. There were no particular rules as to the use of the whip—merely whenever it was needed. The need might come because a slave was lagging behind, talked back to either driver or overseer, or otherwise gave indication of impudence. The whip was the symbol of the disciplinary system in working slave labor on a plantation.

Few Delta plantations were as well organized and as systematically managed as this one, but along the Yazoo bluffs some of the plantations were even more advanced. One of the planters in the older area described the operation of his farm in 1854 in a letter sent to the New York *Tribune*, probably designing it as counterpropaganda to the abolitionist sentiment sweeping the North.

> We now have in this estate 1168 acres of land; on the place 66 Negroes, twenty work horses or mules, five yoke of choice oxen [he wrote]. We plant 270 or 280 acres in cotton, and 125 in corn. We send to the field thirty-four Negroes, old and young, rating them at thirty hands; have one carpenter; a woman who cooks for the above, with all children in charge.

The overseer, he continued, owned and fed his own maidservant; and nine slaves, including seamstresses and two delicate children were fed in the master's own kitchen. For the remaining fifty-six the plantation cook was furnished twenty-two to twenty-four pounds of fat bacon daily, and unlimited meal, vegetables and buttermilk. No cooking was permitted in the slaves' own cabins.

> We do not permit Negroes to stir out before day, nor to get wet if possible, nor do any night work save feeding horses and shelling corn. We give a day or half-day's holiday occasionally during the summer, two to four days at Christmas, and a dance when the young ones desire it.

Whippings were very seldom: "Although very hard work this year, owing to so much rain, no grown Negro has required more than calling his name and telling him to hurry."

The writer's own slaves did not multiply. Within thirty years he lost "five grown Negroes and no telling the number of little ones." Of nineteen children borne by the woman Amy, for example, fifteen died in infancy. He suspended the

pulling of fodder and the threshing of oats when the work proved injurious; he built cisterns as a source of more healthful water than springs; but slaves, and blooded livestock as well, died, despite his care and to his keen distress. Apparently his plantation was in the midst of a disease-ridden area, for the care both his slaves and livestock received was far above the average of the time.

One man stands out as having never lost a day's work except from a case of measles, until a mule's kick laid him upon his deathbed. Thereupon an epitaph was inscribed in the diary: "Peyton is no more: aged 42. Though he was a bad man in many respects, yet he was a most excellent field hand—I wish we could hope for his eternal state."

The slaves were permitted to raise cotton in patches assigned to them and were paid for splitting shingles and doing other jobs in their free time. On the other hand, their liberty was restrained in a measure on Sundays by a requirement that they attend preaching. This rule was a grievance to an overseer named Champion, who said it was "a sin to make Negroes attend, and against his conscience."

The diary of James K. Polk, congressman, governor of Tennessee, and the first "dark horse" President (as well as one of the ablest), gives a good story of the operation of a plantation near the Yalobusha River. Polk began his career as a planter when he inherited a plantation called "Pleasant Grove" in western Tennessee. Too busy as a politician and lawyer to actively manage the plantation, most of the work was done by his brother-in-law, Dr. Silas Caldwell, and his overseer, Ephraim Beanland.

Pleasant Grove proved to be of little profit, and Polk decided to make more money or lose more with a planting venture in the newly ceded Choctaw land of Mississippi. He sold Pleasant Grove in 1834, took the infirm slaves to his homestead at Columbia, Tennessee, bought others to enlarge the able-bodied corps, and in partnership with Dr. Caldwell undertook a plantation operation on a tract of eight hundred and eighty acres in Yalobusha County, bought at a price of ten dollars an acre.

Beanland was commissioned to buy the broadwives (wives of slaves, who were the property of other planters and lived on other plantations), but the owner of the wife of a man named Caesar refused to sell because she refused to migrate. Beanland reported: "I tell Seaser that she does not care anythine for him and he sayes that is a fact."

Caldwell and Beanland in January of 1825 led the trek of twenty-eight slaves, together with mules and cattle, a drove of hogs and a wagonload of equipment. Arriving after a week of travel, the corps built in eighteen days a house for the overseer and his wife, four Negro cabins, a smokehouse and a kitchen.

Caldwell procured cottonseed locally, sent a wagon to Memphis for tools, ordered pork from Cincinnati, directed Beanland to plant his full need of corn and such cotton as he could. He then went home, "much pleased with his situation, and the Negroes only tolerably well satisfied."

The first year of the new enterprise was disappointing. Three of the men ran away and their capture involved expense; another was killed when thrown by a mule; Beanland suffered from malaria; and the cotton crop yielded barely twenty bales. At the year's end Beanland was discharged, and Polk bought out Caldwell's interest in the place.

The successor to Beanland, erring in the opposite direction, demoralized the slaves by indulgence and was succeeded by George W. Bratton, who gradually developed the plantation into a going enterprise. Bratton died in 1839, however, and he was succeeded by John I. Garner.

During Garner's first full year several Negro babies died, and after the cotton-picking three men ran away to Tennessee to complain of his harshness. Polk then replaced

Garner with Isaac H. Dismukes, who held the job for four years. There was still trouble with slaves running away to Tennessee, and he wrote to Polk: "I beleave that they believe that tennessee is a place of parradise and all want to gow back to tennessee so stop them by irong tham and send them back again and they will soon stop cumming to tennessee."

The trouble with the Negroes subsided as Dismukes established himself as a good manager, but Polk began to develop doubts when the overseer asked for the purchase of a barrel of whiskey. In the fourth year reports from Yalobusha neighbors became frequent about the excessive drinking of Dismukes, and a new man was hired.

John A. Mears, at wages of five hundred and later five hundred and fifty dollars a year, took charge in 1845 and continued throughout the fourteen years of the record that was maintained—throughout his employer's term in the White House and in the employ of the widow after Polk's death.

Mears inaugurated several innovations, one of which was individual crops of cotton for the slaves, where they were paid a small cash reward. There was a regular profit yield from the plantation.

Two of the Yalobusha slaves sent messages to their mistress which have been preserved.

Mariah sent a message to her mistress in 1841 "that she is worth at least $30 more than when she left Tennessee. She can spool, warp, and weave, and with a little more practice thinks she will make a first rate weaver."

Harry, the blacksmith, wrote for himself the next year:

> I would wish to be remembered to all my people old mistrs esphhirly Tell the old Lady Harry is hir servent untill

> dath. I would be gld to see Hir one more. I expect to come out a cristmust to see you . . . Dear master I have Eleven children. I have been faithful over the anvill Block Evr cen 1811 and is still old Harry.

Harry was indeed an excellent blacksmith. In addition to the work of the plantation, he earned for his master up to four hundred and fifty dollars a year while hired out to a Coffeeville firm—almost the equal of the annual salary paid the overseer.

One planter calculated the distance his best plowhand walked in a day and found it to be twenty-one miles. One winter he spread forest leaves over a cornfield. He appraised a day's work at forty cents per hand and twenty-five cents per mule, concluding that an increased yield of three bushels per acre for two years would repay the expense of using natural fertilizer.

Cotton was the overwhelming cash crop, but Yazoo plantations were a long way from the one-cropism of later years. Most of the planters attempted to make their farms as self-sufficient as possible, raising as much as possible of the food for their slaves and animals. Plantation records indicate that they were generally successful.

The factor system was a natural result of the remoteness of plantations from the cotton market and the slow transportation available on the river. The system began with the colonial tobacco farmers of Virginia using London factors, but the New Orleans factors brought it to its peak in the hey-day of cotton. Cotton was usually consigned to New Orleans with instructions to hold for the best price, unless a pressing need for cash made an immediate sale necessary. While the factor waited for a better price, he often advanced money or supplies to the planter. This sometimes resulted in a debt, but more often cash surpluses. Usually the planter made use of his factor as a banker, drawing on him for both supplies and cash.

There was general agricultural prosperity throughout the basin. Cotton prices held fairly steady throughout the decade 1850–1860, and the fertility of the soil more than made up for the many inefficiencies of operation. Overoptimism in expanding to new operations and larger holdings was the main cause of bankruptcy and indebtedness. In 1860 the Yazoo planters were generally satisfied and happy with the national economic system built during the years of Southern influence and domination in the Federal government. The election of Abraham Lincoln as President was accepted as a threat of drastic changes in this way of life, and they were ready to resist.

supplies to the planter. This sometimes resulted in a debt, but more often cash surpluses. Usually the planter made use of his factor as a banker, drawing on him for both supplies and cash.

There was general agricultural prosperity throughout the basin. Cotton prices held fairly steady throughout the decade 1850–1860, and the fertility of the soil more than made up for the many inefficiencies of operation. Overexpansion in expanding to new operations and larger holdings was the main cause of bankruptcy and indebtedness. In 1860 the Yazoo planters were generally satisfied and happy with the national economic system built during the years of Southern influence and domination in the Federal government. The election of Abraham Lincoln as President was accepted as a threat of drastic changes in this way of life, and they were ready to resist.

8

Gibraltar of the South

"Mississippi shall be the grand scene of operation"
—William T. Sherman

From the time when Grant first moved on Fort Donelson and Fort Henry, Vicksburg was the goal of the Union war in the West. Vicksburg was the goal because it was the one bastion which the Rebels needed to maintain in order to keep the Mississippi out of enemy hands. To normal military minds it seemed impregnable, and perhaps it would have been if its capture had been the mission of some other soldier than U. S. Grant.

The military historians have found no clear pattern in the development of the Lincoln strategy which made control of the Mississippi River his first major war aim. Perhaps it came in disgust and despair when the back-yard troops, commanded by the glamorous generals like McDowell, McClellan, Hooker, and Burnside, failed to penetrate more than a few miles across the Potomac into Virginia. The early war experience in the Mississippi Valley of Halleck, who became Lincoln's more or less personal chief of staff, had something to do with it. The more likely fundamental cause, however, is the Mid-Western, frontier background of Abe Lincoln. From the time when Thomas Jefferson was ready to fight Napoleon over its control, the Mississippi River was as important to the old Northwest Territory as it was to those who actually lived in the lower valley. The divided Union was a reality when commerce could not move south down the river. Disunity would be all but over when the Mississippi came back into the Union. The Army of the Tennessee fought for cheaper freight rates for wheat, as well as for the Union.

The strategic advantages of Vicksburg were responsible for the settlement of the town. The high bluffs at the river's edge merged into hills dotted with native walnut trees, and the first settlers called their community Walnut Hills. The Yazoo flowed into the Mississippi just eight miles above the original community site, until it was diverted long after the war as part of the Vicksburg harbor. The French governor Bienville erected Fort St. Peter on the Yazoo shore several miles from the Mississippi, but the early settlers went to Walnut Hills.

The bloody battle of Shiloh, which followed Grant's advances through western Kentucky and Tennessee, was a necessary preliminary to the assault on Vicksburg. General Beauregard began to prepare for the inevitable when he ordered construction of gun emplacements on the Yazoo above Vicksburg, at a point where high bluffs commanded the only accessible portion of the Yazoo's south bank. Swampland south to the mouth of the river made any troop landing appear virtually impossible. Beauregard, or whichever staff member directed the order, estimated that control of the Yazoo bluffs, variously called Chickasaw, Snyder's and Haynes', would be essential to successful assault on Vicksburg. The estimate was correct. The successful final siege did not begin until Union troops occupied the point.

Federal gunboats operating out of Cairo cleared the Mississippi south to Memphis, while Admiral Farragut took New Orleans largely by a display of the naval strength brought up from the mouth of the river. By the spring of 1862 the gunboats were able to test the possibility of forcing the surrender of Vicksburg without major land action. The test failed, as the Vicksburg shore batteries proved their mettle.

The first probing gunboats could not even make the run up or down the river past the city. They tried to make the run under cover of darkness. The Vicksburg defenders improvised lights by burning houses at the river's edge. Eventually, the massed fire of fleets combining from the north and south proved enough of a distraction to the Confederates that the gunboats could move back and forth past the city with relative safety. The risk was still too great, however, for unprotected troop transports. Vicksburg was not going to fall to mere shelling from gunboats.

ARKANSAS TRAVELER

The brief success of the Confederate ironclad *Merrimac*, which almost broke the Federal coastal blockade, was no accident. Confederate naval leaders planned the ironclad gunboats from the beginning, but they lacked the time to build them and the time to learn the tactics and strategy of this new type of fighting ship.

Secretary of the Navy Mallory entered into a contract with John T. Shirley of Memphis for the construction of two ironclad gunboats on August 24, 1861, at a price of $160,000. The contract was to be executed in four months, and Shirley immediately began to scour the blacksmith shops of Memphis and Arkansas for the needed iron. A shop at Nashville was able to deliver the bolts and spikes, but even as material rolled in there were not enough skilled carpenters and ironworkers to do the job—too many of the normally small supply in the Memphis area were carrying a rifle in the army.

The boats ordered from Shirley were to be named the *Arkansas* and *Tennessee.* The *Tennessee* never saw battle, but was a casualty burned at the docks by her builders just before Federal troops entered Memphis. The *Arkansas* was far enough along to be towed down the Mississippi to the mouth of the Yazoo and then up to a new Confederate Navy Yard planned at Greenwood. Shipments as far north as Greenwood proved too difficult, however, and the *Arkansas* was towed back down the river to Yazoo City.

The Richmond naval officials were willing to pay heavily to make sure the *Arkansas* would be built. A boom raft was laid across the Yazoo below the city to serve as a temporary impediment to attacking ships, and naval land batteries were installed on the high bluffs east of the river to protect the new shipyard.

Like many another war contract, the original cost in the Shirley contract was lost in the shuffle. On May 26, 1862, after the exploits of the *Merrimac* had thrilled the South with the first setback administered to the Union Navy, Lieutenant Isaac N. Brown, C.S.N., was ordered to take command of the *Arkansas* at Greenwood, and "finish the vessel without regard to expenditure of men or money." Lieutenant Brown was a native Mississippian, but a veteran of the regular Navy who had been building four ironclad vessels at New Orleans which he had had to destroy the day before the arrival of Farragut's fleet.

The Yazoo navy yard became a model of Confederate efficiency. Two hundred carpenters and twelve iron forges worked in shifts around the clock in the struggle to build a ship which might save Vicksburg and the Mississippi River for the Confederacy.

The *Arkansas* was technically a ram, but her design was a combination of the flat-bottomed river boat and the keel-built naval warship. Her bow was armed with a sharp, solid beak of iron, sixteen feet long and ten feet across, bolted to eight feet of solid timber. The iron shield was one thickness of railway iron, laid horizontally over heavy oak bulwarks with cotton-pressed casemating. The wheel was within the shield, but the pilothouse was raised two feet above the shield deck, which was covered with one-inch iron bars. The 180-foot vessel, eighty feet across amidships, drew fourteen feet of water, with a speed of six knots. Her battery included four sixty-four- and two thirty-two-pound rifled cannon, as well as two nine-inch and two eight-inch older type guns. A special defensive weapon was a steam hose to repel boarding parties.

Lieutenant Brown was racing with time on two counts. He had to have the *Arkansas* ready before the Federal fleet landed troops at Vicksburg, and he had to be able to move south from Yazoo City before the late summer low water left him high and dry. The mission was accomplished in July. General Van Dorn, the Confederate commander, ordered Brown to bring the *Arkansas* under the protection of the Vicksburg shore batteries. That meant bringing the ironclad through waters infested by some thirty-five Federal vessels hovering around the mouth of the Yazoo, but Brown steamed on down to test under fire the vessel he had constructed.

Confederate deserters had been keeping the Union fleet

well posted on the progress made in building the *Arkansas*, and they were quick to report when the ship was put out in the Yazoo for trial runs under her own power. The Federal Captain Davis, acting for Admiral Foote and after consultation with Farragut, sent Captain Walke of the *Carondelet*,

with support from the *Queen of the West* and the *Tyler,* up the Yazoo to reconnoiter "and to ascertain, if possible, the whereabouts of the *Arkansas.*"

Captain Walke moved up the Yazoo early on the morning of July 15.

> All was calm, bright, and beautiful [he wrote later]. The majestic forest echoed with the sweet warbling of its wild birds, and its dewy leaves sparkled in the sunbeams. All seemed inviting the mind to peaceful reflections and to stimulate it with hopes of future happiness at home.

Captain Walke's pastoral reflections were suddenly disturbed by the wild shrieking of the steam whistle of the *Queen of the West.* That vessel, in the van of the patrol, had sighted the fearful-looking *Arkansas* steaming down the river. It plunged ahead, continuing to sound the alarm until it reached the Federal fleet in the Mississippi.

The *Carondelet* and the *Tyler* both turned to join the retreat, but they fought a running gun battle with the *Arkansas* for some twelve miles, exchanging shots at ranges that varied from fifty to five hundred yards. The slowness of the *Arkansas* saved them from destruction. The *Carondelet* took thirteen hits and lost thirty men, some of whom jumped overboard when the escape pipes were shot away. The *Tyler* had aboard a detachment of sharpshooters from the 4th Wisconsin and suffered twenty-four casualties among this group.

Despite the warning from the *Queen of the West*, most of the Federal fleet was immobile with banked fires as the *Arkansas* moved into the Mississippi, but all of the ships opened up with their starboard batteries, with spirited answers from the *Arkansas.* The exposed pilothouse had already taken its toll on the Confederate ship. The chief pilot, John Hodges, was killed at the wheel in one of the first exchanges of fire on the Yazoo. Out in the Mississippi two eleven-inch solid shot scored direct hits on the side of the ram, crushing the iron armor and killing ten of the crew.

A Union officer described the *Arkansas's* passage:

> All eyes were now turned in that direction [the mouth of the Yazoo] when the monster shoved around the point, and, a moment later, her huge form lay clearly exposed as all alone she headed boldly towards the whole fleet. Conscious of her strength and invulnerability, she proudly flung down the gauntlet to the whole. There was something grand in this solitary vessel thus sending her challenge to our combined fleet. . . . It was a strange spectacle which those gallant commanders witnessed on that pleasant July morning. The whole fleet had been bearded by a single boat, and it was evident there was mischief in her which must in some way be headed off. Besides her haughty bearing had roused the indignation of the officers and men, and the insult must be wiped out. A general council of war was called of all commanders to take into consideration what should be done. This formidable vessel might make her way to New Orleans and destroy our entire fleet there, and take possession of the city. She seemed more impregnable than the Merrimac, the terror whose name still filled the land. . . ."

At 8:50 A.M. the *Arkansas* reached the comparative safety of the dock at Vicksburg, but Admiral Farragut did not propose to let the potentially dangerous enemy vessel have a chance to be repaired or manned with a fresh crew. That night Commodore Davis's fleet began an exchange of fire with the Vicksburg shore batteries, while each vessel of the Farragut fleet ran down past the *Arkansas* letting loose a broadside as it came abreast. Only one eleven-inch shot took effect, and the next morning thirteen-inch guns were brought up to strike at the Confederate ship, with no success.

The news of how Brown had taken the *Arkansas* through the two massed Federal fleets cheered the whole Confederacy.

On July 18 he was promptly promoted to Commander "for gallant and meritorious conduct."

Commander Brown had been wounded, himself, in the fight with the *Carondelet*, but he went to work at once preparing the *Arkansas* for action on the Mississippi. Wounded crewmen were hospitalized and repairs begun on the loosened iron plating. The Confederates still hoped the *Arkansas* might drive the mass of the Federal fleet from Vicksburg, and the mission might have been accomplished if a Union officer had not been recklessly intent upon building a record that would live up to his father's.

William D. Porter was the son of Commodore David Porter, the famous privateer commander of the War of 1812, the man who first took the Stars and Stripes into the Pacific in the best tradition of Sir Francis Drake. Another son of Commodore Porter, David, became an admiral, and was in the Federal river-boat fleet as a commodore. The most famous of Porter's sons was an adopted one, however—Admiral David Farragut.

William Porter had been in the Pacific when the war began. When his son joined the Confederate forces, brother David was not above accepting the premise that his brother had approved of this action on the part of the nephew. David had raised doubts about his brother's loyalty with Gideon Welles, the Secretary of the Navy, and William was quick to make the same kind of attack on David when he reported to Washington. David Porter, he told Welles, was an intimate friend of Jefferson Davis, and all his sympathies were with the Secessionists. Fortunately, Secretary Welles knew enough of the family failings to take it all with a grain of salt, as revealed in his diary:

> William had, not without reason, the reputation of being very untruthful—a failing of the Porters, for David was not always reliable on unimportant matters, but amplified and colored transactions, where he was personally interested especially, but he had not the bad reputation of William. I did not always consider David to be depended upon if he had an end to attain, and he had no hesitation in trampling down a brother officer if it would benefit himself. He had less heart than William.

William proved his heart as the commander of a gunboat which he had personally converted from a St. Louis river ferry. He named it the *Essex*, after his father's famous privateer. In the assault on Fort Henry the *Essex* sustained heavy casualties, with its severely wounded captain chief among them. He never actually recovered from the wounds, which were one of the causes of his fatal illness at the Brooklyn Navy Yard some two years later.

When the hit-and-run attack on the *Arkansas* at the Yazoo docks failed, Porter volunteered to take the *Essex*, which had just joined the fleet at Vicksburg, for a single-handed attack on the "monster," as the Union sailors termed her. On the morning of July 22 Porter moved under the Vicksburg guns. The shots from shore did not penetrate the pine-reinforced armor plate of the *Essex*, and Porter was able to score direct hits with his nine-inch guns before Commander Brown could get the steam up on the *Arkansas*.

The *Essex* steamed in, determined to deliver a mortal blow with its ram, but Brown managed to move the *Arkansas* aside just in time to avert the blow. The *Essex* missed her target and plowed into the riverbank, stuck fast for several minutes. Fortunately for Porter, the *Arkansas* was so close the shore batteries had to hold their fire for fear of hitting the Confederate ship. The *Essex* managed to let go one volley at point-blank range, before returning to safety out of range of the shore guns, nursing scars from the belated return fire of the *Arkansas*.

Porter had been lucky in the choice of time to attack the *Arkansas*. Brown had less than half of his regular crew aboard. The Confederate armor plate stood up well under the test. Only two shots penetrated, and the damage was repaired by the next day. Brown started out into the river to attack the Federal mortar boats, but his starboard engine failed before he could begin the attack.

Porter was chafing for another chance at the *Arkansas*, and it came in August. Brown had never fully recovered from his wound in the first day's fighting, and he was given a leave to visit his family at Grenada when the Federal forces withdrew from Vicksburg. At Grenada, orders came for the *Arkansas* to support an attack on Baton Rouge by General John C. Breckinridge. Brown set out for Vicksburg at once, but he arrived four hours after the *Arkansas* had been ordered to leave without her commander. Lieutenant H. K. Stevens was in command. The ship also sailed without her chief engineer, hospitalized with malaria, the only man who had been able to nurse her engines along through their installation and repairs.

Just above Baton Rouge the starboard engine failed again. The port engine, operating its separate screw, quickly spun the boat into the cypress stumps at the riverbank. The delay served to keep the *Arkansas* from reaching Baton Rouge that day. New engine failures the next day could not be repaired, and Lieutenant Stevens made the boat fast to the bank while the feverish engineering crew worked on.

Porter and the *Essex* found the *Arkansas* moored, stern in, with the guns covering the river to the right and left. Other Federal gunboats had kept their distance, but Porter moved in and opened fire immediately at five hundred yards. As the fire from the *Essex* began to bound off the armored sides, the *Arkansas's* senior engineer raced to the deck and loudly reported: "The engines are in good order, sir."

The crew cheered; Lieutenant Stevens gave the order to let go the lines; the engines began slowly to move and the *Arkansas* moved into the Mississippi, prepared to ram headlong into the *Essex*. The bell was struck to go full speed ahead. The port engine picked up momentum, but the luckless starboard engine coughed and stopped. The *Arkansas* turned and plowed back into the riverbank, her lightly protected stern toward the *Essex*. The stern guns opened up on Porter's ironclad, but Lieutenant Stevens saw no reason to have his crew blown to bits when a shot reached the magazine through the thin boiler iron at the stern. The crew waded ashore with their small arms. Stevens set the *Arkansas* afire, and a few minutes later it blew up before a Federal party could board it. For want of an engineer, another Confederate dreadnought had been lost, and with it the last chance to stop Federal gunboats on the Mississippi.

Admiral Farragut gave the official credit for the destruction of the *Arkansas* to Porter:

> Although Bill Porter did not destroy her, he was the cause, and thought his shells did the work; for they [the Confederates] would hardly have destroyed her unless he made the attack. I insist that Porter is entitled to the credit of it.

Porter makes one more footnote to the story of the *Arkansas*, again from the diary of Gideon Welles:

> Received a letter from Commodore W. D. Porter stating his arrival in New York after many signal exploits—capturing ironclad steamer Arkansas, running Bayou Sara, etc. Charges from Admirals Farragut and Davis, accusing him of misrepresentation and worse, have preceded his arrival. The War Department has sent me an inexcusable letter, abusive of the military, which Porter has written, and Stanton cannot notice. I have been compelled to reprove him and to send him before the Retiring Board. Like all the Porters, he is a courageous, daring, troublesome, reckless officer.

THE PERILOUS YAZOO BLUFFS

The Mississippi now belonged to the Yankees, but the Confederates determined to hold on to the Yazoo. There was still a chance that the Confederate Navy Yard could turn out a more successful *Arkansas*, but, more important than that, the Yazoo had to be kept out of the hands of Grant, who wanted to use it as the highway to approach Vicksburg from the rear.

The defensive strategy to keep Federal gunboats out of the Yazoo brought another important sidelight to naval history—the first successful use of a naval torpedo in actual warfare. Let acting-Ensign Fentress tell the start of the story from his official report:

> December 13, 1862
>
> Sir:
>
> In obedience to your order I proceeded yesterday morning at 7 A.M. with 20 men from this vessel on board

the steamer Marmora, to act as sharpshooters on an expedition up the Yazoo River. At 7:30 A.M. the expedition got underway, the Marmora taking the lead.

We proceeded up the river very slowly, and met with no resistance. At 10 A.M. we picked up a boat containing a white man and a Negro. At 11 A.M. (or near) we hove in sight of the sunken torpedoes of the enemy.

The Marmora being about 100 yards in advance, her engines were stopped, and the fleet closed up to "close order."

The steamer Cairo came nearly abreast of us, and hailed the Marmora to "go ahead," which order was obeyed and we moved ahead very slowly.

Soon we discovered an object ahead, resembling a small buoy, and I requested Captain Getty to allow me to examine it.

As I approached it, I found a boat from the Cairo on the same errand, and I pushed forward to reach a line I saw on the bank.

As soon as I could, I severed the line with my sword, and a large object immediately arose in the middle of the river. Pulling to it by the line, I soon discovered it to be some "infernal machine," and upon closer examination I found a wire running from it to the shore, and was ordered from the Cairo to cut it, which I did, and towed the torpedo to the Marmora. As I was engaged in breaking it to pieces, I heard an explosion from the Cairo, and on looking up I saw her anchor thrown up several feet in the air. In an instant she commenced to settle, and was run to the bank and a hawser got out; but shortly she slid off the bank and disappeared below the water. Every possible assistance was rendered by all the fleet, while they shelled the banks on both sides of the river. During the time that the Queen of the West was destroying all traces of the Cairo, a party was sent to destroy the remaining torpedoes. At 3:30 P.M. we commenced our decent of the river, and after shelling several places where pickets were seen, we arrived safe in sight of our squadron at anchor off the mouth of the Yazoo river.

I have the honor, sir, to be
Very respectfully, your Obedient servant
Walter E. H. Fentress

The torpedo which sunk the *Cairo* was not a mine of the type still in use today. It was really a homemade "infernal machine," which had to be detonated by a man on shore pulling the trigger by means of the attached line. A Vicksburg craftsman named Weldon built the Yazoo torpedoes, and he was present when artillery Lieutenant Cowan pulled the trigger that sank the *Cairo*. The two men had watched the approach of the Union fleet from slit trenches on shore, then crawled into the near-by woods when the gunboats began blindly to shell each side of the river.

Weldon and Cowan claimed a reward for their inventive genius under the terms of a law which had been passed by the Confederate Congress in April, providing for a reward as high as 50 per cent of the value of ships destroyed by "any machine or engine or . . . new method for destroying the armed vessels of the enemy." The Mississippians had not only destroyed the *Cairo*, but they set a pattern for the destruction of many other Federal warships. President Jefferson Davis ruled that they were not entitled to a reward, however, because they were already in the paid service of the government.

The Federal boats destroyed all traces of the *Cairo*, which had sunk in forty feet of water, because they wanted to keep the Confederates from reclaiming the sunken armor plate and guns. Most of the four hundred crew members of the

Cairo had been saved, but the primary Confederate mission was accomplished—the Yazoo remained in Confederate control until the fall of Vicksburg.

The reconnaissance up the Yazoo by the Union expedition was in preparation for a more important mission up the river. Grant had decided on a two-pronged attack with the mission of occupying the high ground behind Vicksburg and destroying the Confederate army defending the city. The Union commander would move down the Tallahatchie from the north and into the Yazoo. He expected Pemberton, the new Confederate leader, to offer resistance somewhere along the line. The movement would withdraw troops from Vicksburg and make it easier for Sherman to storm Haynes' Bluff successfully. The *Cairo* was sunk as it attempted to clear the path for Sherman's troop transports.

Admiral David Porter assembled a flotilla at Memphis to carry Sherman south with 40,000 men, an overwhelming force with which to hit the garrison of 6,000 at Haynes' Bluff. Grant told Sherman that the success of the attack would depend upon its secrecy. It was the first important independent command Sherman had ever received, but he assembled the army from a nucleus of 5,000 troops at Memphis, loaded supplies and equipment, and moved the expedition away in eleven days' time. Newspapermen were excluded, and he backed up the order by telling his officers to seize any unauthorized passenger and conscript him into military service for the remaining term of the regiment making the capture.

Grant had established headquarters at Oxford and built up a supply dump at Holly Springs for his own push southward through the Tallahatchie and Yalobusha bottoms. The

Holly Springs supply headquarters, including more than a thousand wagons and five thousand draft animals, was a tempting target for the Confederate troops operating in the rear of Grant. N. B. Forrest was operating in west Tennessee, and Earl Van Dorn, replaced by Pemberton after being defeated by Rosecrans at Corinth, was back in the field with a cavalry division.

Colonel Murphy, the commander at Holly Springs, was warned by Grant of his precarious position, but the Union officer probably would have preferred reinforcements to the warning. Van Dorn struck him on the night of December 20. Murphy offered little resistance, surrendering his entire force of 1,500 men. Van Dorn set fire to tons of massed supplies, afraid to keep his small force so close to Grant. He had achieved one of the most successful cavalry raids of the war, for it successfully halted the entire Federal army for some four or five months. Grant could not move without supplies. He had to retreat back into Tennessee, all thought gone of the attack south toward Vicksburg.

The fires at Holly Springs were visible that night in Oxford, but Grant could get no word to Sherman on the Mississippi. Forrest had completely isolated Memphis for a few days by cutting all lines of communication, and no message could be sent down the river by fast packet to delay Sherman's attack.

Sherman reached the Yazoo on the day after Christmas. Admiral Porter turned his fleet into the tributary in the face of a violent rainstorm with the "wind howling like a legion of devils, though which side it was howling for, I have no idea." The river was at flood stage, and the gunboats and transports had to be tied to trees normally out of reach on the banks of the stream. Sherman's corps was landed on the swampy ground south of the bluff.

The secrecy Sherman had sought for a surprise attack was confined largely to the Federal side. The approach of his flotilla down the Mississippi had been carefully reported to Vicksburg. General Stephen D. Lee, the Confederate commander at Haynes' Bluff, had been given 6,000 more troops by Pemberton from Grenada when the debacle at Holly Springs took Grant out of the picture.

On the twenty-ninth Sherman sent his men against the bluffs. The officers carried accurate maps and careful, detailed orders, but they were marching against a waiting enemy. Trees had been felled across the only available field of approach. The Rebel riflemen on the bluff had a clear field of fire, with the Parrott-gun batteries in position for enfilading fire with their murderous grapeshot. The Union gunboats were supposed to support the attack, but they withdrew in the face of counterfire from Confederate vessels further up the river.

Two brigades, one of them commanded by Lincoln's friend Francis Blair, got their forward elements to the edge of the Confederate breastworks, but the length of their advance merely made it possible to lose more prisoners. Sherman reported 208 killed, 1,005 wounded, and 563 captured or missing, against total Confederate casualties of 207. Lee was hesitant in ordering his men out from cover to pursue their advantage and lost whatever chance he had to inflict greater damage when he granted a truce to allow the Union troops to gather their dead.

Sherman feared the river now as much as the Confederates. Watermarks on the trees told him that previous floods had been as high as ten feet over his head, and the rain was still falling. His men were ordered back to the boats, and Porter took the fleet down closer to the quieter Mississippi.

As the drenched and weary troops returned to the boats, Sherman came back to the flagship *Black Hawk* and entered Porter's cabin.

"I've lost seventeen hundred men and those infernal reporters will publish all over the country their ridiculous stories about Sherman being whipped," he protested bitterly after a long silence.

"Pshaw," Porter answered, "that's nothing; simply an episode in the war! You'll lose seventeen thousand before the war is over and think nothing of it. We'll have Vicksburg yet, before we die. Steward! Bring some punch. . . ."

On January 2 General J. A. McClernand, the Illinois political general, arrived to take command of the Corps. It was not a demotion for Sherman, because of his failure at Haynes' Bluff—McClernand's orders originated in Washington, where Lincoln first had pushed him off on Grant in the midst of the clamor from the West for the capture of Vicksburg.

Sherman was correct in his forecast of newspaper reaction to the defeat. Newspapers in the North began to hint that the commander's "insanity" was responsible for the slaughter on the Yazoo. He wrote his wife Ellen:

> Indeed I wish I had been killed long since. Better that than struggle with the curses and maledictions of every woman that has a son or brother to die in any army with which I chance to be associated. . . . Seeing so clearly into the future I do not think I ought to get away.

STAR OF THE WEST

The surprise attack from the Mississippi on the Yazoo bluffs had failed, but Grant still looked on the Yazoo as the route into Vicksburg. Jefferson Davis had sent Joe Johnston to Mississippi as the new western commander, and Johnston was keeping Pemberton with an adequate force at Grenada, on the Yalobusha, ready to stop an attack southward along that river or along the Mississippi Central Railroad.

The second phase of Grant's Vicksburg campaign involved moving down the Tallahatchie, west of Grenada, into the Yazoo at Greenwood. Coming down the Yazoo, the Union troops could attack Haynes' Bluff from the north, instead of having to come over the deadly ground from the south which had been so disastrous to Sherman. The whole plan was as ambitious an amphibious landing operation as ever attempted by American troops before North Africa in 1942.

Some sixty miles south of Memphis, the Mississippi was only about forty miles west of the Coldwater, the major tributary of the Tallahatchie. Before the levees had been built, river steamers had been able to cross from the Mississippi into the Coldwater by way of Moon Lake, Yazoo Pass, and Cassidy's Bayou. Yazoo Pass was an extension of the bayou which filled with water only during flood seasons. It got its name because through it boats could pass from the Mississippi into the Yazoo system. The levee had ended the usefulness of Yazoo Pass, but the levee was defenseless against a heavy charge of dynamite.

Grant planned a new two-pronged attack, making use of the Mississippi floodwaters. He was in Louisiana, supervising the digging of the Lake Providence ditch, through which he expected to bring his transports safe from the Vicksburg guns, for a landing south of the town. To the north, another expedition would blast the levee at Moon Lake, cross Yazoo Pass, and come down for an attack on Vicksburg in conjunction with his forces south of the fortress.

General L. R. Ross was placed in charge of the campaigns. His initial force included 4,500 soldiers on twenty-two transports, escorted by the six boats, including the *Rattler*, *Chillicothe*, and *DeKalb*, commanded by Lieutenant Commander Watson Smith. An additional 25,000 troops were to be poured in behind the assault forces if they succeeded in clearing a path down the Yazoo.

On February 3 Ross breached the levee opposite Montezuma bend. In a few minutes the rush of water from the Mississippi had made a broad break in the levee and a channel into Moon Lake. They found the channel into Yazoo Pass, but the path was not open. Hundreds of pecan, cypress, and oak trees had been felled in the bed of slough. The Confederates had been prepared for the new attack.

Pemberton, at Grenada, had assigned defense of the western area to General W. W. Loring, who set up headquarters at Greenwood. The Tallahatchie and Yazoo meet just above Greenwood to form the Yazoo, but before the Tallahatchie swings east to meet the Yalobusha it nearly meets itself coming back, passing within less than a hundred yards of the Yazoo flowing west. On this neck of land between the two rivers three miles west of Greenwood, Colonel T. N. Waul began to build Fort Pemberton, a breastwork of earth, logs and cotton bales.

Slaves were conscripted to furnish a good part of the labor in constructing Fort Pemberton, while Loring had an important part of his command out cutting trees to obstruct the approaches to Fort Pemberton. Captain Ben Sturdivant, with Lieutenant W. A. Gillespie of the 20th Mississippi, was detailed to handle a major share of the obstruction work, operating from the steamer *J. M. Sharp.* In a one-mile stretch of Yazoo Pass they managed to cut eighty trees, lying from bank to bank, their branches entwined. A less determined man than General Ross might have turned back when he came upon this barrier, for Ross had nearly three hundred miles of Delta streams to navigate even before he reached Fort Pemberton, and as many river miles after that.

Ross ordered out pioneer parties of five hundred men each. They had to cut the fallen timbers by hand, chopping away the boughs and hauling the trunks out of the stream. In two weeks he had reached the Coldwater. The larger stream made the fallen timber obstructions less practical, but Loring had organized companies of sharpshooters for harassment purposes. Heavy rains made it impossible for them to contact the enemy, and Commander Smith brought his boats into the Tallahatchie without a single casualty among Ross's troops. It became apparent that only Fort Pemberton could stop the expedition.

At the last moment it was decided that an additional barrier in the river would be needed to help the Fort hold the gunboats in check. The steamer *Star of the West* had been brought up from Yazoo City to become the barricade. The ship's brief but eventful career was about to end.

The *Star of the West* was built in San Francisco in 1855, a sidewheel steamer considered among the finest of the day. In December, 1860, Major Anderson refused to surrender

Fort Sumter, in Charleston harbor, to the South Carolina troops after that state had seceded. Anderson could not hold the fort without reinforcements and supplies. President Buchanan chartered the *Star of the West* to carry the relief to Fort Sumter—use of a man-of-war would have announced his purpose in advance.

Captain John McGowan brought the *Star of the West* into Charleston harbor on January 9, 1861, carrying a force of two hundred artillerymen and marines, in addition to supplies for Anderson. The South Carolina troops were not willing to let even a merchant vessel reach Sumter, however. A shot was fired across her bow, and the defenseless *Star of the West* turned back to Washington, after having brought on the first shot fired in the War Between the States.

Once the war began, the *Star of the West* was mustered into Federal service as a transport. Her service was brief. In April, 1861, she was temporarily grounded on a sand bar off the Texas coast. Three Confederate cavalry officers, members of a unit commanded by then Colonel Earl Van Dorn, rowed out and convinced the ship's captain that an artillery piece would blow him out of the water if he did not surrender the ship. The horse cavalry thus scored its only success at sea.

The *Star of the West* was rechristened *St. Phillip* as a Confederate ship, but the name did not stick. She was the *Star of the West* again when evacuated from New Orleans and dispatched up the Yazoo to help supply the newly established navy yard. Her cargo included tons of gold and silver bullion from the New Orleans banks for transshipment to Richmond from Vicksburg.

The *Star of the West's* last commander was a Confederate militiaman from Greenwood, Lieutenant A. A. Stoddard, charged with the mission of scuttling the ship across the Tallahatchie three hundred yards above Fort Pemberton. Her engines and other easily removable parts were left behind at Yazoo City, and the *Star's* last voyage up to Greenwood was under tow from the gunboat *Capitol.* At Greenwood, Lieutenant Stoddard took charge with a crew of soldiers and civilian volunteers. They drilled some 250 holes below the water line of the ship and plugged them with crude oak bungs.

On March 11, with the Federal gunboats expected in sight momentarily, the *Star* was brought into the Tallahatchie above Fort Pemberton and moored broadside against the current, held in place by cables attached to trees on each bank. Stoddard gave the signal and his crew quickly pulled the plugs. As the ship settled into the bed of the river one of the cables broke under the pressure and she shifted diagonally across the stream, but the blockade was still there.

The Federal gunboats came into view, but they did not approach as close as the sunken *Star of the West* before they opened fire, preferring a range of eight hundred yards north of the Fort. The big guns of the fleet and the fort exchanged a few lively rounds that day, but General Ross decided to hold his fire for a full scale assault on the thirteenth.

The flood which had held back the Confederate sharpshooters now became a hindrance instead of a help. The high water made it impossible to land troops for an advance against the Fort. Pemberton was a virtual island in a sea of several miles of rivers. Ross did locate one small island of land to which soldiers manhandled two heavy field pieces, but they were merely supporting fire for the gunboats. The navy had to carry the burden of the attack again on the thirteenth, when the gunboats came back from their retreat at

Shellmound, once more within the range of the fort, but the army had added an eight-inch gun to the land battery.

The Confederate gunners proved their mettle against the naval craft and the land batteries. The artillery duel lasted all day, with Loring's men taking less than a dozen casualties. One of Smith's gunboats was disabled and abandoned, and six Union men were killed and twenty-five wounded.

The last of the battle came on the sixteenth. Commander Smith's report reveals its effects:

> On March 16, after having placed cotton bales before the casements of the boats, we advanced at 11:30 and opened fire with the 8-inch and two 30-pounder Parrott guns on shore as the Chillicothe and De Kalb advanced. In less than 15 minutes the Chillicothe was rendered ineffectual, having been struck with a 60 pound shot, breaking through and causing such elevations and depressions in the plates as to render it impossible to slide back the port covers for the purpose of running out the gun.
>
> The report of a board of assistant surgeons informed you of the necessity of my immediate return to a Northern climate.
>
> I left the command to the next senior officer, Lieutenant-Commander James P. Foster.

The records do not show whether the necessity of Commander Smith's immediate return to a Northern clime was occasioned by the final failure of his gunboats.

(In the summer, when the Tallahatchie is shallow and clear, the favorite sport of Greenwood boys for generations now has been probing the river bottom for parts of the *Star of the West*. Occasional shifts in the mud of the stream bed still turn up pieces of timber which are labeled part of the boat.)

The next day General Ross ordered a retreat back to Yazoo Pass. At the pass Ross met General Isaac F. Quinby, coming to his assistance with a brigade of troops. As the senior, Quinby took command, but he also acted on Ross's suggestion that Fort Pemberton might yet be flooded out. Ross reported that the Rebel fort appeared less than two feet above water. If the flood stage could be raised that much, the Confederates would be driven out, and the expedition could get into the Yazoo. Quinby cut the levee at a new spot, directly across from Helena, Arkansas, six miles above the original breach. The Federal fleet again went down into the Tallahatchie, but a quick inspection by Quinby was enough to convince him that the cause was hopeless. The flotilla began the long retreat back to Vicksburg.

Grant, meanwhile, had received no reports from Ross and did not know whether or not Quinby had made contact. He determined to get into the Yazoo below Fort Pemberton, and he chose Cump Sherman and Admiral Porter to accomplish the mission. Once Sherman was in the Yazoo he could attack Fort Pemberton from the south if that fort still held, and then he could lead the combined Union forces at Fort Snyder on Haynes' Bluff from the north.

The Sherman-Porter expedition was another exercise in torturous navigation of Yazoo tributaries. Steele's Bayou was the most western Yazoo tributary, flowing into the river between Haynes' Bluff and its mouth. Deer Creek flowed into Steele's Bayou some thirty miles to the north by way of Black Bayou. During periods of high water Black Bayou was connected with Rolling Fork, and the Rolling Fork flowed into the Big Sunflower, a major Yazoo tributary that could be counted on to take any kind of river navigation. The Big Sunflower reaches the Yazoo about twenty river miles above Fort Snyder. Grant was sending Sherman and Porter on a two-hundred-mile bayou route to save coming under fire of the Fort Snyder guns.

Sherman called most of the route "jungle"—a good part of the area is still dense swampland ninety years later, but navigation is even more difficult in the areas where the streams have not been cleared for flood-control drainage.

On the sixteenth of March, the day Ross was making his final assault on Fort Pemberton, Sherman took one of his divisions up Steele's Bayou on small steamers, preceded by Porter with five ironclads (including the veteran Yazoo ship *Carondelet)*, four mortars and four tugs. The bayou twisted and turned with sudden, narrow bends, around which the gunboats had to be carefully jockeyed. Occasional willow and cypress trees growing in the very beds of the streams would bring delays of hours and days at a time. Sherman's transports followed at about thirty miles to the rear, taking advantage of the channel clearance, but occasionally having a smokestack or pilothouse brushed away by the thick tangle of branches overhead which the gunboats had passed under.

Near the juncture of Deer Creek and Rolling Fork, at the site of the present town of Rolling Fork, Porter first began to brush with the Confederate force under Brigadier General W. S. Featherston, which had been sent out to stop him. Featherston had to stop the attack here, for the rest of the route was open to easy navigation. The Confederates were being supplied by the packet *Sharp* themselves.

Sherman was without the bothers of Porter at this point

in the expedition and had time to reflect on the countryside, musings which he passed on to his wife:

> The trees are now in full leaf, the black and blue birds sing sweetly, and the mocking bird is frantic with joy. The rose and violet, the beds of verbena and mignonette, planted by fair hands now in exile from their homes occupied by rude barbarians, bloom as fair as though grim war had not torn with violent hands all the vestiges of what a few short months ago were the homes of people as good as ourselves. You may well pray that a good God in his mercy will spare the home of your youth from the tread of an hostile army.

Featherston had a heavy blockade of fallen timbers across the Rolling Fork, and he reinforced the obstruction with fire from his sharpshooters and occasional rounds from his two artillery pieces. Porter's uneasiness is very clear from his general orders:

> Every man and officer must be kept below, ports kept down, and guns loaded with grape and cannister, and only fired when an attempt is made to board us or rush upon us. Have all the ports blockaded with hammocks, after ones let down. Put all hands on half rations. No lights at night. . . . Men to sleep at the guns, everything ready to repel boarders. . . . Every precaution must be taken to defend the vessels to the last, and when we can do no better we will blow them up. . . . Every arrangement must be on hand to fire the ships, tugs, and mortar boats, and the commanders will themselves apply the match, having removed the sick and wounded back to the edge of the woods.

On the night of the nineteenth, Porter notified Sherman that he had been attacked by Featherston's sharpshooters and was in imminent peril. Sherman made his way down Black

Bayou in a canoe until he reached the nearest transport. They tried to push the steamer through Black Bayou, but the progress had been so slow by nightfall on the twentieth that Sherman made the troops debark. They pushed through canebrake and swampland, having to light their way with candles for one period of a mile and a half. When the troops, mostly drawn from the 8th Missouri, reached a cleared plantation site, they were rested until dawn. They marched twenty-one miles before midday on the twenty-first, to stage a proverbial "boys in blue" rescue.

After three days of waiting on the scene, Porter and Sherman decided that they could not penetrate the Rolling Fork, and they returned back down into Steele's Bayou and Grant's headquarters across the Mississippi. It was Grant's last failure. He gave up trying to master the Yazoo, and Vicksburg fell before the next attack.

THE LAST ROUND

Newspapers and political seers were clamoring for action to take Vicksburg, scoring Lincoln for sticking to the indecisive Grant as his commander in the West. Except for a brief period when it seemed that McClernand might steal his command out from under him, Grant had been anything but indecisive. His entire strategy of the assault on Vicksburg was built around the premise that the Yazoo bluffs must be taken before the town could be penetrated, and the bluffs still had priority when his main forces were swung south for the final decisive phase of the campaign.

Once it became apparent that Sherman could not put his troops north of Haynes' Bluff, Grant immediately went to work moving his army south through the Louisiana swamps, to a point twenty miles south of Vicksburg opposite the mouth of the Big Black River. The operation took a month. Sherman successfully camouflaged the river crossing by returning to the scene of his defeat at Fort Snyder, landing troops as if for another assault under the protection of eight gunboats. An entire division was put ashore without a casualty. The feint was enough to cause Pemberton to contract his forces in the Vicksburg area, the first success in the Grant strategy to separate the armies of Johnston and Pemberton. Sherman was quickly ordered back south again.

Pemberton had a force at Vicksburg totaling as much as Grant's 45,000 men south of the city. Joe Johnston had 30,000 men at Jackson. If he and Pemberton had been able to combine forces they might easily have thrown Grant south to New Orleans. The obscure but significant battle of Champion's Hill, on the road between Vicksburg and Jackson, prevented Johnston from joining Pemberton.

The victory also sprung Sherman loose to move northwest between Haynes' Bluff and Vicksburg. Panicked at the suddenness with which Grant had blocked the outlets from Vicksburg, Pemberton had set up no plans for the garrison of the Yazoo fortress to resist any attack except from the Yazoo. As Sherman approached, the Fort which had been held so successfully was hastily abandoned, without a pause to destroy either supplies or ammunition. Had Fort Snyder been ordered to resist, a path for the relief of Vicksburg would still have been left open on the Yazoo, now for the first time in Federal hands. Pemberton was caught in his trap, and Grant could take the prize at his leisure, now that his right wing was secure on the Yazoo bluffs.

On the day when the Union troops took over Haynes' Bluff, Grant and Sherman made a sentimental journey to the fortress, pushing their horses up with the point of the advancing column. They were a little too confident in the reports that the Confederates had not remained behind to resist and had to dodge skirmishers' bullets. Grant drew rein on the bluff high above the muddy river overlooking the log-strewn swamp through which Sherman's corps had attempted to advance on December 29. The hazards of the attack were now obvious. Six months before Grant had promised to meet Sherman here on Christmas day. The delay was not long, as military delays go.

"Until this moment I never thought your expedition a success; I never could see the end clearly till now," Sherman admitted to Grant. "But this is a campaign; this is a success if we never take the town. This is one of the greatest campaigns in history."

Sherman rarely waxed so enthusiastic about anything. He had not gained favor as Grant's most trusted general by officious deference to the boss. Grant lighted another cigar without comment and returned to issue the orders for the next day's assault on the trenches of Vicksburg.

In the beleaguered city, Pennsylvania-born General Pemberton had already accepted the inevitability of defeat at this same hour. "Just thirty years ago I began my military career by receiving an appointment to a cadetship at the United States Military Academy," he told a companion, "and today—the same date—my career is ended in disaster and disgrace."

The Federal troops could not just walk into Vicksburg, however. They learned that when full scale assaults were made and turned back on both the nineteenth and twenty-second. Heavy casualties made it evident that a prudent siege would be the wisest way to take the town. Grant had ordered a supply road built from the Yazoo on the day he visited Haynes' Bluff. His troops could be fed without foraging over the countryside, while the Vicksburg garrison was starved into submission.

In the Federal command posts, the monotony of the weary siege was broken by the culmination of the feud between Grant and McClernand, when at last some grounds were uncovered to send the latter packing back to Illinois. Technically, he was charged with publishing an order without clearing it with his commander.

The brass could find amusement in the grim feuds of their commanders, but the siege was fearful monotony for the troops on both sides. During the night they could watch the fireworks of the endless bombardment of the town, but during the day there was enough silence to shout back and forth greetings and taunts between the opposing lines.

Dewberries began to ripen in the gullies between the trenches, and impromptu truces were arranged so that men in grey and blue could come out and pick the berries. Fresh fruit was the best cure for diarrhea.

During one of the berry-picking sprees, a Union officer saw one of his privates toss a shovel into an enemy trench. He came back and explained that "one of them grey devils hit me with a clod." Meetings between kinsmen on opposing sides were arranged—there were a number of relatives in opposing units drawn from Missouri.

After several days of desultory pot-shooting, a private from a Wisconsin regiment suddenly threw down his rifle and announced "I'm goin' out to shake hands with them Rebs."

Calling out as he left the trench, the firing stopped, and a Johnny Reb came out to meet him. As the two shook hands, their respective squads followed. In a few minutes hundreds of men milled between the trenches, swapping tobacco for coffee, complaining about the weather and the errors of their generals. Pocket knives were traded, and tintypes of wives and sweethearts were compared. One Confederate moved away from the group and sat alone and dejected on a log. "I still want to see my Ma," they heard him say.

Union officers had watched the spontaneous demonstration, but eventually one of them became aware of his rank and responsibilities. He clambered out of his trench and cursed the truant soldiers impartially, ordering them back to their respective rifle pits. Within a few minutes, after the last man was back behind a pit, the sharpshooters began to trade shots again with the men with whom they had been trading stories.

With Lee's army roaming Maryland and Pennsylvania, the government in Washington was eager for a victory to report. Grant's army was built up to 75,000 by reinforcements from the north and south when the news came that he had closed the ring around Vicksburg. The additional reinforcements decided Joe Johnston against any last-minute attack from the rear.

The Vicksburg newspaper, printed on wallpaper, kept up a stiff front for the besieged civil and military population as late as July 2: "The great Ulysses has expressed his intention of celebrating the Fourth of July in Vicksburg by a grand dinner. . . . Ulysses must get into the city before he dines in it. The way to cook a rabbit is to first catch the rabbit."

It was bravado more than bravery, at this last minute

of heroic resistance. Mule and rat meat were a standard bill of fare among the population living in caves dug in the face of the hills as the only protection against the constant bombardment. Pemberton had resolved earlier conflicting orders from Johnston and President Davis by postponing a decision. It was long since too late to try to fight his way out, with the deteriorating morale and physique of his hungry army.

July 3 was spent in arranging surrender terms after a flag of truce had been dispatched. Grant stuck to unconditional surrender, but the prisoners were paroled. At 10 A.M. on July 4 the Federal troops occupied the city. It was to be a long time before Mississippi celebrated another Fourth.

9

War on the Plantation

The various aspects of the Vicksburg campaign constituted virtually the entire action of the War Between the States in the Yazoo basin. After Vicksburg, Sherman swept eastward across the central part of the state, but no large Federal garrisons were felt necessary for the interior of the state during the remaining years of the war. Cavalry raids in northeast Mississippi sometimes reached as far as the Tallahatchie and Yocona bottoms, but the action was usually remote and little felt, except for the burning of Oxford in 1864.

The Yazoo farmland had its day on the battle scene before the Federal troops turned to the system of living off the land in their advances across the South. Grant first began to forage for food and horses when he retreated north after Holly Springs. If he had known beforehand how unnecessary it was to be completely dependent upon a supply base, Holly Springs might not have been of such value in the defense of Vicksburg. In the long run, the retreat did convince Grant that there was little risk in crossing the river at Grand Gulf, with no immediate supply base, and marching inland with plans to live off the land.

Sherman, the very symbol of the ravages of war in the

Confederacy, set a completely different example in the Delta during his abortive expedition up Deer Creek behind Porter's gunboats. The relatively idle troops raided near-by farms for food, and some of them carried away animals and plantation equipment. Sherman ordered everything returned to the planters. He wrote General Steele, a division commander:

> War at best is barbarism, but to involve all—children, women, old and helpless—is more than can be justified. Our men will become absolutely lawless unless they can be checked. . . . I always feel that the stores necessary for a family should be spared and I think it injures our men to allow them to plunder indiscriminately.

The battle scene shifted, but the people at home in the Yazoo country felt the trials of war even more. Foraging parties from both armies made regular visits, impressing livestock, grain, cotton and anything else in the hands of a farmer that might be useful to the command. Deserters from both armies drifted into the inaccessible bayou country and carried on organized robbery and pillage under the guise of impressment for the fighting forces.

Impressments by the Confederates, and sometimes by the Federal troops, were supposed to be paid for in cash or warrants against the government, usually the latter. Exercising its full right as a state, the Mississippi legislature in December, 1863, authorized impressments by state agents without concurrence by Confederate authority. This had the effect of further inflating the existing prices. Usually the state agents won when they were bidding for supplies in direct competition with the Confederate agents, for they were not restricted by the price ceilings established by the Richmond commissary department.

Although food for the farmers at home was usually plentiful, shortages of various items normally brought in from other areas made life considerably more primitive. Game was more abundant than ever in the forest, with a shortage of the normal supply of hunters. Before the end of the first year of the war the supply of salt practically vanished. With no salt to cure hams, the pork supply rapidly increased. More and more hogs were turned loose in the swamps to shift for themselves. Slaves and landowners both would catch them as they were needed to fatten. Various substitutes for salt were used in attempts to cure the meat—ashes and lime was the most common, but nothing seemed to work satisfactorily.

The salt famine led to such acute complaining that Governor Pettus arranged for an exchange of cotton for salt brought through the blockade. Planters flocked to Jackson to get a share of the supplies, only to find that Confederate authorities had stopped the exchange as trading with the enemy. Another plan was devised whereby French and English agents would provide the salt, but Richmond said this was a polite subterfuge for direct trade with occupied New Orleans. The enforcement powers of Richmond were limited, however, and a trickle of salt came through the lines until 1864, when the Federal occupation commanders clamped a tighter lid on contraband trade themselves. The salt was beginning to reach the Confederate army.

The hardships of war and occupation were not without compensations, one planter wrote his brother, in the return to the simple life. "Our civilized conventionalities must once more give place to primitive necessities and simplicities," he sad. "Every man, woman, girl, and boy must again do his own building, cooking, washing, and mending, soap-making, dish-cleaning, and all the little and big decencies of sober primitive life."

In the summer of 1862 a detachment of Confederate partisan rangers summarily executed eight members of a party they caught on the west bank of the Yazoo, returning from trading with Federal boats. This period at the beginning of the Vicksburg campaign was about the only time stringent efforts were made to prevent trading with the enemy in the Delta country, however. All the proof needed of the extent of trade was the flood of greenbacks which came into the Delta in 1863. From that time on, enemy currency was more valuable than Confederate.

Memphis became a boom town after its capture by Federal troops, as Yankee merchants established forward headquarters here for trade behind the Confederate lines. Cotton was what the Northern business interests wanted, and they managed to get it in fairly good quantity, playing havoc with the plans of Jefferson Davis to gain support for the Confederacy in Europe by withholding all cotton from the market. One legend is that Grant first conceived of the Yazoo Pass route from the Mississippi to the Yazoo when he was told that it was the principal route for contraband being carried to Friars Point, on the Mississippi, for shipment north to Memphis. After Vicksburg fell, the Yazoo became the principal outlet for all trade with the enemy in north Mississippi. Plantations which had been deserted in 1862 were back in limited production in 1864, with a ready market for the cotton down the river. A Confederate scout reported that as many as five hundred bales of cotton were passing through

Vicksburg in a single day in March of 1864—obviously cotton produced in earlier years and stored against the time the market would be restored.

The Federal purchasing agents for cotton were usually women, and they came out regularly from Vicksburg to contract for purchases. When planters were reluctant to trade, quite often Federal troops would appear in a few days and seize all available farm produce. As soon as it became clear that Union forays followed the appearance of the cotton agents, cotton sales came quicker and with less haggling.

The Confederate Congress moved in 1863 to keep cotton out of enemy hands by establishing a produce loan. J. D. DeBow, the editor of the famed *DeBow's Review*, was agent for the Congress in Mississippi, and his report after a trip up the Yazoo reveals the troubles better than anything still of record.

DeBow found cotton in a deplorable condition. Large plantations were abandoned, and cotton, both ginned and fresh picked, had been left in sheds, destroyed by cattle and vandals, stolen by runaway slaves or white thieves "with whom the country abounds." Cotton was being carried off in wholesale quantities "trading it to the Yankees, or hiding it in inaccessible places—they do it at night, or even in broad daylight, as there is little law in the country." Even some of those planters who were selling cotton to the Confederate government would "sell it again to the Yankees . . . on the pretext that they will replace it from the next crop." Confederate soldiers were "implicated in their guilt." General demoralization prevailed throughout almost the entire section, DeBow declared, reaching to every class of citizen.

"Trade with the enemy is universal. The temptations to fraud are overwhelming. Even our own agents are often charged with complicity. It is impossible to stop depredations."

There were approximately ten thousand bales of government cotton still in Mississippi in this district, DeBow reported, and because of the continuing increase in price, its value to the government would be sufficient reimbursement for the heavy losses in cotton destroyed and stolen. He estimated that the Confederate army had destroyed thirty-five

thousand bales, the Federal forces ten thousand, and five thousand had been accidentally destroyed by civilians.

DeBow was irritated most by the "wildest and most irrational manner" in which cotton had been burned and destroyed by the Confederate army. Tens of thousands of bales had been destroyed which the enemy could never have reached. Often the soldiers would burn the ginhouse, as well as the cotton bales. Other cotton in the path of the enemy had been turned out of the warehouses and then not burned. He cited individual examples of military carelessness in the field. More than one thousand three hundred bales had been collected and stored at Goodman for protection, and then more than half of it was destroyed by incendiaries among the civilian population. Six thousand bales had been used in the construction of Fort Pemberton. DeBow arrived on the scene after the Fort had been abandoned and began to rebale the cotton. A roaming cavalry outfit showed up and burned it all. General Pemberton had advised DeBow to remove all the cotton from the Yazoo basin and to store it in east central Mississippi between Morton and Meridian. DeBow noted with satisfaction that if he had followed this suggestion the cotton would have been gathered neatly in the direct path of Sherman's sweep across the state.

The planters in the area were not without their own hardships. Teams were needed to produce the new crops, and "horses, mules, and wagons had been taken by both armies. To impress other supplies would intensify the discontent and increase the demoralization." DeBow could not secure his own transportation through the area by payment of Confederate currency. He had to barter for it by offering sugar and salt.

The cotton agent eventually relented and himself proposed a form of trade behind the lines. He told the Richmond committee that he had means of sending agents to Memphis or New Orleans to "transact with foreigners or their consuls" for the sale of cotton for gold or sterling. DeBow's agents would be "citizens of high character." Such a trade policy was almost universally backed in the area as "the true one for the government," and he had "almost official" assurances from the Federal commanders that they would not interfere.

Trade with the enemy brought no more death penalties after the summer of 1862. It became so respectable that the Mississippi legislature narrowly defeated a bill to repeal the state ban against it. As one local observer put it, the times were "too utilitarian for such Quixotic patriotism as some preached but few practiced."

When Federal garrisons moved in, the housing of Union soldiers in a town was occasionally long enough to break down some of the normal barriers, which divided the invading army from the civil population. In 1864, at Holly Springs, a Union officer was quartered in the home of a family which included a marriageable daughter. One of the items in the parlor was a "Memory Book" in which the daughter had placed tintypes and sentiments inscribed by a long series of beaux when they departed for the wars. Besides the pictures and signatures, there were notations like "killed at Shiloh, April, 1862." When the Union officer had departed, this additional inscription was found in the memory book:

To Miss Clemmie

'Tis certain, Miss Clemmie, whether Fed or Confed,
In the plain course of nature, you're destined to wed.
Some "Lord of Creation" will lovingly kneel,
And pour forth his tender and fervent appeal,
If the Feds and Confeds will cease this vain strife,
And leave a man living to make you his wife.

Fed

Despite the absence of so many menfolk from home and the confusion and chaos which existed all over the area, the slaves remained remarkably peaceful all through the war. When Mr. Lincoln's army first came they deserted the plantations to flock to the rivers, as if some homing instinct told them where the Union army would be. Many never returned to the farm, but as many more did, or never left at all. There was generally more assurance of food and shelter on the plantation than in the Freedman's Camps established to handle the newly freed slaves who crowded behind the Yankee army.

Masters and mistresses were not betrayed, but the Negroes were a useful source of information for the Federal raiders. In June, 1864, a detachment of Marines from Vicksburg were ordered to destroy the Confederate steamship *H. D. Mears*, reported hidden in Indian Bayou, on the Sunflower River (at the present site of the town of Indianola). The Marines came north by way of the Mississippi, debarked at Greenville, and went east across Deer Creek. At Bogue Phalia they had to stop to construct a ferry to get across the narrow but deep stream. Across the Bogue they found plantation country where Yankee soldiers had never been before. While the troops were feeding their horses and appropriating chicken, hams, and bacon, plus wagons to take them back to their ship, Captain Isaac Newell was called to the quarters of General Alfred W. Ellet, commanding. Let Newell tell the rest of the story:

> I was called to the General's tent, about midnight, and found the General cross-questioning a grinning darkey, who had been brought in from the picket line. The darkey reported two lots of Confederate officers, some four miles away, in two different houses. In the first house, he said, there were only four or five officers fast asleep, while in the second house there were some 12 or 15 having a dance, with

the house full of southern ladies. The General said: "Captain, we want those fellows. You will take your company, or so much of it as you deem necessary, and go after them. Your force will go on foot, taking only one horseman in case you get into trouble and want reinforcements in haste. You will take this darkey with you as a guide, and if you are ambushed or led into any trap, be sure and kill him the first thing you do. Make your capture quietly, and if possible without firing a gun. We are in a strange country, and I don't know what may be in here. If you succeed, throw out pickets, and stay there until daylight, and then come in."

It was one of the darkest nights I ever saw, or seemed to me so. Much of the road lay through, or along the edge of, a heavy timber. I sent Lieutenant Guildemeister with six men as advance guard, with the darkey as a guide, and between this advance and the company I intervened another small squad. The first house, as I learned from the darkey, was just beyond a bridge, and surrounded by a high rail fence. Accordingly, I told Lieutenant Guildemeister to go to the bridge, and there wait until I came up with the company. Reaching the bridge, I gave instructions to the men to cross over in perfect silence, and then line up along the fence, and when I gave a certain signal all, without regard to any particular order, were to go over the fence and surround the house as quickly as possible, permitting no one to escape. With the house surrounded I went to the front door, knocked and demanded admittance. The door was not opened, and no response to my demand was made, but I heard a shuffling that sounded very much like men getting hold of their sabres and pistols, so I kicked the door open, and lo, and behold! here were five rebel officers fixing for fight. I ordered them to throw down their arms, and told them my men were all round the house, and they surrendered.

It was a mile or more to the next house, where the dance was going on. Putting the captured men in the rear under guard, we went on. It was a hot summer night. The house brilliantly illuminated, was filled with men and women, and the windows all up. The dance had ceased for a time, because the fiddler had broken one of his strings (made of silk because catgut could not be obtained) and was repairing it. We tarried just a minute to take in the scene, and then, at the signal, the men went pell mell over the fence and around the house. The rebel officers within heard us coming, and rushed to the hall, where they had stacked up their arms. I ran up to the door and cried out: "My men are all around this house; think of your women. If you fire a shot you take the responsibility. Lay down your arms and retire from the hall!" One of the rebels said: "Boys, I guess we are in for it." I ordered in a guard and took possession of the arms. As I remember it was thirteen men with their horses and arms captured here, making eighteen in all. I asked the darkey, who guided us, how he knew that we were in the neighborhood, while the white people seemed not to know anything of our presence, and he said, "Wy Marster, I knowed when you uns crossed de fust hosses ovah de bayou." "Well," I asked, "but how did you know?" "Wall I des got er 'spatch ovah de grapevine telegraf." "Well," I said again, "How many of the darkeys round here knew we were coming?" And he replied, "Wy all de darkeys in de country know it." They had closely kept the secret of our advance.

The isolated Delta swamp country became a haven for deserters or draft dodgers, even though the region as a whole had one of the better records for loyalty to military service of the Confederacy. There were complaints, as always, about the inequities of the calls to army service. A group of Yazoo City citizens petitioned the Governor to call the legislature and conscript more soldiers in November, 1862. "Our thinned camps are every where confronted by strong armies of abolitionists while our towns are full of *non*combatants . . . our railroad trains are crowded by those who should be soldiers.

The time has come for all to fight." A similar petition was received from Carroll County, but most of the complaints about shirking service came from elsewhere in the state.

In 1864, with the prospects of victory gone, the complaints of the patriots grew more bitter. "I am truly sorry to know that the counties of Leake, Attala, Neshoba, and Winston and other counties are now and have been for the last six months emptying their filthy, base, disloyal, deserting, stealing, murdering population into Yazoo," one man wrote in a letter passed on to Governor Clark. They ought to be hanged, the writer, Circuit Judge R. S. Hudson said. The objective of this "base and worthless set" was to "avoid our army, plunder, steal, and be with the Yankees." Judge Hudson submitted a list of names among the disloyal, and suggested that the Governor "dispose of them without gloves."

Typical of the group Hudson listed was Joel Williams and his sons and sons-in-law. Except for the father, who was too old, they were all "deserters for the 2nd and 3rd time," and they had "danced in joy over the downfall of Vicksburg." There were hundreds more settled in the out-of-the-way hills and swamps, "abolitionist spies, deserters, liars, thieves, murderers, and everything foul and damnable."

Hudson's protests produced some action in Jackson. Governor Clark had a squad of cavalry sent into Yazoo County to check the names given him by the judge. Using the list, Sergeant Hightower, the troop commander, arrested ten deserters. "Finding sufficient evidence of the treason and other crimes of the party, he ordered them shot," and then crossed the Yazoo into the western part of the county in pursuit of another band of deserters reportedly in the Atchafalaya swamp area.

The arrests and executions did not drive the deserter bands out of Yazoo County, although Hudson pointed out that most of them had come into the area from other counties. They turned their abuses on Judge Hudson as the man responsible for the raids, burned one of his crops, and threatened to bushwhack him. The Judge was especially aroused at the civil officials who took no action against the lawlessness. Many of the officeholders were too busy speculating in various trading schemes with the enemy, he charged. When Hudson secured the indictment of officials who were allowing the deserters to run free, the disloyal groups were bold enough to enter their own candidates in some of the county elections of 1864. At one backwoods precinct on election day, twenty-seven deserters marched out of the woods armed with guns, pistols, and bowie knives, cast their ballots, and departed.

The terrorism spread to loyal men. Soldiers home on furlough were afraid to go back to the army and leave their families defenseless. Others listened to unhappy wives and decided to stay at home. Judge Hudson was especially vehement against the disloyal women—"the women are far worse then the men and are responsible for most of it."

In the state as a whole the desertion problem was so great that several proclamations of amnesty were offered to bring the AWOLS back into service. An entire regiment of state troops was furloughed home in the hopes that individual members could persuade backsliders to return to the colors. Demoralization among the civil population increased as the war dragged on, and it was always immediately felt among the soldiers.

In the summer of 1864 a Federal detachment occupied Yazoo City for a few weeks, and a staff officer confided some of his tribulations to his diary: "I could tell a strange tale of the destitution and privation among the people here. They rush around like mad, and try all kinds of schemes with the commissaries and sutlers. The great cry is 'flour—flour! Only let us have flour.' Women beg, urge, plead, and it has been my duty to listen to these appeals and decide what must be done."

Among the majority of the citizens in the Yazoo, loyalty to the Confederacy persisted down to the bitter end, long after hope for the cause of secession appeared hopeless. The daughter of a Delta planter told how the news of final defeat came to her home:

> I had stolen off with a book to my favorite retreat under a big oak when I saw Pa and Brother Tom talking to Ma on the back porch. Both men looked so silent and stern and Pa handed Ma a telegram to read. I could see by their faces that something DREADFUL had happened and ran to the porch where the telegram was being handed around for all the family to read. Yes, it was all over. Lee had surrendered at Appomattox! Like a thunderbolt it fell on us. We were stunned. I remember feeling astonishment that we were not dead. Buddy was playing with his dog out on the steps; it seemed a desecration. Why, our Country was dead . . . !

10

The Woman's War

On many Yazoo plantations the entire management and operation during the war was left in the hands of the planter's wife and the family slaves. The much-maligned "twenty Negro" law, which allowed farmers who owned that many slaves to escape conscription, was taken advantage of by some, but Captain Benjamin Grubb Humphreys was typical of the larger group who took up the burden of war despite dependents and large farming operations at home.

Humphreys was the grandson of a Revolutionary officer from Virginia who had settled in the old Natchez district on the Bayou Pierre after the Revolution.

Like another young Mississippian of the same period, Jefferson Davis, an appointment to West Point was secured for young Ben, where his classmates included Joseph E. Johnston and a Virginian named Robert E. Lee. During Christmas holidays Ben, with a number of other cadets from distant states stranded at the Point because the trip home and back was too long, enlivened their period of boredom with a rock-throwing contest, using the door of the commandant's quarters as their target. They were all promptly brought before the commandant. Most of them pleaded that they had had too much Christmas cheer and escaped dismissal because the disciplinary board believed the enforced stay at school over the holidays was an extenuating circumstance. Young Ben feared the wrath of his father back in Mississippi more than that of the United States Army, however, and told the board that he had been cold sober when he threw the rocks. So Cadet Humphreys was expelled, along with thirty-eight other members of the class.

Ben Humphreys came home to take over the management of his father's holdings. He became a leader in community affairs, and was elected to the State Senate in 1839, the same year he married sixteen-year-old Mildred Maury, whose Virginia cousins included Matthew Fontaine Maury. They lived at the Hermitage, the old family home for which Andrew Jackson had named his own mansion, and extended their land holdings to include other plantations on the Big Black. But the ancestral acres were fast losing their fertility, and, following several crop failures, Senator Humphreys took a trip by river steamer up into the Yazoo wilderness to look for a new farming opportunity in the Choctaw cession.

He found the place on Roebuck Lake, a stretch of old channel the river had discarded a few miles west of Greenwood, in the then Sunflower County. Bringing a group of slaves up from his plantations during the winter, when boats could pass from the Yazoo into Roebuck, he began the long task of clearing farmland from the wilderness. Old Claiborne County friends became interested in the project, and the first of them began to acquire land in the area two years later.

Humphreys had established a permanent winter residence, "Lucknow," in Claiborne County, and did not bring his family to the wilderness until he completed the building of a substantial home in 1857, christened "Itta Bena," the Choctaw words for "Home in the Woods." The walls of Itta Bena were made from logs felled in clearing the plantation, plastered and painted. It was the earliest substantial residence built in the wild Yazoo country and was the center of activity for the plantation's many hundred acres. (Today Itta Bena is a thriving small town, commonly pronounced "Etta" Bena, because of some early corruption. The main portion of the original Humphreys home is still in use as a residence.)

Although his views in opposition to secession were well known, former Cadet Humphreys, the community leader from the time settlers first came into the area, organized a company of militia when it became apparent that the break with the Union was coming. The troops drilled on the Yazoo banks at Sheppardtown, named themselves the Sunflower Guards, and elected Humphreys as their captain. Captain Humphreys made preparation for war. His wife Mildred was ready to take over the operation of the plantation. Like many of the farsighted Southerners, Humphreys had years earlier made provisions for his slaves to be freed and provided for upon his death.

The Sunflower Guards were called into service immediately upon the outbreak of hostilities. They took the steamer *Dew Drop* down to Vicksburg and were shipped with other Mississippians to Virginia, where they were merged into the 21st Mississippi Regiment. The 21st saw action in all the major Virginia campaigns through four years of war. Captain Humphreys of the Sunflower Guards eventually became the Colonel commanding the regiment and was made a Brigadier General after Gettysburg.

Back at Itta Bena, Mildred Humphreys, his wife, took

on new responsibilities on a relatively greater scale. The transition from plantation wife and mother to farm operator at Itta Bena tells in good part the whole story of the Yazoo country in wartime.

Plantation mistresses as well as one-mule-farm wives had to learn to make ersatz coffee from parched corn, okra, or dried sweet potatoes; tea from raspberry leaves; soda from sour milk; vinegar from leaves; and corncob lye. Candles could be made by adding quicklime to hog or mutton suet, with a few pear leaves to harden the mixture; ink and dyes were normally from berries and tree bark; and horse collars could even be plaited out of corn shucks.

Most of the ladies were able to stretch out their ante bellum clothing, with varieties of additions and transformations, for their own personal wear, for social activity was at a minimum all the war through. Hats of home-knitted wool and plaited fern leaves were an exception. Looms and spinning wheels were brought back into service, as well as the craftsmen who could make the scarce items. The planter's wife, or an outside teacher, if she didn't know how herself, trained slave women in spinning and weaving, which was the first time many of the Negroes had ever done anything save field work. Even if the plantation wife was fortunate enough to have enough leftover finery to last out the war, homespun garments had to be provided for the soldiers and the slaves.

In 1862 Mrs. Humphreys raised a highly successful corn crop at Itta Bena, and her gristmill supplied a great deal of the surrounding area with meal. In February, 1863, she wrote her husband in Virginia a long letter which best tells the story of Yazoo women at war. (An early transcription of the letter deleted many names for local consumption. There was no need to rub old sores. The "Tom" of the letter is a Negro servant. "Uncle Gus" is Colonel Humphreys's body servant, who was sent home regularly to carry letters and messages back and forth.)

My Dear Husband—

Barnes was sitting by me reading night before last when Tom came running in and said, "Uncle Gus has come." I asked where you were. Tom said, "He's coming, too." We all flew out of the hall to the south gallery and then to the north, calling Gus and asking where you were, but receiving no answer and not meeting you. I ran across the yard to the loom house, and there met Gus, who told me that he had left you in Virginia. I came back into the house and found the children on the gallery, dancing and singing, "My Pa's come! My Pa's come!"

It was a happy note to be so suddenly changed. You can easily imagine our disappointment. The next morning it was the first thing that David thought about, and he commenced crying because his Pa had not come. Gus led me to believe that you would certainly get a furlough, until I read your letter, which crushed our hopes of seeing you at home soon. If two field officers are required to be with the regiment, there is no prospect of your coming, as the Twenty-first has but two.

Gus looks well; says he does not know whether he is to remain at home or return to Virginia. Suppose Captain G . . . knows, of course.

You are so comfortably quartered in Fredericksburg that the Yankees will have to fight harder than they did before to drive you to the woods. Suspect you have heard by this time that a Yankee fleet has passed through the Yazoo pass and the Coldwater, perhaps by this time in the Tallahatchie. The fleet consists of five gunboats and seven transports. Gen. Pemberton is making an effort to prevent their descent into the Yazoo. Fortifications are being made and troops concentrated at different points on the Tallahatchie river very near Beck's Ferry. You know the two rivers are only a few hundred yards apart there. Twenty-five hundred troops are there. The Negroes from this region of the country are doing the work; eleven from this place are there.

You see the Yankees are right in the midst of us, when we thought ourselves very secure. Persons living on the river are moving their properties into the woods and other places they think secure against invasion. Mr. . . . and . . . are building shanties in the depths of the woods on the island to be used in case they have to run. I do not think the Yankees will leave their boats far if they should succeed in passing our battery. They may, if successful this trip, bring in reinforcements and devastate the whole country. If the batteries fail in checking their progress, they will certainly provoke them to devilish deeds. If they come to Roebuck Lake they will be sure to find me at home. I think my presence may check them in the destruction of property. I will have the meat, hogs, and cattle taken to the woods and put in houses or pens and watched day and night.

Some of the Negroes might tell where it was, and the labor would be lost. I will therefore make the men go to the woods, too. I feel no fear or uneasiness about the approach of the Yankees, and hope they may be soon at the bottom of the river. I think they will then find themselves right where Banks says his army has gone. You know where that is, I suppose. We are all afraid our own soldiers will eat us out of house and home while they are camped so near. They certainly ought to be fed as long as there is food to be had. Starvation is a sorrowful object to look at, even a prospective view of it.

I want you to write me whether you sold any cattle to . . . and what sort of claim he has to oxen and other cattle on the island. Perry says he knows of but 35 head of cattle on the island now, and the last beef I sent him to kill, . . . told him they were his and he must not kill any more of them. If they are mine, I do not like to have my rights disputed. The stock of cattle on this place has been much diminished; many have been used for food, many more have been stolen. Do not fail to write me fully on the beef question.

I think Lee wears out a team of oxen and then turns them out and picks up a fresh one, and when the old ones are brought here and got in good order, he tells . . . they are his, and have been taken away from him. . . . perhaps knows as little about them as I do. Mr. . . . is at Port Hudson; is in good health and fat, he writes me. He was sent to . . . county in January to get some deserters or truants or delinquents. I do not know what name they give to such folks in that county of chivalric democrats.

The middle of January Mr. Foote started . . .'s Negroes from High Hills to this county. Their teams were poor and broken when they started, from bad management probably, as they had corn for sale. After traveling two weeks through rain, snow and mud, they camped fifteen miles south of Moore's Ferry. Many of the Negroes were sick, out of food, and teams completely broken down. Foote came to me for assistance. He said . . . told him if they broke down, no matter where, not to go back to Claiborne, but to come here for aid. I sent Wash with his wagon and Tom with his. After an absence of more than two weeks they returned with all of the Negroes. Most of the six yoke oxen they started with are dead; both of their wagons left on the road in consequence. My own teams were so much worsted by the trip I would not send back after the wagons and contents, which were left near Lexington in charge of Steven. By next Monday Wash and teams will have to start for them. He will not agree to trust his oxen to Steve, as he killed all his own. The wagon belonging to . . . was left below the Big Black, and will have to be left there. Mr. . . . can send for it at his leisure.

The Negroes have been working on their houses ever since their arrival. They will not have time to prepare ground for much of the crop. If they had been sent in November, when they ought to have been, . . . would have been spared all this loss and trouble, and could have been ready to put in a full crop. I would Mr. . . . had to pay for all the losses. This is the manner in which he attends to the property of his wards.

Mrs. . . . writes from a little town in Claiborne Parish, La., graphic descriptions of their dangers, anxieties, fears, and troubles, and winds up by saying she thinks those who stay at home have more trouble and suffer more than those who go to war. Mr. . . . , in addition to all other troubles, has some office, (is a sinecure, of course), which I suppose does not more than pay his family's expenses. Mrs. . . . , like a great many others, persuades herself that all of her troubles and her husband's are for their oppressed and bleeding country. Mr. . . . is at home, and likely to remain there. It would not be safe for anyone to tell his wife he ought to go to war. Someone said in her presence that she thought every man who voted for secession ought to be in the army, and she soon found herself in hot water; she got out by saying she was not alluding to her husband, that she did not know how he voted.

Work is progressing satisfactorily. Two hundred acres will be planted in cotton according to your directions. The old plows were considered sufficient to make this crop, so no new ones were made. We have had rain, snow and sleet almost incessantly since Christmas, which have impeded farming operations very much, made the roads about as bad as they ever got to be, and all the streams very high. Another great overflow is expected by everyone.

I had the first piece of cloth taken out of the loom yesterday, and hope to have the Negroes clothed in homespun next summer. Mr. . . . has not made any shoes for me yet. He was applied to for them in October, November, and December, and failing to get them, I wrote to inquire of him if he would let me have hides corresponding in number and weight to those I sent him, to which he replied in the negative, saying he had shoes made for me, but as I failed to apply for them, he had let others have them. He will get his dues when the Yankees hang him.

I have seven hides at a tan yard in Yazoo county, deposited there last summer, thinking the proprietor an honest man. I will send all I have there in a few more weeks and expect to get shoes enough in exchange for next winter. He pays three pairs of shoes for a hide. I have sold 3,200 bushels of corn. It has not all been taken off yet. It was bought by the neighbors. I have received a thousand dollars only yet, but the rest will be paid soon. I must reserve 4,000 bushels and I think there are not more than 2,500 or 3,000 bushels now for sale, as I think an abundance ought to be reserved for home use. We have a great many young hogs, and it will take a large quantity of corn to keep them in good condition. There are 350 acres of new ground on the island ready for the plow. The logs are cut all over the place, if not rolled. None of the log heaps have burned much in consequence of wet weather. Everything is ready for starting the plows when the ground is dry enough.

Cotton will be planted in gin field and in the new ground on this side of the lake.

So many cattle have been lost on the island that I have concluded to have a fence made across the Narrows, and at the water falls have a log and rail fence made down to the low water mark. What do you think of it? It will take about 1200 rails, most of which are now made.

You have no idea what close watching and nursing it takes to prevent the hogs and cattle from being stolen and devoured. I'm going to have a lot enclosed with oak pickets ten feet high, two by eight inches, fastened to rails with wooden pins, wedged inside. In this lot I will have the hogs driven every evening and locked up. Tucker can call them and drive them to any place without any trouble. There are about 250 of them. They grow and fatten every day.

There are some few cases of sickness among the Negroes all the time, from colds generally. Bob has been quite sick with pneumonia, but is well now. Briant, Baxter, Wallace and Simon are at Yazoo City at work on fortifications. I do not know how long they will be gone. I was very sorry to see them go, but think it was my duty to send them. This government has taken off fifteen of our best hands, which will interfere very much with the crop. Maunel, Willis, and Allen are with those at Beck's Ferry.

Barnes and Lily came to me and told me to give their best love to you before they went to bed. Dave Smith is asleep, too.

A few nights since, after Lily said her prayers, she said, "Mama, when I ask God to bless everybody, am I praying for the Yankees? For I wish old Lincoln was dead." I must confess I could not tell her she must pray for these enemies.

You and Jim must wipe your mouths and kiss each other for me. Give my love to him and ask which he likes the best—picket duty or wood chopping.

May God bless and preserve you both, is my prayer,—

Yours affectionately,
Mildred.

The war was to come much closer to her. A few weeks after Mildred Humphreys wrote this letter she was supplying the garrison at Fort Pemberton with one hundred bushels of meal a day. She gave all her coffee, several barrels of this rare commodity. Cotton bales, representing the entire crop from Itta Bena, were manhandled seven miles overland by her slaves to the site of the Fort, where they formed the foundation of the breastworks. The *Dew Drop*, the steamer which had taken her husband and his company to Vicksburg, was brought up to the pass between Roebuck Lake and the river and sunk as obstructions to bar Yankee gunboats.

The end of the war brought her further trials instead of

relief. General Humphreys was chosen Governor in 1865, and sought to bring Mississippi back into the Union under the original reconstruction plan enunciated by Lincoln and Johnson. Humphreys had been a Whig before the war, always opposed to the secessionist firebrands. He did not seek the governorship, but was drafted for the job by old army comrades who wanted a moderate man to lead the state during the perilous period ahead. It was not until after his election that Humphreys received the Presidential pardon necessary before ex-Confederate officers could accept civil office.

Carl Schurz, the liberal Republican leader, was one of the special commissioners appointed to check into the operation of the Presidential reconstruction plans. Schurz inspected Mississippi after approximately a year of Governor Humphreys's administration, and reported "the people had reorganized their government and were yielding obedience to the laws and Constitution of the United States with more willingness and greater promptitude than could reasonably be expected under the circumstances; they evinced a laudable desire to renew their allegiance to the government, and to repair the devastation of war by a prompt and cheerful return to peaceful pursuits. The demoralizing effects of the war had occasioned disorders in some cases, but they were generally local in character, and rapidly disappeared as the authority of the civil law was extended and sustained."

The Reconstruction Congress paid little heed to the Schurz report. In June, 1868, Major General Irwin McDowell, the Military Governor of Mississippi, ordered Humphreys to vacate his office and turn it over to Major General Adelbert Ames. Humphreys refused to vacate his post voluntarily, but the removal was accomplished by military force. McDowell sent a detail of Negro troops to the executive mansion to enforce the order.

Mildred Humphreys, given the responsibility of holding the mansion, had her family possessions packed in advance, but to no avail. When the troops arrived she marched out of the house between files of soldiers armed with fixed bayonets. Ignoring the gathered Federal officers and onlookers, she walked straight ahead, disdaining to glance to the right or the left, to the carriage which would start her on the long journey back to Itta Bena.

11

Picket Line of Freedom

With the end of the war for Southern independence, the Yankees rode the steamers up the river from Vicksburg. Often they were on hand with the last straggling, returning Confederates.

But they came not as carpetbaggers—they were the adventurous postwar G.I.'s of the War of '61, reluctant to turn from the power and prestige of Army officer rank back to the small-town obscurity that had seemed their fate in prewar years. The idle Southern plantations were a fine opportunity for aggressive young men with initiative; the Southern owners obviously could not handle them under the new system of free labor. Many of the impoverished landowners were actively seeking buyers or renters for their lands from among Union soldiers who had high hopes and perhaps a little capital saved during the war years by their families at home.

It was a time of confusion among the remnants of the postwar plantation owners. Most of them had only land, with no prospect of capital, and no idea of a system for labor now that there were no slaves. Many, like the family of Jefferson Davis, decided not to get into the struggle. The Davis family plantation, a few miles south of the mouth of the Yazoo, was sold to Isaiah Montgomery, a newly freed black man who had once been the slave of the President of the Confederacy.

Despite the confusion among the old landholders, the big river ports like Vicksburg were full of bustle in 1865. The productive land of the region had been idle too long, and energies spent in war were being turned toward peaceful commercial pursuits.

Discharged Union officers mingled with officers still in uniform, who had asked for garrison duty in the South as a means of looking into postwar opportunities. The cloud of Reconstruction had not yet risen, and the conqueror and conquered mingled in general friendliness.

Two of these fortune seekers from the North were Albert and Charles Morgan, late a brevet lieutenant colonel and a captain, respectively, of the Union army, by the original route of a Wisconsin volunteer regiment. Albert was only twenty-three, and conspicuously aware of his record of advancement from private to field officer after he entered the army from his college preparatory course at Oberlin.

The Morgan brothers listened to the propositions of the various land agents and finally decided to rent on a three-year lease Tokeba Plantation, some four or five hundred acres on the Yazoo a few miles north of Yazoo City. They closed the deal with the owners after visiting in their home.

Young Albert's comments upon the family library indicate his years at Oberlin, or in the Union army, had given him a good indoctrination in abolitionist sentiment. They also indicate a lack of realism that was to spell his failure as a farmer and his tribulations as a politician.

> . . . The literature of the family library was quite ancient. Dryden, Scott, Shakespeare, Pope, Swift, Byron, and Johnson were to be found there. Also Voltaire and Paine, Adams, Madison and Jefferson were there; but Calhoun, Webster, Clay and Benton appeared to be the favorites. . . . Of course, I looked in vain for a scrap from such advanced thinkers as Gerrit Smith, Garrison, Phillips, Sumner, Lowell or Whittier, or even Seward or Emerson.

Although Charles was ten years his senior, Albert was the dominant figure in the partnership. Neither was particularly successful as a farmer at Tokeba. During the first year the cotton crop was not very good, and only a small portion of the land was put into cultivation because of a scarcity of labor. The Morgan brothers paid the "freedmen" (as they referred to the Negroes) $15 per month, but they had trouble in keeping an adequate number of workers available during the periods of heavy farm work, or keeping the number on the payroll down when the need for labor slackened.

There would have been no income from Tokeba in 1866, if their Wisconsin experiences had not suggested a logging operation. They put a sawmill to work and soon were able to pay a portion of their rent with the returns, as timber was thick in the uncultivated swamplands of the plantation.

Early in 1867 the rising waters of the river put most of their timber land under water, and the sawmill operation had to be temporarily shut down. Charles voiced the universal complaint of farmers along the river, and suggested a system of levees to protect the lands. (Nearly a century later, the levees are still not there, and the Yazoo still haunts the farms of the area.)

In the evening before dinner, Albert and Charles formed the habit of ascending to the cupola of the Tokeba plantation house. In the winter, with the trees bare of leaves, their view carried for miles over the flat land of the rich Yazoo Valley to the north and west.

Pointing to the expanse of fertile land, Charles would exclaim:

"Yonder lies an empire surpassing India, surpassing the Nile; unequaled."

But the floods which made the Delta land fertile joined in the seeming conspiracy of trouble in the path of the plantation operation of the Morgan brothers.

The conflicts between the theories of Gerrit Smith on the handling of freedmen and the reality of making a crop on Tokeba were too much for the Wisconsin farmboys. Only a few skilled farmworkers were left among the Negroes available for hire at Tokeba, and all of them needed close and experienced supervision, which Albert could not supply. After the Yazoo had flooded the land, the late cotton crop of 1867 was attacked by army worms, killing the cotton plants by stripping them of leaves.

The native Southern owners of Tokeba had not received all their rent for the previous year, and they stepped in with a writ of attachment on the property to secure back payments. This action made it necessary to shut down the sawmill, the one source of revenue. Morgan fought back with a writ of replevin, but eventually all of his holdings on the farm were ordered sold to help satisfy the debt.

The brothers had taken a loss of nearly fifty thousand dollars, but there still remained the debt to the Negro farm hands, few of whom had been paid their back wages. According to Albert, all of the freedmen forgave him the debt upon his surrender of the property.

Charles moved away from Yazoo County, but there was still opportunity in the South for former Union soldiers in the field of law and politics, to which Albert Morgan now turned. He began reading law while still on the farm and was admitted to practice law in 1867. The bar examiners were good Republicans and also migrant politicians, late of the Union army.

There were nineteen ex-Federal soldiers in Yazoo County, most of them engaged in farming. Albert decided to band most of them together to furnish the leadership for the Freedmen in writing Mississippi's Reconstruction constitution. Running on a ticket with a Negro blacksmith and another ex-Union officer, he was elected as a delegate to the convention.

Following the constitutional convention in 1867, the Reconstructionists began to take hold in Mississippi politics. The old-line Democrats were too weak to enter a ticket in the 1869 election, but they attempted to throw some support to one of the Republican factions which nominated as a gubernatorial candidate Lewis Dent, a brother-in-law of President Grant who had married a Mississippian. Another faction nominated James L. Alcorn, a native Mississippian who had been a leader in Delta politics before the war. Prominent on the Alcorn ticket was James Lynch, a Vicksburg Negro nominated for Secretary of State.

From the beginning, Albert Morgan cast his lot with the Alcorn faction and became a candidate for State Senator. The bitterness of the campaign was reflected in some doggerel verse printed in the *Yazoo Banner:*

Old Morgan came to the Southern land
Old Morgan came to the Southern land
Old Morgan came to the Southern land
With a little carpet-bag in his hand.

(*chorus*)

If you belong to the Ku Klux Klan
Here's my heart and here's my hand.
If you belong to the Ku Klux Klan
We're marching for a home!

Old Morgan thought he would get bigger
Old Morgan thought he would get bigger
Old Morgan thought he would get bigger
By running a sawmill with a nigger.

The crop it failed and the sawmill busted
The crop it failed and the sawmill busted
The crop it failed and the sawmill busted
And the nigger got very badly wusted.

The campaign in Yazoo County was more than a song. As in most of the other areas of Mississippi, the contest was to secure the allegiance of the mass of freedmen, most of them illiterate and primarily interested in the help or handouts which could be secured from the local office of the Freedmen's Bureau. A scheduled debate and political meeting at Dover's Crossroads turned into a gunfight, with one white man killed and a Negro badly wounded. Blood was to continue to flow in Yazoo County until Albert Morgan departed, but he was easily elected State Senator through the solid vote of the ex-slaves.

Albert, as a veteran of the constitutional convention, was one of the leaders of the Reconstruction Senate. He won some cautious words of praise from the Vicksburg *Herald*, a leading Democratic organ, which observed that he was a "prominent radical in this state—a man whom we can respect as a man—one whom we know, at least believe, to be as near conscientious in his political convictions as any sane man, who is a member of the radical party, can be."

The young abolitionist had occasion to put his theories on race relationships to a personal test during his service at Jackson. He met Carolyn Victoria Highgate, a native of Syracuse, New York, who had come to Mississippi as a missionary and teacher among the freedmen. Carrie was a quadroon whose father had been a mulatto freedman. The best evidence of her beauty has been given to us in the recollections of conservative Democratic leaders in the fight for overthrow of the Radical Republican rule, who often referred to the "beauteous Miss Carrie Highgate."

Young Senator Morgan had quickly established himself as a leader in the legislature. The Radical Republican group had no excess of brilliant leadership, and there was plenty of room for men at the top. The old-line conservatives respected him, too, for he demonstrated at once that he would not blindly accept the Radical leadership. When Albert began to consider marriage with Carrie Highgate, he had to face the reality of an end to further political advancement, even among the Radical Republicans.

There was another obstacle. The state law forbade miscegenetic marriages. Senator Morgan introduced a bill for repeal of the ban, and it passed with little comment at the time.

Building the new sea wall at Vicksburg, Mississippi. September, 1953.

Carrie and Albert were married on August 3, 1870. A few days after they returned to Yazoo City, which was Albert's official residence now, a large group of the colored women of the town came to visit Mrs. Morgan. The dark jezebels were bedecked in fashionable, but faded and flashy, clothing which made their calling obvious. The former schoolteacher quickly and politely got rid of the guests and told her husband that the visit had been prompted by a group of white women of the town, who had also supplied the discarded finery worn by the callers.

They would not be back, Carrie said, because "there is no social equality except among equals."

Yazoo City had changed considerably since Albert Morgan first came up the river on the steamer *Martin Walt* in 1865. There were forty-one liquor stores and saloons in a town of less than two thousand five hundred people, and the regular mercantile establishments all kept a supply of liquor on hand to give to their customers. Carpetbaggers, white and black, as distinguished from those who originally came in as farmers like the Morgans, had flocked in. Brawls and violence were the order of the day, in both politics and business.

The income of a State Senator and lawyer without clients was limited, even though he also took over the job of president of the County Board of Supervisors. Albert became a candidate for sheriff, the prize political job of the county, in the elections of 1873. He was the Radical Republican candidate, and his platform was temperance and law and order.

The law and order candidate won at the polls by an overwhelming majority, apparently getting even some of the votes of conservative white people. A man named Hilliard, another former Union soldier, was the defeated candidate.

Although Hilliard had first gone into office through appointment by the governor, upon Morgan's recommendation, he determined that the law and order candidate would not take office without violence. For several days he refused to yield possession of his office.

Albert, his new deputies and other assorted followers, finally took over the office by force. Hilliard returned with a group of his henchmen and was killed in the ensuing gun battle. The reports of the fight over the county gave the Morgan enemies a rallying point. Warrants were sworn out charging Sheriff Morgan with murder and presented to the chancellor for the district, a conservative holdover opposed to the Radical Republicans. The chancellor ordered Albert arrested and jailed, refused him bail, and appointed a Democrat as acting sheriff.

As word of the fight and Morgan's arrest spread out over the county, freedmen began to flock into town to defend their leader. They concentrated in some empty lots across the street from the jail, and Yazoo City began to take on the look of a divided armed camp. Down in the business district, groups of native whites were making plans "to clear the town of niggers."

The Democratic sheriff proved his mettle as a peace officer. No spark was allowed to light the flame between the two camps, and in a few days Albert was transferred for safekeeping to Jackson, the state capital. From Jackson, the arm of the Reconstruction Governor, General Adelbert Ames, made itself felt. Albert was released from jail and restored to his office. A grand jury investigated and refused to return an indictment against him.

There was outward peace for a few months, but the

battle for the sheriff's office and the resulting show of force by the Negro freedmen had marked the end of efforts to reach a peaceful solution to the Reconstruction conflict in Yazoo County. The Negroes who had gathered across the street from the county jail, armed and apparently ready to fight, were an ominous sign to the bulk of the white population of Yazoo County, more fearsome than the Federal bayonets available to Governor Ames.

Three military companies were organized and the members began to drill secretly in isolated parts of the county. Most of the leaders were Confederate veterans, but the members were generally boys who had been too young to wear the grey uniform. They took the following oath:

> We, the undersigned citizens of Yazoo County, Mississippi, hereby pledge our word and honor that we will support and protect each other and our families through this present condition of excitement and danger; and that we further pledge our honor to send our aid and assistance to any part of the State that may be suffering from such danger; and we firmly declare that we do not assemble in arms for the purpose of violating any of the laws of the United States or of the State of Mississippi, but for the purpose of protecting our homes from the hands of ruthless bands of armed men that have been reported to us as assembling in this county and adjoining counties, contrary to the laws of the United States and the State of Mississippi.

It soon became obvious that the approaching state general election of 1875 would likely be settled by both bullets and ballots. During the summer of that year the following letter was published in Democratic newspapers throughout

Mississippi, after having reportedly been intercepted in Alabama:

> Yazoo City, July 21, 1875
>
> Mr. Thompson My Dear
> friend, it is with Pleasure I write you this to inform u of some Politocal newse. They are preparing for the Election very fast & also for riots. They is a little place just 15 miles Below hear by the name of Starttia the colored people are buyin amonnition in Yazoo City. The colored folks have got 1600 Army guns All prepared for Bussness. I wish you were out hear you must Be sure and come out this fall if you please. Be sure and send me all the newse and other Papers and that Rosgam off of the Pine Trees. I am still your wife.
>
> Benjamin Franklin Eddin

Both the authenticity and the accuracy of Benjamin Franklin Eddin's letter are subject to question, but there is no question about the reaction to the letter. The white military companies were spurred to new activity. A caucus of Republican members of the legislature was held at Jackson, and Morgan told of the military companies of his county. Similar reports came from other strongholds of Republican officeholders, but the Negro legislators rejected the suggestion that the governor organize and arm a loyal militia to meet the threat. They did not want to further arouse racial antagonisms, and they saw no victory in a blood bath. Perhaps the President, General Grant, would save the day by ordering in new garrisons of Federal troops, but the Negro leaders believed that nothing else would quench the bonfire.

Yazoo County came to a boil on September 1, at a rally of the Yazoo City Republican Club. The Republicans present were all colored men, with the exception of Morgan and three or four "native white Republican" officeholders.

The meeting attracted some of the bolder elements among the local Democrats. With the leaders on both sides armed, there was no long delay in provoking a gun battle in the midst of Sheriff Morgan's speech. The first casualty was an ex-Confederate captain named Mitchell, who had turned Republican officeholder. Morgan escaped through the exchange of shots, but it was his last public appearance in Yazoo County. Indicted for attempted murder in Yazoo County, he spent the rest of the campaign period in Jackson and Holly Springs,* Mississippi, where he had sent Carrie and the children for safekeeping earlier in the summer.

The Democratic Party was restored to power in Mississippi in the election of 1875, and Albert Morgan and his family joined the list of Republican "refugees" who flocked to Washington for largesse from the Republican administration after having been turned out of office in the South. The Negro Senator from Mississippi, Blanche K. Bruce, secured his appointment as a clerk in the pension office, with the help of Angus Cameron of Wisconsin.

In 1884, Albert published the story of his experiences in Mississippi in a long, but readable, volume entitled *Yazoo; or On the Picket Line of Freedom in the South.* The author states that he intended it to be one of the campaign documents of 1884, but he had to publish it himself, from his sixteen hundred dollar pension-office salary.

Perhaps the Democrats thought this contribution to the

* Seventy-five years later Holly Springs was a place of peace and refuge during a period of racial tensions. During a race riot in Illinois in 1951, a Negro physician sent his wife and family to Holly Springs for safekeeping.

bloody-shirt side of the Cleveland-Blaine campaign worthy of some attention, however, for they relieved Albert Morgan of his pension-office job a few months after coming into power in 1885.

The pension-office files provide the only record remaining of the quixotic Morgan and his bride Carrie. With a family of four daughters and two sons, they moved to Lawrence, Kansas, in 1886, where Albert engaged in several business ventures over the state, all of which apparently failed. Silver mining in Colorado seemed to offer an opportunity, and Albert went to that state in 1890, while Carrie remained in Topeka with the four daughters. The girls were all beauties, and, as one of them later told the story to the pension office:

> We went on the stage, and Mama was our chaperon . . . then she lived with Angela—as she has with one of us, ever since—mostly with Angela. . . . Mama was so convinced that it was her mission to be with Angela and help her in giving the world her beautiful verses. . . . For 27 years her home was in New York City. She never remarried. . . . Mother became a mental healer, Christian Science lecturer and dramatic reader. Those are her professions, but she is wonderfully equipped in all phases of literature, art, and religion. . . .

Angela's career took her to England, and Carrie was living there with her when she applied for a widow's pension in 1923.

Albert Morgan lived in Colorado for thirty-two years, prospecting for gold and silver and operating a "School for Money" in Denver. Apparently, his one source of income was the small Civil War pension. From the record there is no indication that he ever saw Carrie again or had any other dreams of the wealth which might have been in Tokeba. The bright shaft of the young idealist, who rewrote the statute books to marry Carrie, who wanted to remold an entire regional culture in a day, had been blunted beyond repair in the Reconstruction politics of Yazoo County and the confining pressures of raising a family as a pension-office clerk.

12

Cotton Takes Its Last Kingdom

Before the War Between the States a few plantations in the tradition of the Southern seaboard, or the Natchez area of Mississippi, had been carved out of the Indian cession wilderness, but in the main the Yazoo region was still too much a frontier to gain any other appellation before 1861.

The end of the war left most of the planters with their land and little else. The freeing of the slaves had wiped out a major portion of their capital investment. Most of them were the owners of worthless Confederate bonds and currency. Small farmers were in the same fix. They had the land and nothing else, even if their losses had not been so great. Cotton was the only money crop they knew, and the world shortage of cotton occasioned by the war sparked their natural inclination to go back to its production full scale.

The slaves who had manned the farms and plantations were given token help by the government through the Freedmen's Bureau, but their only opportunity to earn a living was through the one skill that most of them possessed—plowing, chopping and picking cotton. It was inevitable that the Negroes would return to the farm, even without the forty acres and a mule of which many vainly dreamed after fraudulent promises.

The production of cotton requires land and labor as essential items, but credit is just as essential when both the landowners and laborers are penniless. The improvised credit system, established to meet the first necessities following the end of the war, soon gained the strength of custom and law. It firmly established the shackles of a cotton economy on the Yazoo basin, more strongly than it did in any other area of the South. The lack of an adequate agricultural credit system strengthened the hold of all the undesirable features of the plantation system on the cotton economy of the region, with the resulting erosion of both land and people.

The people were not suffering from hunger at the end of the war, but the breakdown of the farming system made the actual threat imminent. Even where the farms had been kept in operation to raise food or to trade through the enemy lines, large areas had usually gone to waste because of shortages of labor and livestock. Plows and wagons were as scarce as mules, with no means to buy new ones. The cavalryman fortunate enough to have been paroled with his horse or mule upon surrender was the envy of his neighbor without even this basic farm equipment.

For the former slaves of the plantation, the vision of freedom had been synonymous with idleness in their dreams of when the great day arrived. Few of the free white men they had known in the days of bondage had been required to engage in physical labor, and the newly freed Negroes imagined that freedom would provide a seemingly effortless existence for them, too. For most of them, the illusion was completely shattered in the cold and hungry winter of 1865-1866. They flocked back to the farms seeking any kind of work that would provide food and shelter, but still they were far from the training and the self-discipline needed to work for any goal beyond the day's reward.

The hardships of the first postwar winter in Mississippi were accentuated by the casualties of war among the white farmers. A newspaper correspondent reported attending a meeting of three hundred men, at which at least one hundred were minus either an arm or a leg as tokens of Civil War surgery. Before the Reconstruction government took power in 1866, one fifth of the state revenues for the year were spent to supply Confederate veterans with artificial limbs. More than one third of the Mississippians in Confederate service were killed in action or died of wounds or disease, and more than half of those who returned are estimated to have brought back some war disability. The number of breadwinners for the farm had been sharply cut back for a generation.

The returned soldiers were not malcontents. Release from the army, even in the despair of defeat, was enough for most of them. One ex-Johnny Reb explained that if he could just get along until dewberries were ripe he could make out then until fruit and roasting ears came in; when these gave out he had a good possum dog and could pull through the remainder of the year. The man with a dog and powder for his rifle could be assured of a constant supply of game meat, for hunting had been greatly neglected during the war all up and down the rivers. Quail and doves were plentiful, and deer and bear roamed the swamps and river bottoms. Wolves had gone unmolested so long that a pack attacked a man on the Coldwater in the winter of 1866.

Yankee greenbacks had become the only solid currency in the Yazoo country in the latter days of the war, but there was little around for even the man who had credit. The only

Southern currency still with any substantial value was a Mississippi state script, supported by cotton which the state had bought, called "cotton money." Some of the Southern railroads which continued in existence after the war had issued script, which, too, maintained a dubious value. In April 1866, an auction at Hernando of some of this "Southern money" with a face value of $11,088.50 brought in a total of $1,663.50 in Yankee greenbacks, gold and silver.

The sharecropper, or tenant, system did not begin to develop until there had been detailed experimentation with various schemes for farming with wage hands. Most of the farmers who used this system in 1866 offered to pay a year's wages of one hundred and fifty dollars for a full (adult male) hand, payable at the end of the year, together with doctor's bills. Two hundred pounds of pork distributed over the year and a peck of meal each week would be furnished free. Housing was always understood to be part of the bargain.

The Freedmen's Bureau, the government agency established for the announced purpose of helping the Negroes make the adjustments between slavery and freedom, took the lead in urging the former slaves to accept farmwork contracts. The Bureau proposed, however, that the contracts should be for fifteen dollars per month, payable monthly. The Bureau also urged the Negroes to secure contract provisions for a supply of flour and molasses in addition to the meal and pork, together with the use of a plot of ground for each family, and Saturday afternoon off for the cultivation of vegetables on the garden plot.

Most of the planters able to finance the arrangement adopted most of the wage system proposals of the Bureau, for labor was scarce in 1866 and the Bureau had obtained something of the status of an employment agency. Moving into the wage system was not simple. When the plantation grapevine indicated that the planter might be short of money, the hands would become suspicious and watchful, cautious as to the quality of the flour and meal furnished them, severely critical of the pork, and perfect almanacs as to the approach of payday. The Saturday-afternoon-off system became an accepted part of the plantation practice, but from the first it was more commonly used for going to town than for hoeing gardens.

The plantation commissary began to make its appearance during the wage-hand period. Planters found it was easier to get credit for food and clothing to be supplied the hands than for cash wage payments. Many farmers were forced to begin to pay wages in part in scrip or "tickets" good only at the commissary, and the bookkeeper was on his way to becoming a more and more important part of each farming operation. Occasionally scrip was issued in town for the stores which advanced the credit.

Credit was available only to those planters who were lucky. One ex-Confederate general went north to his native Pennsylvania to make arrangements to finance his 1866 crop. He managed to borrow eight thousand dollars, under terms which required payment of four thousand eight hundred dollars in interest within the year. Few planters had connections in Pennsylvania, and most crops were made in good part on capital scavenged from personal possessions and family heirlooms.

Before the war, credit for cotton production had been no problem. The demand for cotton had always been so certain that moneylenders competed spiritedly for the planter's business. There was simply no such capital available in the South after 1865, even though the cotton demand still held. The normal sources of credit were wiped out by the war, and solvent banks outside the South were slow to come into an untried field when other opportunities were readily available throughout the rest of the country.

It was inevitable that conditions would make for a farming system under which the laborer agreed to work for the privilege of living on the land and getting a share of the product, while the landowner supervised the labor and marketed the cotton. No bank would lend the laborer money to live through the year; his only source of credit had to be the landlord. The existing banks could not finance the landlords, and so the merchant entered the picture as a banker, by furnishing food and equipment for the production of a cotton crop. In many districts there were no banks worthy of the name. Planters of means and substance could secure loans only at an interest rate averaging above 20 per cent, and small farmers often had to pay as much as 100 per cent. The merchant advanced credit at this extreme interest rate, and the planter passed a good portion of the rate on to the tenant for whom he had borrowed the money to supply through the year.

The tenant-credit system entrapped all who used it. A merchant-factor of the period was asked if the 100 per cent interest rate he was collecting was not exorbitant.

"It's a large profit," he replied, "but it is profits on the books, not in the pocket."

Crop failures, improper equipment and management, plus lackadaisical labor, all combined to sink the Yazoo cotton country further down into the mire of the tenant-credit system. The evils of the credit system intensified the weaknesses of those who lived by it. The vast majority of the Negro tenants were illiterate, with no ability to comprehend the ordinary principles of a commercial transaction. It was too easy to assume that the end of the season would wipe the ledger clean. If it did not, a man could always move on to a new landlord. The landlord, appalled at the paper profit his creditor made off him, began too often to think in terms of the profits on paper which could be made at the expense of the tenant who had no comprehension of his accounts. Without losing his land, the farmer could not walk away from his debt in the manner of the tenant, so he began to seek restrictive laws to hold the tenant to his obligation beyond the year when his crop "didn't pay out."

The wage-hand system rarely occurred again on the plantation after 1866. Credit requirements began to establish firmly the tenant-credit system, and for the plantation it became the sharecropper system, as distinguished from other forms of tenancy. Under the "share" system, the tenant or "cropper" would agree to furnish the labor of himself and his family while the planter furnished the land, seed, housing for the family, usually the farm implements and animals used, and provided the merchant with security for any supplies advanced during the crop year. The cropper's share of cotton and other crops produced would normally be from one fourth to one third and sometimes as high as one half, depending upon the individual arrangement and the mules and implements which he furnished for the operation.

Merchants who often began as country storekeepers entered the plantation finance picture when the banks and old-line cotton factors disappeared in the postwar days. The merchant furnished the various supplies necessary to make the crop, including staple food and clothing for the tenant, collecting with the sale of cotton at the end of the year. Sometimes the merchants furnished both planter and cropper direct from his own shelves. This was the system most prevalent in the hill areas, where the crossroads storekeeper could handle both the furnish and the bookkeeping for the big and little farmer. In the Delta area the plantations gradually shifted to a furnish system supplied by large "wholesale" firms located at river towns like Vicksburg, Yazoo City and Greenwood. The river-town merchants would ship the supplies to the plantation commissaries, and the planter would sell them in turn on credit to his tenants. River merchants at Vicksburg built up vast trading areas over the entire Delta, whereever boats could navigate the Yazoo and its tributaries. They owned and operated their own river packets or else held part interest in shipping lines.

The merchant protected his investment of "furnish" for a planter through a crop-lien system. The farmer gave the merchant a mortgage on his growing, or to be planted, crop as security. Part of the agreement was usually for the pledged crop to be put on the market and sold by the merchant. Additional security was made available in the form of mortgages on farm animals and equipment and eventually upon the land itself. The lien system was financial bailing wire for the cotton economy, and orthodox merchants and bankers from the outside still have trouble in comprehending a system under which an unplanted crop can be pledged for a loan of unstipulated amount which will be advanced in pork, plowpoints, calico and hay instead of money.

The procedure for enforcing the lien system was written into law by the Mississippi legislature in February 1867, in a bill entitled "An Act for Encouraging Agriculture." The law also authorized a provision in the contract which could make the merchants' accounts incontestable. Northern farmers secured credit through a simple mortgage, but this system was impossible in Mississippi, a merchant explained, because "merchants can't furnish goods on property that would be an incumbrance to own. Unless they can get some guarantee of receiving crops for supplies, the supplies will remain in New Orleans." The price of making a crop was considered of more value than the land.

It was not possible to turn to banks for a simpler adjustment of the problem, because the banks were largely nonexistent at the beginning of Reconstruction. The National Banking Act of 1862 was written with two thirds of the agricultural states out of the Union, and the banks, first revived in the South under its terms, did not have the financial structure designed to make agricultural credit easier. The dividends from the war between industrial and agricultural economies began to come in early.

The farmer had been starving for want of credit and had welcomed the Mississippi lien law as the means of relief, but his contentment under the domination of the supply merchant did not last long. One Delta planter termed it "extortion, genteel swindling, legitimate larceny . . . a plan of dealing which held the landowner as an insignificant factor. . . . . The negro and poor white men of the country make nothing; the factors and the country merchant are the divinities presiding over the agricultural interests . . . the landlords are out in the cold ignored even by their tenants; lands are being worn out."

The farmers' grievances against the supply merchant

were numerous. Once the lien had been signed, the farmer had no choice but to buy from the lien holder. No competing merchant would sell him a yard of calico on credit, for the only acceptable security, his crop, was already assigned. By the same token, there was no way of acquiring cash to make outside purchases. There was traditionally a two-price system for everything the farmer bought—cash and credit. At one time, for instance, the cash price of corn was seventy-five cents a bushel while planters were feeding their mules at the $1.25 credit price. On most items a cash price was never set, for there were no buyers. In addition to the credit markup, there was a standard interest rate charged against the amount owed. The total cost of supplies at the end of the crop year was often more than 100 per cent above what a running cash price would have been through the year, or even under normal credit arrangements.

Even with his crop harvested, the planter still suffered new tribulations. After paying for the production of his crop in the highest market, he usually would have to sell it in the lowest, for the merchant usually settled with the farmer at the peak of the marketing season, when prices were normally below the average for the season. The farmer who did not "pay out" to his supply merchant when his crop was turned in was bound by the terms of the lien to renew it for his next crop with the same merchant.

> When one of these mortgages has been recorded against the southern farmer [wrote a contemporary observer] he has usually passed into a state of helpless peonage. . . . With the surrender of this evidence of indebtedness he has also surrendered his freedom of action and his industrial autonomy. From this time until he has paid the last dollar of his

> indebtedness, he is subject to the constant oversight and direction of the merchant. Every mouthful of food he purchases, every implement that he requires on the farm, his mules, cattle, the clothing for himself and family, the fertilizers for his land, must all be bought of the merchant who holds the crop lien, and in such amounts as the latter is willing to allow.

A song, sung to the tune of the top Confederate patriotic melody, "Bonnie Blue Flag," became popular among some of the same housewives who had sung the popular Confederate patriotic melody:

My husband came from town last night
As sad as a man could be,
His wagon empty, cotton gone,
And not a dime had he.
Hurrah! Hurrah!
'Tis queer, I do declare!
We make the clothes for all the world,
But few we have to wear.

The supply merchant was roundly damned by all cotton producers, from the man with five acres in cultivation to the one with five thousand, but hindsight today makes him no more a villain than most of the other participants in the economic life of the cotton country. The merchant, too, paid outrageous interest to the financiers further up the economic ladder, and in general he was merely another way station on the belt-line which drained agricultural wealth from the hinterlands to the centers of credit in the North and East. Floods and crop failures were part of his regular risks, just as much as the erratic price of cotton and the natural fallacies of farmers. One successful merchant confided that he had "to make enough every third year to carry me over for the two out of three when I go busted."

Yazoo planters joined most other farmers over Mississippi in making the lien law a major political issue for some twenty years after it was enacted, but they were too busy opening new ground to join in great numbers with the farmers' political revolt which began to spread over the South around 1880. Eventually most of the planters took up part of the system of the supply merchants in distributing supplies through their own commissaries. In the Delta the man who was lucky enough to own land outside the range of the more frequent flood stages usually turned in a good enough average return to the merchant that competition for his business would bring better terms. His commissary made the regular markup, but the favorable rates he received from the wholesale house as a large buyer made his prices comparable with any other credit store.

The Negro tenant had to confine his purchases to the plantation store, and commissaries began to stock goods besides the regulation staples—meat, meal and molasses. Canned goods like sardines and mackerel, and stick candy, rings and pins exercised an irresistible charm. The opportunity to make an extra profit out of the plantation store, both by liberal credit policies and heavy stocks of flashy luxuries, often was more costly than profitable. The sharecropper's debt was no good unless he made a crop big enough for him to "pay out" with his share. Crop failures, poor management and lazy labor all could prove doubly costly to the landowner when he was too generous with the credit advanced through the commissary.

Fancy bookkeeping became part of the system of the unscrupulous farm operator and has given rise to many an item of plantation lore, such as the order to the bookkeeper: "Charge up another barrel of flour to all the tenants. I had another bad time at the poker game last night, and I can't have my wife and children paying for it." Or the story at settling time, when the shrewd Negro is shown the books and told that they exactly balance. "Then I don't owe you nuthin', Cap'm?" "No, you don't owe me a cent." "An' you don't owe me nuthin'?" "You saw the books." "Then what's I gonna do with them two bales I ain't done hauled in yet?" "Well, what do you know! Just look at that! Here's two pages stuck together. I'll have to add this whole account up again."

The temptation for sharp practice was great for a farmer dealing largely with illiterates and often beset by similar sharp practices on the part of the people who furnished him. Offsetting this was the competition for capable labor which always existed. The Negro tenant might not be able to read the entries on the ledger, or add the columns of figures, or know what price his cotton brought on the market, but he had an unfailing sense of the degree of fairness and justice in the general conduct of the farming operation by the planter. The farm with satisfied labor inevitably had a better production record, other things being equal. The Negro's methods of security might be devious, but he always had them.

The greatest evil of the tenant-credit system was its destruction of the land. The improvised credit system which put the land back into production was the basic cause of the farm practices which turned rich acres into gullies and washed countless tons of irreplaceable topsoil down into the Yazoo and eventually to the ocean. Inertia and ignorance had a part in establishing the one-crop system, but the fundamental cause was the lack of farm credit. Contributing factors like the lack of markets, absence of marketing and storage facilities, and undeveloped transportation facilities could be traced back to the over-all poverty of the region. The farmer who was willing to buck all of these obstacles was still faced with the one insuperable barrier—no one would advance him money to make anything but a cotton crop.

The effects of erosion were first felt in the hill country along the Tallahatchie and Yalobusha. Repeated planting of nothing but cotton for cash and corn for the mules drained more and more life out of the soil each year. The ignorant new freedmen, less supervised as tenants than they had been as slaves, persisted in plowing up and down hill, to speed the topsoil on its way. The farm owners themselves rarely had any better knowledge of conservation practices, even though most of them were the sons of men who had come west when the soil began to wear out on the seaboard. In debt most of the time, his only salvation was to hope for a year when he hit the lucky combination of a good crop and a good price. Merchants were naturally interested first in a cash-crop return, and, besides, they made an extra profit selling food to farmers who did not raise it. As the riches of the soil were washed down into the river, or eaten up by the hungry cotton, the farmer plowed deeper and deeper to make up for the loss in production and thus accelerated the vicious cycle.

Great gaping red gullies, the "grand canyons of Mississippi," began to appear all up and down the Yazoo bluffs, from the old Confederate fort at Vicksburg north to the site of Van Dorn's victory at Holly Springs. These red scars of erosion are often washed more than fifty feet deep, by the same processes that made the great canyons of the West.

These were made in a generation instead of a thousand years, however. In sunrise or sunset their red clay banks become dull gold walls. Grotesquely shaped masses of sandstone on the floors offer other miniature patterns of wild mountain country. The broken farmer has no opportunity to transform this imagery into beauty. Deserted homesteads began to be visible along the roads with the same frequency as during the war. The dogtrot cabin, and sometimes the stately mansion, would usually burn down before it rotted away, and after a few years an occasional patch of chinaberry trees might be the only symbol of the old habitation. The eroding lands, plus the other handicaps of cotton farming, marked the end of the great ante bellum plantations of the bluff hills country like the one which Greenwood LeFlore had built as an inland empire around his capitol at Malmaison.

The farm still owned in 1880 by the family which had owned it in 1860 became the exception rather than the rule. One observer estimated that more than two thirds of the farms had changed hands, with still others reduced in size. In the Delta, erosion did not have the same immediate effect. The flat land could not wash away into gullies, and it was considerably richer to begin with. Sheet erosion began to take its gradual, deadly toll, however, and even the operators in the American Nile began to see production averages fall, unless there was generous use of fertilizer. Floods and other risk factors in cotton farming worked to make landowner mortality almost as great as in the hills of the upper part of the basin. But there were always new owners ready to come into the Delta, and both planters and sharecroppers streamed in from the gullied land they had worn out in fifty years to try their luck with the new hazards of the swamplands.

The plantation system, established on the basis of urgent expediency after the end of the War Between the States, gradually began to eliminate itself through its own shortcomings in the hill country of the upper basin, and along the bluff hills to the South. With the exception of a few bottomland areas, the self-defeating combination of costly credit, erratic crops and prices, and erosion effectively abolished the storied planter from the area. Unfortunately, when the land changed hands, the evils which had bankrupted the plantation owner continued to beset those who worked the land. The unending battle against farm poverty took its toll in people. The withering land could not support all the children it spawned.

"Gone to Texas" was a more familiar closing to uncollected accounts in country store ledgers than it was as an epitaph for participants in neighborhood scandals. The hardworking farm family might grapple enough from the eroding earth to bring up the standard large number of children, but the farm could never furnish the livelihood for the children's families. Many of the surplus young people joined the unending movement to the cities, and others went to Texas, but the majority just moved down to the Delta, where new ground cleared each year offered sustenance for more people.

For seventy-five years, as the swampland was gradually released, new farmland put into production and new towns created, the Delta absorbed the surplus population of the rest of the basin, both black and white. Cotton remained supreme in the bluff area even while its corrosive effects were destroying the established plantation system. In the Delta the fertile soil made cotton yields so high that the destructive effects of the one-crop economy could be postponed further and further into the future. The Delta type of plantation economy set the social and economic pattern for half a million people, until the revolution of the 1930's.

Flood and disease, plus alternating stages in the value of cotton, acted as natural brakes on the opening up of the Delta, but there was always an unsatisfied demand for more farm labor than was on hand. Farms throughout the rest of the state were the usual source of labor. White men as well as Negroes came into the Delta to work on plantations where there was a generous advance of furnish money. Before long laws had been written into the statutes against "enticing" labor, but the steady shift to the flatlands continued without noticeable letup.

The fertility of Delta soil was the major difference in the strength and stability of the plantation system in the Yazoo Delta during the two generations following its establishment. Delta planters and Delta tenants gained a far better living from the soil, as a whole, than any of the other chattels of the Southern cotton kingdom. Some of the burden of the credit system was eased in the Delta by natural competitive laws long before any relief was found elsewhere in the South. Beyond these minor changes, there was little difference between the plantation system of 1875 and that of 1925. Both had the seeds of self-destruction, and the agriculture depression of 1930 became the impetus for revolutionary changes.

The vast natural richness of the Delta country ameliorated the hardships of the cotton economy sufficiently to provide a distinctive way of life for all in the region. The plantation system could have lasted nowhere else but in the Yazoo Delta.

13

Go Down, Moses

Life was better in the Delta for the Negro sharecropper than it was in the hills, but it was not the promised land the new freedman still dreamed of in the first years after freedom. The same vitality which made Delta cotton and corn grow made it harder for the chopper's hoe to keep ahead of the grass. The bayous and sloughs were good for fishing, but they always had the gnats and mosquitoes which came with water. Swamp fever made life uncertain even when crops were good, and the knowledge of yellow fever epidemics hung over the land.

During the laying-by time of 1878, an eloquent Negro revivalist known as "Dr. Collins" came out of nowhere with an answer to many unexpressed longings. His message was about a modern-day promised land in the new country of Liberia, where food grew on trees and no one had to work, where black men made the laws and set up the rules. Delta Negroes who wanted to go should get ready for the boat that would be up the river after them before very long. Of course, it would be helpful to make sure of space on the ship to Africa by paying a small donation to Dr. Collins, the new Moses with a promise of a land of Canaan.

In some areas the date for the boat's landing was set, either by Dr. Collins or by the strange osmosis of rumor. A dozen or more Negro families would appear at the river landing on the appointed day, quietly waiting for the boat. Careful not to raise too many questions with the white men of the town, they sometimes maintained their vigil for days at a time, but Dr. Collins's Ark never did arrive.

Perhaps it was all a mistake of geography. Richly illustrated pamphlets began to appear, telling the story of the rich land in Kansas, begging for someone to take it. The Kansas land companies said the holdings were for sale, but the pictures and the big print made it seem that the sale price was almost giving it away. Letters began to be circulated around, signed with names nobody knew, but making it clear that Kansas was the new Canaan for the colored man. Vague rumors started and finally became specific details about a boat or a train for Kansas. The boats or the train always left from some other town, so some five thousand Delta Negroes decided not to wait. They paid their own way to Kansas in the early months of 1879. They went in almost religious frenzy to the land where John Brown was the hero. Only the lack of train fare held back thousands of others who sought to make the trip. The others had high hopes of going after they made one more crop.

New and authentic letters from Kansas came in the summer of 1879. Most of the migrants had not been able to buy farms or even to find farmers who would sign them as tenants or sharecroppers. Occasional farm-labor jobs were the only protection against starvation. Money was needed to come back home. The land companies were in disrepute with many other Kansans because of the penniless Negroes who had been brought in. The great exodus came to an abrupt halt as the full story of the conditions in Kansas began to spread. There was to be no new mass migration of Negroes from the Delta until the stirrings which came with World War I.

One of the evils which accompanied the ever-recurrent labor shortage in the Delta was the convict-lease system, which had its beginning during the Reconstruction period. Edmund "Ned" Richardson cleared thousands of acres in the central Delta through use of convict labor and soon acquired the title "Cotton King of the World." Reaction against the lease system began as soon as it was instituted, and the first political opposition came from the Delta. A convict lessee was discovered attempting to smuggle eighteen prisoners back to the penitentiary in a covered wagon after they had been disabled by frostbite and disease. Even greater scandals were uncovered in railroad construction in South Mississippi, and the lease system was outlawed in the new state constitution adopted in the convention of 1890.

The Negro population of the Delta, from the time the first slaves were brought in, always greatly exceeded the white. Before mass migration began, the ratio averaged five and six to one. On the plantations it mounted from twenty-five to one to two hundred to one. The new pattern of plantation life inevitably became the pattern of Negro life in the Delta.

Down through the years the Negro and the white man in the Delta have lived together in greater harmony and mutual respect than perhaps anywhere else in the traditional Southern black belt. The attitudes of the leaders of the white community have never been such as to inspire the praise of national Negro leaders from Frederick Douglass down to

Walter White, but neither have they gained favor with the Ku Klux Klan. Writing of Negroes, William Faulkner, who has chronicled a major portion of the history of the region has put it this way:

> "Because they will endure. They are better than we are. Stronger than we are. Their vices are vices aped from white men or that white men and bondage have taught them; improvidence and intemperance and evasion— Not laziness: evasion: of what white men had set them to, not for their aggrandizement or even comfort but his own—" and McCaslin
> "All right. Go on: Promiscuity. Violence. Instability and lack of control. Inability to distinguish between mine and thine—"
> and he
> "How distinguish when for two hundred years mine did not even exist for them": and McCaslin
> "All right. Go on. And their virtues—" and he
> "Yes. Their own. Endurance—" and McCaslin
> "So have mules": and he
> "—and pity and tolerance and fidelity and love for children—" and McCaslin
> "So have dogs": and he
> "—whether their own or not or black or not. And more: what they got not only from white people but not even despite white people because they had it already from the old free fathers a longer time free than us because we have never been free—"

The plantation year was built around the cotton crop and the financial arrangements to produce it. March 1 was Limit Day, on which the first allowance was made by the plantation commissary for the rations through the year. There was no obligation of the planter to extend credit before this date, for before that time too many interferences might develop which would prevent the particular tenant or cropper from making the crop with him. If the tenant was on hand and ready to accept credit on March 1, the prospects for making a crop would be good. For permanent tenants in good standing, limit day was relatively unimportant, for the planters honored their credit all through the winter. Even for these, however, limit day was enough of a symbol to end the long spending fast that might have lasted since Christmas. It at least meant a new calico dress for the wife, at least some piece goods for clothes for the children, and maybe a little sweetening a step above molasses for the table.

Farmers have traditionally been poor, but they have usually been well fed, except in times of crop failures. The cotton-tenant-credit system did not even provide an adequate diet for people who worked at nothing but cultivating rich land. Pellagra and ills resulting from dietary deficiencies were commonplace in the Yazoo basin in the floodtime of the old plantation system, thanks to a combination of ignorance, poverty, and farm policies controlled by a shortsighted insistence on cotton production only—first, last and always. Dietary diseases would have run roughshod over the majority of the Negro population, but for the saving grace of collard greens and fish and their ready availability.

Tenant rations were traditionally restricted to the three "M's"—meat, meal and molasses. The meat was inevitably salt pork, white side meat with rare streaks of lean, called also "fat back" or "sow bosom," with "buttons" along the rind. It was fine for seasoning greens, or black-eyed peas, but its nutritive value was at the lowest level for meat. Fat back supplied the grease for cooking bread without milk from white cornmeal, very lacking in vitamins. The molasses was usually sorghum, which supplied quickly exhausted fuel. Molasses made from sugar cane instead of sorghum was sweeter and tastier and was also a source of sweetening for other foods, but it was also more expensive and rarer.

Oh, I gits my stren'th frum white-side meat
I sops all de sorghum a nigger kin eat.

(An interesting sidelight on post-World War II farm prosperity was the new problem encountered in marketing "fat back" by the major meat packing houses in the South. This symbol of malnutrition was the one meat product which offered major marketing difficulties. The farmer had been able to raise his own meat or buy the lean cuts. He had a refrigerator or icebox to hold fresh meat and thus removed another one of the selling points for salt pork.)

In the normal small-town or rural understanding of the term, it is likely that no more than one tenant in fifty maintained a full-scale garden. No more than half raised any vegetables at all. The basic difficulty was the fact that food crops matured at the same time as cotton, and labor was not available. Greens could grow at odd seasons, and sometimes an energetic tenant maintained a good supply of these from makeshift strips of land, but usually lethargy of the sharecropper restricted this small activity, if the landlord did not.

Probably an average of one third of the tenants had a cow during at least part of the year. The initial investment for a cow was a heavy sum, pasturage was rarely available, and landlords knew that they presented an irresistible temptation to steal food intended for the mules which were the working stock of the cotton operation. For the tenant who did have a cow, the temptation to dispose of it for cash during the lean wintertime was often too great. Hogs were rarer than cows. They had to be kept closely penned to prevent any destruction to the cotton crop, and that was a task beyond normal indolence.

The combination of self-defeating, pyramiding factors worked to make pellagra endemic over the area. There was a sharp decline in malnutrition during good crop years and immediately afterward, when credit was easier, and it was possible to buy the canned salmon, sardines, tomatoes, corn, and hoops of cheese at the store, and the cow could be fed through the winter. Otherwise, ignorance and indolence added to the burdensome restrictions of cotton raising and kept the farmers of the most fertile fields in America on a substandard diet.

The one bright spot in the whole picture for the tenant was hunting and fishing. Through the long winter every man had to have a shotgun of some description. The game was small—quail and dove and rabbit and squirrels—but it was tasty meat. The fly in the ointment was the fact that shotgun shells cost money. Sometimes a squirrel or a bird was not worth the nickel that the shell might cost. Skilled hunters could occasionally make an arrangement with white folks in town for them to furnish the shells in return for half the kill, and those able to make such arrangements were often the only farmers able to hunt all year without the restraint of the pocketbook.

Fishing was something else again. Poles were always available in some near-by cane thicket. Lines and hooks might cost a few cents, but they were long enduring, just as worms and crickets were ever available for bait. There was hardly a tenant's cotton patch in the whole Delta not within easy walking distance of some place to fish. If no actual river or lake was nearby, there was a bayou or slough certain to contain some catfish, for brackish ponds without outlets were usually replenished with fish by the annual spring high water. The yellow Yazoo would hold no attraction to a hip-booted sportsman searching for trout beneath the foam and rocks of a mountain stream, but the sportsman probably knows nothing of the need of a Negro farm wife to have some meat on the table for supper, or the fine relaxation of sitting in the shade on the bank and gossiping if there is a neighbor about. Fish were food, but even Delta fish bite only in spells. The close-riding planter who would let the tenant wives leave the fields for a few hours' fishing found his morale problems reduced.

From limit day to laying-by time were days of work. There were not enough hours of the sun for the good farmers to get in all the plowing and hoeing that a good stand of cotton demanded. Wet days could be fishing days, but if the riding boss was on the job, the tenant and all the working members of his family needed to be in the fields from before daylight until after dark. The long hours could be made endurable by the knowledge of the rest that would come with laying-by. Until then, the work was ceaseless.

Laying-by time came in the late summer, when the cotton had grown too big to plow or hoe, when there was nothing to do but sit back and let the bolls mature and open in the blazing sun and sultry nights. Once the bolls were open, the long job of picking had to begin, but there was time for rest and relaxation in between. The relaxation had to be something with a minimum of expense—there could be no money until the cotton was picked. Credit was almost always strained to the breaking point by this time, even if crop prospects were looking very good. The revival, or the "protracted meeting," became the institution of the laying-by period. Every plantation had at least one church, for which the landlord usually donated land and lumber, and no church could be without a meeting during the laying-by period.

During the year lay preachers from the neighborhood usually filled the pastor's role, for most sharecroppers were beyond the luxury of paying for a regular preacher. The revivalists came out from the towns and down from the hills. The successful preacher had to be as much a master of emotionalism as a knowledgeable theologian, for he had to bring religion to people who regarded it as an emotional experience. The mountebank and the charlatan had great opportunities, as did the traditional "brother" who was seeking always an opportunity to get to know better the "sisters" of the congregation.

Cindy Mitchell, an old woman who operated in Leflore County, was an early-day Aimee Semple McPherson, who held a large following in sway as the Good Shepherd of her "sanctified" congregation. Cindy planned, as a climactic performance to a long summer-end meeting northeast of Greenwood, to walk on the waters of the Yalobusha River. Without advising her congregation, she secretly erected a wooden platform at water level out into the river, counting on a normal rise of the river to conceal the structure under the muddy water. On the appointed day, Cindy was rowed out to her platform by boat, but long minutes of prodding with the paddle failed to find the platform. It became evident that the stream had not only covered the special platform—it had washed most of the planking away. The boat was ordered back to the bank, and Cindy debarked. "I ain't goin' to walk," she declared. "Th' Lawd Himsef' done said, 'Don't do it, Cindy, not befo' folks ain't got th' faith of a mustard seed.' "

For the moment the congregation accepted the challenge, and began a frenzied demonstration of new faith in Cindy, but her failure to live up to the promised supreme demonstration of faith had its effect. Cindy's following went into a sharp decline, and never again was as high.

(Experts in the field of American folklore say that the story of Cindy's walking on water is a retelling, with a new locale, of a folk tale which has survived down from Colonial America. Perhaps this is correct, but Leflore County Negroes who profess to have heard eyewitnesses tell of Cindy's misfortune say that this was a case of folklore becoming actuality.)

For every Cindy Mitchell, however, there were many more called to preach who made up in sincerity and faith any lack of learning and literacy. The muddy waters of the Yazoo have washed away the countless sins of thousands of sinners. On the appointed Sunday afternoon of a great baptizing, the chosen candidates are assembled along a river sand bar, along with crowds from every church in the neighborhood. The preacher, clad in a white gown and cap, moves out into the river until he finds a spot with good footing that brings the water at least above his waist. Two able-bodied deacons join him, to protect the candidates from being lost in the water. Another pair of deacons alternate in leading the candidates from the bank, unmindful of the havoc being wrought on Sunday clothes. The preacher intersperses a scriptural admonition as each candidate comes before him, before putting his hand on his head, and exclaiming, "I baptize thee," as he quickly bends the member back to complete immersion under the water. On the bank the congregation is singing the ancient spirituals in their natural setting with full-throated beauty. It is no great trick of imagery for the Yazoo to become the Jordan, as the words of "Go Down, Moses" and "Let's Go Down to the Jordan" echo through the willows in the fading summer sunset. The river has become a sacred baptismal font.

Burying the dead was a community responsibility until the day of the burial insurance firms which began to appear on the scene about the time of World War I. The crop lien allowed no margin of credit on a coffin, and by general agreement the plantation carpenter supplied it, built with lumber usually furnished by the planter, with the labor of any neighbor or relative possessed of carpentering skill.

The funeral itself was a community gathering, with people on hand from miles around unless the weeds were mighty high in the cotton. It was usually preceded by a a night of vigil in the cabin attended from time to time by representatives from all families on the plantation who brought with them the dishes of food served the mourners. Burial was in the plantation cemetery, at the churchyard.

The day of burial associations brought a change in the burial system—the plain pine box disappeared, and with it the funeral wagon. The social aspects of the funeral made everyone desire to be buried "in style," which meant a lacquered coffin and an automotive hearse. Most planters tried to keep the burial association agents off their premises, but resisting them proved impossible. Town Negroes paid their burial association dues before they would buy food or clothing or pay the rent, and plantation Negroes eventually followed suit. The first Negroes to amass wealth in the Delta were wily undertakers who could not only sell the burial policies, but also an extrapriced ornate coffin to the grieving widow or widower whose crop prospects looked good enough to pay the extra fee.

School usually began in August to make possible a month of work before a general recess that lasted through the peak of cotton picking. Education for the children of Negro farmers was almost entirely a matter of one-room schoolhouses serving neighborhoods within walking distance. Quite often the schoolhouse was a church. County funds for Negro schools were severely limited, and the only major building programs before the days of WPA and PWA were the result of grants from the Rosenwald Foundation. Sears Roebuck money come back to the South bridged an almost fathomless gap in Negro education. The one-teacher schools carried their pupils all the way up through the capacity of the teacher, but there was rarely enough interest or opportunity for boys or girls to progress as far as the equivalent of high school education. The length of the school year was gradually increased as more funds became available, but the term was always shorter than standard.

Cotton picking comes after laying-by. It has always been hard, back-bending work, but it is also a social activity for the Negroes on the plantation and especially for those who came out from town as part of the picking crews. It brought the first trickle of cash money for many since limit day, and perhaps as far back as Christmas money or the last fall's settling time. Saturday in town had been a privilege all the year, but after picking began it could be a time of money to spend. Hot fish at the corner colored café would be within reach, instead of the year-round staple of a nickel or a dime's worth of soda crackers and cheese.

Settlin' time has already been covered in the story of the plantation credit system. It brought both good news and bad, but generally the tenant or the sharecropper had a good notion of the outlook long before the day of actual accounting. Settling time was followed closely by moving time, and both parties to the settlement remembered that. The planter had to have an adequate supply of labor to work his place during the coming year, and movement was the standard course of action for the sharecropper unsatisfied with the conditions on a particular plantation. The sharecropper was a continual migrant.

Moving might be for some fancied advantage or might be for a better house or school. It might be the only way to answer the urge to hit back at the landlord for some slight, real or fancied. It might be for no other reason than search for the cheapest luxury for all the family—the pleasure of something new and a little bit different. Part of the reason was because grass is always greener a little farther down the road, but there were always other factors.

The average sharecropper and his wife would normally make several moves during the first years of their family existence. They might try a year of "public work" in town and stick with it if a good enough job, or series of jobs, opened up. "Public work," by the widest definition, was any type of wage job outside the field of farming. When their children began to grow old enough to take on a share of the farming operation, the tenant family would move to a new operation large enough to accommodate the increasing size. As the children would mature and strike out for themselves, the parents would gradually reduce the size of the tract they worked. On the largest plantations, landlords could shift tenants around to fit these varying needs if they were anxious to keep them on the place. Ninety per cent of moves by tenants were to and from farms within a few miles of each other. They might have hope of a more fertile patch of land, a better house, or some comparative advantage over the old location, or they might be moving because the old landlord was too dissatisfied with their work to let them stay, but they rarely wanted to get out of the general neighborhood. Delta Negroes might migrate to Memphis, or further north, but they never moved back to the hills to continue farming.

Moving might take place any time between settling and limit day, but it generally came before Christmas. Liberal advances of "Chrismus money" made the difference for many a planter between an adequate labor supply and a shortage. Spending habits throughout the fall inevitably reduced all but the most prudent tenants to a penniless state by Christmas, and no money for Christmas finery and festivity, plus peppermint sticks and oranges for the children, could wreck the morale of any tenant.

Oranges were a standard Christmas delicacy for the poorest of families. Santa Claus tried to get one in each child's stocking. If the mother was a good cook, she ordered the peeling saved for flavoring a Christmas cake or pie. If Christmas was a good one, there was a coconut or two for Christmas cooking. Saving the lower half of the shell was something of a mark of the prestige of having had coconuts, and many a shell was saved as a decoration or a dipper because of this.

The Christmas advances were normally charged against the tenants' accounts for the coming year's crop, but occasionally they were written off as a bonus after a good year, or as a bonus for recruitment when the new tenant was an especially good farmer.

The temptations for parting a tenant from cotton-picking and settlement money were always abundant during the fall season. The small-town merchants had special attractions for "Saddity" which was traditionally the Negroes' day all over the Delta. Saturdays were always social as well as spending occasions. For the young women it was dress-up time, for the clothes a little too spectacular for Sunday church wear. Folks went to town in the morning, or early in the afternoon, which meant that many a girl had to carry her shoes in her hand to protect them from the dust of the turn-rows, and to save from punishment feet unused to binding. Many a party dress, often trailing to the ground in imitation of the latest white society style, had to withstand a day on the streets and in the stores. An additional round trip to the cabin or wagon was almost always too far, no matter what the social occasion was in town.

The circuses and the minstrels always toured the cotton country in the fall, but they never missed the Delta at the height of the cotton-picking and the crop-settling time. Special trains brought in the crowds from up and down the railroad on circus day. The minstrels had to be content with less, but they worked the field more thoroughly.

Like Delta white folks, Delta Negroes absorbed the tradition of free spending when the money came. Living on a credit system, a furnish was as good to spend as a settlement, both for planters and tenants. The custom of living on as much money as could be borrowed, instead of as much as could be made, was easy to adopt when there was always a certainty of a furnish and by no means an assurance of a settlement for everyone along the cotton ladder. Neither the tenant nor the planter had much opportunity to exercise or develop the virtue of thrift. When the cotton crop did bring in an income that paid off both furnish and debts, it was no more than natural to regard the money as a windfall and treat it as such.

Delta people, white and black, were usually more "liberal" about liquor and gambling, as well as with the general spending of money. Other people over Mississippi might point the finger of scorn at easy-going ways, but there was all too often a note of envy in the strongest indictment of the manners and morals of Delta people.

Liquor and gambling were common ingredients in Negro social life that helped to make life cheap. When they were mixed with switch-blade knives, commonly in every town at least every Saturday night, the mortality rate was certain to be high. The white community, which made and enforced the laws, was usually not greatly aroused by Negro crimes against Negroes. Cutting and shooting scrapes in town usually meant that somebody was jailed and sent to Parchman, but out on the plantation they might mean no formal punishment from the county. Plantation owners or managers usually didn't call in the law unless the crime was murder, or unless they wanted to put away a bully who was making life miserable for the other tenants. A tendency for the courts to treat lightly Negro crimes against Negroes developed, with its resulting reaction in over-all law enforcement problems.

As mobility among plantation tenants increased with the

steady development of the plantation system, the autonomy of each plantation began to break down. But even as the practices of plantation discipline began to pass, the planter still assumed responsibility for tenants arrested for minor law violations, especially during busy work seasons. The planter from the first was called upon to settle family quarrels, maintain peace and order between neighbors, arbitrate disputes, protect wives from the punishment of irate husbands, reconcile other couples who left each other, procure marriage licenses and divorces, build churches, and bury the dead.

The planter loaned his mules and wagons for Saturday trips to town, and the mules alone for week-night social visiting. He usually provided the supplies for the annual plantation barbecue and had to be a generous contributor to church picnics and fish fries. All of these were incidentals in the efficient plantation system. Where they were lacking, there was usually an unsuccessful farm operation. Morale was not a word that either planter or tenant was likely to know, but it had to be present on a plantation to get the best production year in and year out.

Most sharecroppers and tenants in the Delta, down through the years, were Negroes. Many planters experimented by bringing in white tenants from the hills from time to time, but the general consensus over the years was that Negro farm labor was most satisfactory. Most of the white migrants from the hills took up salaried jobs and wage work in the towns, although a great many white farmers who left worn-out hill land made fresh starts in the Delta as sharecroppers or tenants and eventually became successful plantation owners. The rags-to-riches story became harder to find, however, as the troubles of the cotton plantation system began to pile up. In the 1920's and the early thirties, the percentage of white tenants and sharecroppers began to increase at a rapid rate, until it became obvious that few of them were making the transition from cropper to landowner or operator. In the Delta, as elsewhere, tenancy was rapidly increasing during the last days of the old plantation system.

The successful plantation owner rode his land instead of doing his farming in town, unless he had an operation big enough to afford an efficient manager. The good planter was not only a landlord and capitalist, but an agronomist, diplomat, veterinarian, and social arbiter as well. His contribution to the plantation had to be both from the pocketbook and from the brain. Both he and the tenants profited if he was skilled at all the varied tasks.

The tenant supplied what might be called supervised brawn, but it was not the rote of a machine or the blind response of a serf. With native farming skills acquired through a lifetime of work, he had to have intelligent supervision to make the best use of his energies. On the rich Delta land, under good management, there was probably no system that provided a better return for unskilled labor during good crop and price years. But even when the planter and tenant both made the best and fullest contributions, they were bucking against a system which irresistibly beat them down in the long run. The cotton kingdom was not producing enough wealth to give anyone a fair division, and the inequity became acute when a major portion of the wealth was drained off through the credit system.

14

The Yaller Dawg

Moorhead is a small plantation town in the gumbo land between the Sunflower River and its tributary, the Quiver. In the days since the decline of the railroads, Moorhead is best known as the home of Sunflower Junior College, one of the dozen or so two-year colleges spotted over Mississippi, supported jointly by county and state to provide a start toward a college education for even the poorest high school graduate.

Moorhead started as a timber town, taking its name from one of the operators who came in during the 1880's. Chester Henry Pond of Illinois built a stavemill at the townsite, and later a cottonmill and cottonseed-oil mill. Pond's sister founded a college for Negro girls at Moorhead in 1891, to establish caste for the town among Delta Negroes. The Methodist Missionary Society of New York supported the school for some thirty years.

Once upon a time, Moorhead was the best known small town in the South—certainly the best known among the Negroes. The town was, and still is, the site of the most famous railroad crossing in the world, "where the Southern crosses the Yellow Dog." W. C. Handy was an obscure Clarksdale musician, conductor of a Knights of Pythias band, until Yazoo-

Delta Negroes taught him that the folk music of his race had a combination of haunting appeal and rhythm to make top-quality popular music.

According to the acknowledged Father of the Blues, the "Blues" were born in the Delta. In 1903 Handy's Knights of Pythias orchestra, which dressed in military uniforms and confined its musical numbers to the latest Broadway hits, played for a white society dance one night at Cleveland. Until after midnight they had played nothing but conventional dance music. The dancers were beginning to thin out, when there was a call to "play some of your own people's music." The Handy band played a slow drag, "Peaceful Henry," but there was no enthusiasm. As a demonstration, one of the Bolivar Countians brought in three local Negroes with a guitar, mandolin and bass viol. The rustic trio played a rough back-yard "over-and-over," which brought the loudest applause from the crowd for the whole evening, and, more important, a larger collection of tips than the fee which had been agreed upon for Handy's professionals.

A few weeks later Handy was at the depot at Tutwiler, another small town south of Clarksdale, waiting for the train back home. Out under the baggage shed a lonesome Negro was picking a tune with a knifeblade from a battered guitar, moaning some words about "Gwine where de Southern cross de Yaller Dawg." Handy made a note of the words and the tune. He still had no conscious plan of attempting to develop something of commercial value from this music which he had been enjoying all his life. The sheet music, the piano rolls and the phonograph records which sold were traditional waltzes, Broadway ballads, and ragtime, not the down-to-earth Negro blues.

Handy left the Delta for the metropolis of Memphis, but the blues followed him north from the Delta. In 1905, when the Handy band was first organized, it was hired to provide the music for the advertising and street corner rallies for a young reform candidate for mayor, E. H. Crump, another migrant to the big city from the Yazoo country. For such occasions there had to be a special song. To write it, Handy went back to the idiom of the blues wafting up from the Delta. "Mister Crump," of course, was the name of his song, one verse of which ran as follows:

Mister Crump won't 'low no easy riders here,
Mister Crump won't 'low no easy riders here.
I don't care what Mister Crump don't 'low,
I'm gwine to bar'l-house anyhow—
Mister Crump can go an' catch hisself some air!

The first blues had been committed to paper, although it was not to be actually published for another seven years, and then under the title "Memphis Blues."

The blues moved north from the cotton fields to Beale Street, not along the river, but on the railroad system which had developed to connect the hardwood mills of Memphis with the lumber camps and sawmills of the Delta during the long years when the "new ground" was being cleared between Reconstruction and World War I. In the fall, excursion trains did a heavy business each weekend during settling time, but through the year only sawmill men and an occasional levee worker had the cash money to ride the Yellow Dog to Memphis and the joys and glories of Beale Street.

For the vast majority of Delta Negroes, Saturday night had to come in the little Delta towns, and Moorhead, where two railroads met in a perpendicular crossing, was one of the best. They gave most of the words, and the basis of a tune, to Handy:

E'er since Miss Su-san John-son lost her Jock-ey, Lee,—
There has been much ex-cite-ment, more to be,—
You can hear her moan-ing night—and morn.
Wonder where-my Easy Rid—er's gone?
Ca-ble-grams come of sym-pa-thy,
Tel-e-grams come of sym-pa-thy,
Let-ters come from down in "Bam"-
And ev-'ry-where that Un-cle Sam-
Has e-ven a ru-ral de-liv-e-ry.
All day the phone rings—But it's not for—me.
At last good ti-dings—fill our hearts with glee,
This mes-sage comes—————from Ten-nes-see.

Dear Sue your Eas—y Rid-er—struck this burg to—day
On a south boun' ratt-ler—side door Pull-man car.—
Seen him here—an' he was on the hog.
Eas-y Rid'er's got a stay—a-way, so he—had to vamp
it—but the hike ain't far.—
He's gone where the South-ern—'cross' the Yel-low Dog.

I know the Yel-low Dog Dis—trict—like a book,—
In-deed I know the route that Rid-er took;—
Ev-'ry cross-tie, Bay-ou, burg-and bog.—
Way down where—the South-ern cross' the Dog,—
Mon-ey don't zact-ly grow on trees—
On cot-ton stalks it grows with ease;
No race horse, race track, no grand stand—
Is like Old Beck and Buck-shot land—
Down where—the South-ern cross' the Dog.

Ev-e-ry kitch-en there—is a cab-a-ret—
Down there the boll-weevil works—while the dark-ies play—
*This Yel-low Dog Blues———the live long day.**

The Yellow Dog Line ran from Tutwiler to Yazoo City. Like all the other north and south railroads in the Delta, it was, or became, a branch of the Yazoo and Mississippi Valley, in turn purchased as a branch of the Illinois Central. The years of the opening up of the Delta were the years when the first railroads came into the Delta country. One line, the Mississippi Central (which became the main line of the Illinois Central), had been built in the 1850's down across the high ridges through the Tallahatchie and Yalobusha country, but the Delta had to stick to the river boat for transportation until sawmills and new plantations began to develop far inland from the navigable streams.

Memphis was the largest hardwood market in the world by 1890, and most of the hardwood came from the Yazoo-Delta. Even after the war, most of the Delta was still virgin forest. Most of the timber could have been taken out by river boat, under different circumstances, but the Yankee lumber tycoons wanted to make Memphis their base of operations. They bought timber rights to vast plantations as cheaply as twenty-five cents an acre, because farmers wanted the land cleared for crop planting.

Dummy line railroads into the timber-cutting operation was the usual setup for logging in the Delta, and branch lines like the Yellow Dog were established to reach into all the timber pockets between the larger streams. The origin of the name "Yellow Dog" is lost in confusion. One story has to

* Copyright 1914, by W. C. Handy. Copyright renewed, 1942, by W. C. Handy.

do with the contract under which the railroad workers were hired; another is the term of contempt from a rival line. There can be no question that the nickname was ever intended to be complimentary.

Branch line railroading was a rough, frontier operation, because logging has always been one. The Delta lumberjacks were largely Negroes. Black men were the only readily available labor supply, and traditionally only black men could work in the swamplands amid the distractions of heat, mosquitoes, bugs and snakes. The Delta loggers were called "flatheads," and most of their work was done from lumber camps built around a railroad spur where a few boxcars, converted to a cookshack and bunkhouses, had been parked. Some of the logging firms brought coaches down the line to take the flatheads to Memphis on payday Saturdays, while others used the more convenient Delta towns. Few camps were complete without crap games and moonshine whiskey under the supervision of the foreman; it was good business to keep the Saturday night brawl in camp and have the labor still available on Monday. There might even be a profit in the sale of the liquor and a cut of the dice game. Levee construction camps were to follow these precedents in future years.

The logging boom has long since gone forever, but today hardwood is beginning a comeback in the Yazoo bottomlands. Agronomists with the Department of Agriculture say that about one third of the Delta land—that acreage in the lowland swamps and sloughs, or in the high water channels—is economically best suited for timber production. With severance taxes, fire protection programs, and more knowledge about the advantages of selective cutting, landowners are be-

ginning to think in terms of Yazoo hardwood as a cash crop, instead of cream to be skimmed off once in a hundred years. The Delta National Forest, part of the "jungle" which Sherman and Porter tried to penetrate in the spring of 1863, is providing a sound example of what scientific timber management can provide. Some of the timber cut in this new hardwood operation is once more riding the Yellow Dog.

The heyday of the Yellow Dog was during the first twenty-five years of the twentieth century, before the day of the highway and the automobile. Regular excursions to Memphis, and sometimes to Jackson and Vicksburg, filled special trains on weekends and after weekends in the fall. Excursions were designed to appeal to both the white folks and the colored, but the Yellow Dog would never have survived if it had been forced to depend upon the business of white people alone. A round trip to Memphis at $1.50 was usually too costly for more than one trip a year for the Negroes who lived along the Dog, but a year without the trip was as bleak as a Sunday afternoon in town with the rain too heavy to go down to the station and watch the train come in.

The Columbus and Greenville connection with the Southern Railroad has little romance in its history, other than its crossing of the Dog at Moorhead, but it made one spectacular trip that is part of Delta folklore. The "last train out" of Greenville before the Mississippi flood of 1927 brought both human and animal refugees to safety in the hills.

Next to the crossing at Moorhead, the Yellow Dog line's other fame has come largely because it is the railroad which serves Parchman, the vast penal farm of the State of Mississippi in northern Sunflower County. The Yellow Dog passes right through Parchman, and it was the Yellow Dog which brought in the Midnight Special before the automobiles and buses put it out of the passenger business. In the old days every fifth Sunday at Parchman was visiting day, and the convicts' wives and sweethearts from the south and central parts of the state would gather at Jackson on Saturday night for the special train which left at midnight in order to reach Parchman at dawn and lose none of the visiting time. The Parchman inmates still have a song about the train from the "free world," even though it doesn't run any more:

Midnight Special, shine yo' light on me,
Gonna brang my woman, a pardon in her han'
Gonna say to de boss, I wants mah man,
Let the Midnight Special shine its light on me.

Parchman is a giant cotton farm—sixteen thousand acres. There are no stone walls or cell blocks, but blockhouse type camps divided about the farm to fit the agricultural operation. Parchman would probably take no prizes for scientific penology, but as occupational therapy for prisoners from an agricultural state, farm work is not at all out of line. Parchman's operations not only feed the prisoners, but in good cotton years return a substantial net profit. Progressive administration since World War II, with co-operative governors and legislators, has brought many prison reforms.

In the old days, all the work of guarding the prisoners was done by trusties known to the men they guarded as "shooters," because of the shotgun they carried always ready for use. The nontrusties still call themselves "gunmen," not because of past crimes, but because they work in the fields always "under the gun." One of the Parchman abuses which has been eliminated is the old system of awarding a pardon to shooters who killed or wounded a prisoner who was attempting to escape.

Parchman has long been recognized by authorities like official researchers of the Library of Congress as one of the best sources of American folk music. Parchman visitors report today the disheartening news that commercialized "folk music" of the sort typified by Eddy Arnold and Gene Autry is crowding out the genuine product. But at the Negro camps, songs from the cottonfield still mingle with New Orleans jazz improvised on a banjo, and at the white camps "ballets" (the hill name for ballads) of almost pure Anglo-Saxon derivation and hymns from the Sacred Harp can still be heard amidst the Tin Pan Alley cowboy tunes.

John Lomax and his son Alan, most extensive collectors of American folk songs, made some of their most successful recordings at Parchman. They found Joe Baker, better known as "Seldom Seen," at one of the colored camps. Joe told them, "I never had been in no trouble wid de law, but one fellow kept messin' up my homely affairs, so I blowed him down." Then Joe sang:

Heah I is, bowed down wid shame;
I got a number instead of a name,
Ninety-nine years, in prison for life,
All I ever done was to kill my wife.

Fiddles, French harps, jew's-harps and banjoes still give accompaniment in the white camps to songs which came from down the river and across the hills and sometimes originated in Parchman. They tell of "The Blue-Eyed Boy" who "has broken every vow"; "That Waxford Girl" who was "an expert girl with dark and rolling eyes," or perhaps of their famous fellow prisoner now escaped to the free world, "Kinnie Wagner," who "shot the sheriff, kissed the prettiest girl in town," and left "to live a life of sin."

Some of the Negro songs reflect the philosophy of the prisoner interviewed by Governor Mike Conner on an inspection trip. The Governor asked:

"What are you here for?"

"I was shootin' craps, cap'n, an' killed a nigger," the prisoner answered.

"Why did you kill him?"

"I made my point, suh, and he wouldn't recognize it."

In general, however, the colored songs reflect the fatalism that is inevitable in prison songs everywhere, with death and melancholy always present.

Oh Death he is a little man,
And he goes from do' to do'. . . .

15

The Adventures of Mike and Bob Hooter

B'AR IN THE CANEBRAKE

John James Audubon, the great naturalist of the Mississippi Valley, toured the Yazoo before the Indian cessions, and, because of this, wildlife of the "Yazoo Swamp" has been preserved in *The Birds of America.* Audubon also wrote something of his travels with his interspersed "delineations of American scenery and manners." From these delineations we have an account of one of the first hunting expeditions of white men on the Yazoo.

On the Coldwater river Audubon found a squatter from Connecticut who was willing to accompany him "through the great morass" as he searched for birds, plants and animals to paint. When the squatter reported that a "painter" (panther to the American, cougar to the European) was killing his hogs and robbing him of deer, Audubon suggested a hunt for the cat. A date was set for the hunt, in order to bring in several neighbors who lived a few miles away and would add needed numbers to the pack.

> The hunters, accordingly, made their appearance one fine morning at the door of the cabin, just as the sun was emerging from beneath the horizon. They were five in

number, and fully equipped for the chase, being mounted on horses, which in some parts of Europe might appear sorry nags, but which in strength, speed, and bottom, are better fitted for pursuing a cougar or bear through the woods and morasses than any in that country. A pack of large ugly curs were already engaged in making acquaintance with those of the squatter. He and myself mounting his two best horses, waited whilst his sons were bestriding others of inferior quality.

Few words were uttered by the party until we had reached the edge of the Swamp, where it was agreed that all should disperse and seek for the fresh track of the Painter, it being previously settled that the discoverer should blow his horn, and remain on the spot until the rest should join him. In less than an hour, the sound of the horn was clearly heard, and, sticking close to the squatter, off we went through the thick woods, guided only by the now and then repeated call of the distant huntsman. We soon reached the spot, and in a short time the rest of the party came up. The best dog was sent forward to track the Cougar, and in a few moments the whole pack were observed diligently trailing, and bearing in their course for the interior of the Swamp. The rifles were immediately put in trim, and the party followed the dogs, at separate distances, but in sight of each other, determined to shoot at no other game than the Panther.

The dogs soon began to mouth, and suddenly quickened their pace. My companion concluded that the beast was on the ground, and putting our horses to a gentle gallop, we followed the curs, guided by their voices. The noise of the dogs increased, when all of a sudden their mode of barking became altered, and the squatter, urging me to push on, told me that the beast was *treed*, by which he meant that it had got upon some low branch of a large tree to rest for a few moments, and that should we not succeed in shooting him when thus situated, we might expect a long chase of it. As we approached the spot, we all by degrees united into a body, but on seeing the dogs at the foot of a large tree, separated again and galloped off to surround it.

Each hunter now moved with caution, holding his gun ready, and allowing the bridle to dangle on the neck of his horse, as it advanced slowly towards the dogs. A shot from one of the party was heard, on which the Cougar was seen to leap to the ground, and bound off with such velocity as to show that he was unwilling to stand our fire longer. The dogs set off in pursuit with great eagerness and a deafening cry. The hunter who had fired came up and said that his ball had hit the monster, and had probably broken one of his fore-legs near the shoulder, the only place at which he could aim. A slight trail of blood was discovered on the ground, but the curs proceeded at such a rate that we hardly noticed this, and put spurs to our horses, which galloped on towards the center of the Swamp. One bayou was crossed, then another still larger and more muddy; but the dogs were brushing forward, and as the horses began to pant at a furious rate, we judged it expedient to leave them and advance on foot. These determined hunters knew that the Cougar being wounded, would shortly ascend another tree, where in all probability he would remain for a considerable time, and that it would be easy to follow the track of the dogs. We dismounted, took off the saddles and bridles, set the bells attached to the horses' necks at liberty to jingle, hoppled the animals, and left them to shift for themselves.

Now, reader, follow the group marching through the Swamp, crossing muddy pools, and making the best of their way over fallen trees and amongst the tangled rushes that now and then covered acres of ground. If you are a hunter yourself, all this will appear nothing to you; but if crowded assemblies of "beauty and fashion," or the quiet enjoyment of your "pleasure-grounds," alone delight you, I must mend my pen before I attempt to give you an idea of the pleasure felt on such an expedition.

After marching for a couple of hours, we again heard the dogs. Each of us pressed forward, elated at the thought of terminating the career of the Cougar. Some of the dogs were heard whining, although the greater number barked vehemently. We felt assured that the Cougar was treed, and that he would rest for some time to recover from his fatigue. As we came up to the dogs, we discovered the ferocious animal lying across a large branch, close to the trunk of a cottonwood tree. His broad breast lay toward us; his eyes were at one time bent on us and again on the dogs beneath and around him, one of his forelegs hung loosely by his side, and he lay crouched, with his ears lowered close to his head, as if he thought he might remain undiscovered. Three balls were fired at him, at a given signal, on which he sprang a few feet from the branch, and tumbled headlong to the ground. Attacked on all sides by the enraged curs, the infuriated Cougar fought with desperate valour; but the squatter advancing in front of the party, and almost in the midst of the dogs, shot him immediately behind and beneath the left shoulder. The Cougar writhed for a moment in agony, and in another lay dead.

The sun was now sinking in the west. Two of the hunters separated from the rest, to procure venison, whilst the squatter's sons were ordered to make the best of their way home, to be ready to feed the hogs in the morning. The Cougar was despoiled of its skin, and its carcass left to the hungry dogs. Whilst engaged in preparing our camp, we heard the report of a gun, and soon after one of our hunters appeared with a small deer. A fire was lighted, and each hunter displayed his *pone* of bread, along with a flask of whisky. The deer was skinned in a trice, and slices placed on sticks before the fire. These materials afforded us an excellent meal, and as the night grew darker, stories and songs went round, until my companions, fatigued, laid themselves down, close under the smoke of the fire, and soon fell asleep.

I walked for some minutes around the camp, to contemplate the beauties of that nature, from which I have certainly derived my greatest pleasures. I thought of the occurrences of the day, and glancing my eye around, remarked the singular effects produced by the phosphorescent qualities of the large decayed trunks which lay in all directions around me. How easy, I thought, it would be for the confused and agitated mind of a person bewildered in a swamp like this, to imagine in each of these liminous masses some wonderous and fearful being, the very sight of which might make the hair stand erect on his head. The thought of being myself placed in such a predicament burst over my mind, and I hastened to join my companions, beside whom I laid me down and slept, assured that no enemy could approach us without first rousing the dogs, which were growling in fierce dispute over the remains of the Cougar.

At daybreak we left our camp, the squatter bearing on his shoulder the skin of the late destroyer of his stock, and retraced our steps until we found our horses, which had not strayed far from the place where we had left them. These we soon saddled, and jogging along, in a direct course, guided by the sun, congratulating each other on the destruction of so formidable a neighbour as the Panther had been, we soon arrived at my host's cabin. The five neighbors partook of such refreshment as the house could afford, and dispersing, returned to their homes, leaving me to follow my favourite pursuits.

Aububon hunted the panther, and everyone along the Yazoo hunted deer and turkey, but bear hunting was the favorite Delta sport throughout the nineteenth century. It would be yet, but the plow and blade clearing new ground have taken away the countless canebrakes in which the bear lived. The bear hunt was a thing apart to the Deltans and to their neighbors in the hills who came down to join them. Ordinary hunting for deer and quail and the like was a necessary and pleasant diversion, but it had no spark of danger. Panthers were dangerous, but a successful kill brought only satisfaction that a barnyard pest had been eliminated. The bear could provide a contest, and sometimes he won it. He was never an easy victim. His hide made a good rug or robe or coat. His meat was succulent eating, drippings from bear tallow were ideal seasoning for other meats and for turnips and collard greens, and bear grease itself was a prime necessity around any farm, both house and yard.

When ex-President Teddy Roosevelt, vilified by Delta editor James K. Vardaman more than any other public figure, came South to hunt bear in the last wild swamps of the Issaquena and Sharkey Counties, the Delta forgot its grudge to embrace a fellow bear hunter in complete forgiveness. To testify to the institution of the Bear Hunt, William Faulkner's greatest single story, *The Bear*, is about a group of Yoknapatawpha Countians on their bear hunt in the Tallahatchie bottoms.

In the days of new ground clearing, bear hunting was a sport for relaxation after the toils of lumbering and plowing. Bear roads were cut through the canebrakes to get closer to the hunt. From the roads the dogs would be sent along the cane paths. The hounds would let out a great bellowing. Then the bear would roar and snarl back, beat his way up against the tall cane, bending it down for a foothold from which he would start running over the top, crashing and crackling the dry canes like a forest fire. With luck the dogs would corner him and provoke the desperation measure of climbing a tree. Sometimes the hunters shot the animal down from the tree. Sometimes they had to pick him out of the center of a snarling pack of dogs. (Mongrels with a mixture of redbone hound were the best bear dogs.) Sometimes the bear had to be stopped at the last perilous moment as he charged the hunters themselves in his torment. Usually a sin-

gle rifleshot was not enough to stop him, and therein lay the question of the outcome of the hunt.

An otherwise unimpressive Indian mound north of Isola, east of the Sunflower River in Humphreys County, is called the Prentiss Mound, because the fabled orator Seargeant Smith Prentiss used it as a rostrum in 1841 during a bear-hunting trip of lawyers from downstate. The recollection of Prentiss's Rabelaisian stories from the Indian mound became part of the Prentiss legend, and the mound was famous among people who had no idea of its location.

Hunters who are not hunting talk about hunting, and the tall stories of hunting and fishing began on the Yazoo with stories of a b'ar in the canebrake. Mike Hooter, sometimes called Mike Shouter to provide a more accurate description, lived at Satartia. When he was not hunting, he was in one of the local saloons talking. Mike can best tell his own bear stories:

> "You see," he continued, "my wife wanted a new bar-skin petticoat, and Sal, that gal of our'n, kept pestering me 'bout some bar's ile to slick her har with, (as the fellers didn't like to see her mommock her head with taller,) so as how I couldn't rest. Well, one Sunday morning, I took 'Brown Betsy,' my old two shooter, and all the dogs, and off I sot for the cane brake in the hollow, over back of Ike Hamberlin's, the steam doctors'—for I know's Ike would be tarnation riley if I kilt a bar any where close to his clearin, and that made me sorter ambitious like. I hadn't got fur into the woods afore I hearn the all-firedest crackin' 'mongst the cane that ever you hearn any whar, and sez I to the dogs, sick 'em Bose. I know'd it must be a bar, for I saw 'bundance of Sign scattered all 'bout, and sorta stirred up fresh, kinder.
>
> "In the puppies went, yowling like mad, and talkin' to

him most perticler musical. Go it, old Bumper, says I—speak to him, Echo—and they did speak to him, I swan. And sich music! Tom Goin's fiddle and my Sal's singin, and all the camp meetin hallelujahs you ever hearn, warnt a patchin to it. Oh! man, but it was *some*. But it wasn't no time before the barkin critters begin to play another tune, and the furst thing I spied was they all comin terin like flinders through the cane, right plumb sock whar I stood, and the bar, drot his pictur! close at their tails, puffin and blowin like a young steamboat, with his eyes shot close together, and his har all turned the wrong way! Whew! wasn't I mad? I haint been so riled afore since Parson James preached my best sermon down at Dilly's Post Office, and when I 'tacked him about it, swanned it was his'n. My dander *was* up, I tell you, and my har stood straight out like the bristles on a tom cat, when he's kinder techy. I let you know I was dangerous then, and it wouldn't er done for one o' them are Cole boys to cross my path. I was wrathy, you may know, and I fotch one jump up in the fork of a dogwood saplin 'bout ten foot high, jest to have a good sight at him. Skeered? Was that you, Mose Bonny, said 'skeered?' Oh! the bar was skeered? Well, he warn't nothin' shorter, and if you'd seen him when I blazed away at him with both barrels, right plump slap in the countenance, you's opinionated he was gwine to kingdom come quicker than my Sal can tote a sommerset. What? Didn't he roll and wabble and play kerwallop 'mong those ar canes and briars? He hadn't no more use for his feet nor a toad for a side pocket? But he didn't lay thar long 'fore the dogs they 'gan to chaw at his hide and kinder tickle the hind sights of the varmint; and the crittur, seein' as how 'twouldn't do to play possum no longer, gin to grabble about for his walkers; and when he seed he wasn't perzactly dead, he sorter picked hisself up simultaneously like, and toted off through the cane, like flujuns. Cracky! didn't he travel! Talk about your railroads and your telegraphs! They aint a circumstance. Away he went. Wait for the waggin, says I; but the varmint thought 'twarn't no time for swappin' knives, so he mizzled. 'Go it, steamboat,' sez I, and me and the dogs up and follered. But he hadn't run fur afore his bilers gin to git sorter kinder hot, and the fust thing I diskiver, he fotch up kerlumpus down in the water in Cole's creek. When I cum up, I knowed I had him, for he was circumsurroundified by the dogs, and his hine parts kerslap up agin the tallest kinder bank.

"You see, then, I could afford to be perlite a few; so I takes off my coonskin cap, and kinder scraped my foot, and bowed somewhat at him. Sez I, 'Good mornin,' Mister Bar. How did you leave Misses Bar and all the little Bars? Takin' a bath, I diskiver, with your breeches on!' He didn't pay no 'tention to what I was sayin', but looked kinder glum; so I riled up and begin to show mad a circumstance. Sez I, 'You look hearty, Mister Bar. Good livin' up in Jim Stewart's punkin patch, I spose?' Then he begin to turn his head sideways and look at me pertickler queer, like he smelt what I was thinkin' 'bout. I *was* not, I tell *you*, so I thought I'd harry his felins a little speck afore I made bacon of him. Sez I to him, sez I, 'the ile what's in your hide would slick the har of all the gals in our neck o' the woods 'til the cows comes home. You carry a most too much dead capital in that ar skin of yourn, any how; and if it's the same to you, I'll jist peel the bark off'n you, and larn you the rudiments of perlitical economy.' And, sez I to him, 'Mr. Bar,' sez I, 'the tail of your jacket is a trifle too short for cold weather, and a feller might kalkilate the tailor that made your coat was an idee sparein of his cloth,' sez I. And at that he got most allfired ugly, and pickin hisself up from the water sorter permiscuously, he begin rearin and rampagin; and arter a while, he cum at me on all fours, a rippin and a tearin! Whew! I wasn't skeered! The cane was so thick he couldn't get away without comin right by where I stood; so when he got agin me, I grabbed him—I wont say whar—and then we had it, up and down; first one and then tother; who should and who shouldn't; first one on top and then tother on the bottom, and sich a fight you never did see!"

Here Mike, rolling in his jaws his huge quid of tobacco, picked up his coonskin cap and was about to retire. "But, Uncle Mike," queried Mose, "which one holler'd 'nuff?"

"Why, you see," said Mike, "he was the most tarnationest, rampagin bar ever you *see*. The bar was down on Big Black ain't none of 'em a primin to him. Thar we had it; up and down, nip and tuck; who should and who shouldn't, 'til you'd er thought the very yerth a comin to an end——"

"But, Uncle Mike," again chimed in Mose, "which whipped?"

"Why," said Mike, "the cane was monsos thick, and thar we had it, first one and then tother; nip and tuck; pull Dick, pull Devil, and—and, if you will have it, I got all-fired tired, and jist slid down into the creek and *div* out of the varmint's way, or I'm blow'd if we hadn't er fout plumb on to Christmas! Come boys, let's liquor."

"It's no use talkin's," said Mike, " 'bout your Polar Bar and Grisly Bar and all that sort of varmint what you read about. They ain't no whar, for the big black customer what circumlocates down in our nect o'woods beats 'em all hollow. I've hearn of some monsos explites kicked up by the brown Bars, sich as totein off a yoke o' oxen and eatin humans raw, and all that sort o' thing; and Capen Parry tells us a yarn 'bout a big white bar what 'muses hisself climin up the North Pole, and slidin down again to keep his hide warm; but all that ain't a circumstance to what I've *saw*.

"You see," continued Mike, "there's no 'countin on them varmints as I'se ben usened to, for they comes as nigh bein' human critters as anything I ever see what doesn't talk. Why, if you was to hear any body else tell 'bout the bar fights I've had, you wouldn't b'leeve 'em, and if I wasn't preacher and couldn't never lie none, I'd keep my fly-trap shet 'tell the day of judgment.

"I've hearn folks say as how that Bars cant think like other human critters, and that they does all the sly tricks what they does from instink. Golly! what a lie! You tell *me* one of 'em don't know when you've got a gun and when you ain't? Jist a minit, an my privit 'pinion is, when you've hearn me through you'll talk tother side of your mouth.

"You see, one day, long time ago, 'fore breeches come into fashion, I made a 'pointment with Ike Hamberlin, the steam doctor, to go out next Sunday to seek whom we couldn't kill a Bar, for you know bacon was skace and so was money, and them fellers down in Mechanicsburg wouldn't sell on 'tick,' so we had to 'pend on the varmints for a livin.

"Speakin' of Mechanicsburg, the people down in that mud hole ain't to be beat no whar this side o' Christmas. I've hearn o' mean folks in my time, an' I've preached 'bout 'em a few; but, ever sense that feller Bonnel sold me a pint of red-eye whiskey—and half ov it backer juice—fur a coonskin, an then guv me a brass picayune for change, I've stoped talkin'. Why, that chap was closer than the bark on a hickory tree; an ef I hadn't hearn Parson Dilly say so, I'd ov swor it wasn't er fac, he was cotch one day stealin' acorns from a blind hog. Did you ever hear how that hoss fly died? Well, never mind. It was too bad to talk 'bout, but heap too good for him.

"But that ain't what I was spoutin' 'bout. As I was sayin' afore, we had to 'pend on the varmints for a livin'. Well, Ike Hamberlin, you see, was always sorter jubous o' me kase I kilt more bar nor he did; an', as I was sayin', I made a 'pintement with Ike to go out huntin'. The Ike he thought he'd be kinder smart, and beat 'Old Preach,' (as them Cole boys used to call me); so, as soon as day crack, he hollered up his puppies, an' *put!* I spied what he was 'bout, fur I hearn him larfin' to one o' his niggers 'bout it the night afore—so, I told my gal Sal to fill my privit tickler full o' the old 'raw,' and then fixed up an' tramped on arter him, but didn't take none o' my dogs. Ike hadn't got fur into the cane, 'fore the dogs they 'gin to whine and turn up the har on their backs; an' bime by, they all tuck'd tail, an' sorter sidled back to whar he was standin'. 'Sick him!' sayd Ike, but the cussed critters wouldn't hunt a like. I soon diskivered what was the matter, fur I kalkilated them curs 'o his'n wasn't worth shucks in a bar fight—so, I know's thar was bar 'bout, if I *didn't* see no *sine*.

"Well, Ike he coaxed the dogs, an' the more he coaxed, the more they wouldn't go, an' when he found coaxin' wouldn't do, then he scolded an' called 'em some o' the hardest names ever you hearn, (sich as 'son-of-er b—h,' and sich like,) but the tarnation critters wouldn't budge a peg. When he found they wouldn't hunt no how he could fix it, he begin a cussin. He didn't know I was thar. If he had er suspicitioned it, he'd no more swore than he'd er dar'd to kiss my Sal on er washin' day; for you see both on us b'longed to the same church, an' Ike was class leader. I thought I should er flummuxed! The dogs they sidled back, an' Ike he cussed; an' I lay down an' rolled an' laughed sorter easy to myself, 'til I was so full I thought I should er bust my biler! I never *see* enny thing so funny in all my life! There was I layin' down behind er log, fit to split, an' there was the dogs with ther tails the wrong end down, an' there was Ike a rarin' an' er pitchin'—er rippin' an' er tarrin'—an' er cussin wus nor a steamboat cap'n! I tell you it farly made my har stand on end! I never see er customer so riled afore in all my born days! yes I did, too, once—only once. It was that feller Arch Cooly what usen to oversee fur old Ben Roach. Didn't you know that ar' hoss fly? He's a few! well *he* is. Jewhilliken! how he could whip er nigger! and swar! ! whew! Did you never hear him swar? I tell *you*, all the sailors and French parrots in Orleans an't er patchin' to him. I hearn him let hisself out one day, an' I pledged my word he cussed 'nuff to send twenty preachers like old Joe Slater an' Parson Holcom, an' them kind er Judases, right kerlumpus into hell!—an what was wus, it was all 'bout nothin', for he warn't mad a wrinkle. But all that ain't neither here nor thar. But, as I was er sayin' afore, the dogs they smelt bar sine, an' wouldn't budge a peg, an' arter Ike had a 'most cussed the bark off'n a dogwood saplin' he was standin' by, he le'nt his old flint lock rifle up agin it, an' then he peeled off his old blanket an' laid her down, too.

"I diskiver mischief was er cumin', fur I never *see* a critter show wrathy like Ike did. Torecly I see him walk down to the creek bottom, 'bout fifty yards from whar his gun was, and then he 'gin pickin' up rocks and slingin' 'um at the dogs like bringer. Cracky! Didn't he link it into 'um? It minded me o' David whalin' Goliah, it did! If you'd seen him, an' hearn them puppies holler, you'd er thought he'd er knock'd the hine sites off'n every bitch's son of 'em! But that ain't the fun yet. While Ike was er lammin' the dogs, I hearn the allfiredest cracklin' in the cane, an' I looker up and thar was one of the eternalist whollopin' bars cumin', crack, crack, through the cane an' kerlosh over the creek, an' stoped right plumb slap up agin whar Ike's gun was. Torectly he tuk hold er the old shooter, an' I thought I see him tinkerin' 'bout the lock an' kinder whistlin' an' blowin' into it. I was 'stonished I tell you, but wanted to see Ike outdone so bad that I low an' kept dark, an' in about a minit Ike got done lickin' the dogs an' went to git his gun. Jeemeny, criminy! —if you'd only bin whar I was! I *do* think Ike was the madest man that ever stuck an ax into a tree, for his har stuck rite strait up, an his eyes glar'd like two dogwood blossoms! But the bar didn't seem to care shucks for him, for he jis sot the old rifle rite back agin the saplin', an walked off on his hine legs jist like any human. Then, you see, I gin to get sorter jealous, an' sez I to myself, Mister Bar, sez I, the place whar you's standin' aint perzactly healthy, an' if you don't wabble off from thar purty soon, Misses Bar will be a widder, by gum! With that, Ike grabbed up ole Misses Rifle, and tuk most pertickeler aim at him, an' by hokey, she snapped! Now sez I, Mister Bar, go it, or he'll make bacon of you! But the varmint didn't wink, but stood still as a post, with the thumb of his right paw on the end of his smeller, and wiglin' his tother fingers thus [and Mike went through with the gyration]. All this time Ike, he stood thar like a fool, er snappin' and er snappin', and the bar he lookin' kinder quare like, out er the corner o' his eye, an' sorter larfin' at him. Torecly I see Ike take down the ole shooter, and kinder kersamine the lock, an' when he done that, he laid her on his shoulder an' shuk his fist at the bar, and walk to'ard home, an' the bar he shuk his fist an' went into the cane-brake, an' then I run off."

Here, all the Yazoo boys expressed great anxiety to know the reason why Ike's gun didn't fire! "Let's licker fust," said Mike, "an' if you don't all caterpillar, you can shoot *me*. Why, you see," concluded he, "the long an' short of it is this, that the bars in our neck o' woods has somethin uv the human in 'um, and' this feller know'd as much about er gun as I do 'bout preachin', so when Ike was lickin' the dogs he jest blowed all the powder outen the pan, an' to make all safe, he tuk the flint out too, and that's the way he warn't skeered when Ike was snappin' at him."

FISH STORY

When men in the Yazoo country are not hunting or fishing, they are almost certain to be talking about hunting and fishing. The stories they tell have emerged from many a deer camp and fish fry, and they have been collected in their best form by Bob Hooter, a great-grandson of Mike Hooter and legendary Delta character since the time of his struggle to save the Brunswick stew pot on Mossy Lake.

Bob had been chosen to prepare the stew for a fishing party one afternoon, and he had a big double-sized galvanized iron washpot in which to brew it. In the midst of his preparation, the wind shifted and brought in a swarm of mosquitoes fresh from the swamp across the lake. There was no time to turn the tide with a pine-knot fire, and Bob chose an immediate defensive measure. He turned the heavy pot over and crawled in under it.

The raging mosquitoes did not give up the fight. They swarmed over the kettle, plunging their bills right through it after a succulent bite of Bob. The wily Bob kept fighting back. As fast as a mosquito plunged a bill through, he braided it firmly on the inside. His fight was in vain, however. Struggling to free themselves, the mosquitoes flew off with the pot. Bob says he never would have survived if that swarm of mosquitoes had not been fresh hatched—still pretty small as Delta mosquitoes go.

Bob is naturally an expert in the difficult art of coon hunting. Nowadays just finding one somewhere in a slough or swamp is a satisfactory conclusion for most hunts, but Bob and the three coon dogs he always keeps are never content with anything less than a coon den.

One night he was walking along a road near his house with two companions, when two of the dogs raced past on the heels of a fleeing coon. Bob and his friends quickly grabbed some tree limbs that would serve as clubs and followed up the chase. They found the dogs barking at the foot of a large tree on the edge of a slough. A hole at the bottom of the old oak was the only entrance and exit to what they agreed was a large den.

Bob rapped on the trunk with his club several times, and that started a stampede of the trapped coons. They poured out in a steady stream, and Bob and his friends lined up at the entrance and proceeded to give each one a healthy lick as it emerged. The coons continued to come out for a solid hour, to make a total that was estimated variously from one to five hundred.

When the last one had come forth, the hunters built a fire to check on the results of their endeavors.

"We didn't kill a coon," Bob says, "but we did beat off four hundred pounds of fur."

No man has a healthier respect for rattlesnakes than Bob. One day he was making one of the very infrequent inspection tours of his farm when he encountered a rattlesnake pilot coiled at the edge of a turnrow. He ran back quickly and grabbed a hoe leaning against the side of a tenant's house.

The regular hoe handle had been broken and in its place was a sassafras sapling. Bob took the makeshift hoe and swung at the snake. But the rattler had already begun to strike, and Bob missed him. The snake sunk its fangs into the handle, and, Bob concludes the story, "That handle swelled up so big that we split it up and made four fence posts."

Bob was telling the boys down at the barbershop why he had laid by his cotton crop so early in the summer.

"One night I heard a big noise in my back yard and got up to see what it was all about. A big boll weevil had a little one across the wood block and was giving it a beating with an ax handle because it couldn't strip more than one row of cotton at a time. I figgered then and there that I'd better hand it all over to them, or they might take it out on me."

During the duck season a few years back, Bob came down with a case of pneumonia that some of the town gossips attributed to a little bout with the weather and alcohol. I am inclined, however, to agree with Bob's version of the cause of his illness.

He was duck shooting one subzero morning, and while standing up to reload his gun struck a log and was plunged into the icy waters. Despite the handicap of a heavy overcoat and hip boots, he managed to make his way to the top, only to become encased with a solid covering of ice. But luckily, he was near a bank, and managed to struggle in to its safety.

On the bank, however, he realized that he would soon freeze to death in the ice-coated clothes, so he set out toward the warmth of camp in a steady trot. Before he had covered much distance the heavy boots caused him to trip over a tree root and fall sprawling to the ground.

As Bob tells it, "When I fell down, all my clothes but those rubber boots broke up into little pieces, and I had to run the rest of the way with nothing on but that frozen rubber."

There are few chances for turkey shoots in the Delta any more, but it hasn't been many years since a man could get a turkey dinner by spending a few minutes in the nearest patch of woods.

Bob and a friend were on a turkey hunt one morning when one of his near perfect calls pulled one strutting gobbler out into the open. Bob and his friend crawled to the edge of the bush that screened them from view. The cautious bird came as far as a log twenty yards away and stuck up its head.

Bob was using a rifle, and it was decided that he should take the shot, because the noise of his friend's shotgun might scare away any near-by birds. He carefully drew a bead on the gobbler's head and fired. The turkey ducked down immediately, and for a few seconds not a sound was heard. Then the head showed up again and Bob cracked down for the second time. Seconds passed, and then the head was up again—was up once more for another shot from the hunter.

The whole action was repeated nine times more, with each attempt bringing new curses from Bob over the failure of his usually perfect accuracy. After the twelfth shot he decided to get a better look at the turkey with the charmed life. Moving slowly out to the log, he quickly peered over. Scattered over the ground on the other side were twelve gobblers, all shot in the neck!

On a warm day Bob was fishing for perch in the middle of Round Lake. His luck had been so bad that he had to rely for his sole amusement on the quart of liquid refreshment that was part of every fishing trip. By the time half of it was gone he had become rather unsteady, and it was fortunate that half of the remaining pint was spilled into the minnow bucket.

Bob baited his hook with a fresh minnow several minutes later and dropped it listlessly over the side. The line started a wild dash out and around the boat, and a few seconds later he felt the tug of a speckled two-pounder, which he immediately pulled in. The fish had not swallowed the hook in the attempt to get the minnow, however. The pleasantly alcoholized minnow had bitten the big perch in the back of the neck and pulled him in with the assistance of the line.

In half an hour, with the assistance of several refreshing rests in the minnow bucket, the bait had dragged in the day's limit.

Telling the story about the fish scales is the only way to quiet Bob. The scales came into prominence when one of Dan Taylor's annual offspring came into the world.

Dan took a notion all of a sudden to see how much his new son weighed. Bob Hooter was his nearest neighbor, so Dan went up the road to see if he had any scales. Bob was out fishing, and the only thing Mrs. Hooter could find around the house was the pair that Bob used when he weighed his fish catches. They put the baby on these scales, and it weighed thirty-seven pounds.

During a long spell of wet weather on his farm, Bob discovered that his hogs were pining away and about to die. He investigated and found that they were suffering from insomnia. As they walked around, the ball of mud on each critter's tail kept getting bigger until finally it was so heavy that it stretched their hides so tight that they couldn't close their eyes, and so they got no sleep!

Bob had a great bird dog that was his pride and joy and the subject of endless bragging about his merits. There was some question, however, on the day the dog came to a point right on the main street of the county seat. There wasn't even a sparrow in sight, and Bob called to the dog, at first quietly, and then half mad, but still Tige made a perfect point.

Finally Bob had an idea. There was a stranger loafing in the shade across the street, and Bob approached and asked his name. The man answered, "My name is Bob White," and that explained everything.

Another one of Bob's prize dogs was a hound that he called the best coon-and-possum dog in Mississippi. All he had to do was to show the dog a board, and the dog would go off and find a possum or coon whose hide would fit the board. This saved Bob the trouble of hunting up a board to fit a hide, and he never had to worry about the quality of the possum or coonskin.

One day, though, the dog disappeared and when he had

been missing for three days, Bob took to the woods himself to see if he could find any trace of the faithful animal. After hours of searching, he found the dog, so worn out and exhausted that Bob had to carry him home in his arms.

The incident puzzled Bob for a while, but he finally figured it out. His wife had left the ironing board out leaning against the back porch, and the dog saw it and went out in the woods and wore himself out trying to find a possum or coon with a hide big enough to fit the ironing board.

Speaking of coons and coon dogs, Bob tells about the one where the pack treed a coon after a long chase, but there was no way to get him out except for one of the boys in the hunting party to climb up and knock him down. In the midst of the climbing, a rotten limb gave away, and the boy fell to the ground, sustaining a broken neck.

His companions bore the boy home sadly, but the injured youth's father received the news philosophically.

"It coulda been worse," he observed. "George mighta fell on one of the dawgs."

But on the subject of remarkable bird dogs, Bob says that one he heard of in Texas should take a few prizes. The specialty of this dog was to run a covey of quail down a prairie-dog hole, put his paw over the opening until the hunter was ready, then lift his paw just long enough for one bird at a time to fly out.

Bob is especially fond of talking about the gwinters of Carroll County, just about the most remarkable animal that Mississippi ever produced. A gwinter was something like a goat, but the most remarkable thing about him was his legs—the two on one side were longer than the two on the other side.

This met with the gwinter's approval, because he would keep grazing while walking around a hill, and so his body was kept on an even keel as he walked with his longer legs on the down side of the hill.

The Indians, who once hunted the gwinters long years ago, had to perfect a defense from the charges of the animal. They couldn't run, because the gwinter was too fast. The only defense was for the man to stand his ground until the gwinter was about four paces from him, then to jump quickly to one side, preferably downward. The gwinter would then have to run clear around the hill to get a step lower, and by then the Indian could be safely away from his adversary.

According to Bob, the funny thing about the gwinters was the existence of two specimens—not all of them had their long legs on the same side of their body. There were right gwinters and left gwinters. The right gwinters went around a mountain in one direction and the left gwinters in another.

Sometimes the gwinters of opposite types would meet on a hill and, of course, neither could pass the other, and that often led to fights in which both participants were killed.

"And that's why they are extinct, or soon will be," Bob Hooter says.

On a fishing trip one spring, Bob had been fishing all day in one spot before he decided to move on to a better location. The sum total of his catch up to then was a slender little eel, but even an eel tastes good when there is nothing else to eat at camp, so he tied it to a string and left it dangling in the water near the bank, planning to come back by and get it on the way in.

Coming back in the late afternoon, Bob reached down to pull in the eel, which he was going to have to use after all. The minute he took the line in his hand, his arm was nearly jerked out of its socket. Fighting hard to keep from going into the lake after the eel, he finally got a foothold and began a tug-of-war with whatever was on the other end of the line. After a twenty-minute fight, he pulled in a twenty-pound catfish. The eel was still on the line and wiggling happily!

It took a minute to figure out what had happened. The catfish had tried to swallow the eel, but the eel had other ideas about the matter. It had slipped out through the cat's gills after the big fish had taken it into its mouth, and then coiled the line around tightly enough to hook the fish with complete effectiveness.

When somebody brings up the subject of the wild boars in the Smoky Mountains and talks about how fierce and tough they are, Bob snorts. He says there never has been a boar that would be a match for one of the wild razorback hogs of Arkansas. And he can back up his sneer with a number of hard-to-get-around stories which he swears are the gospel truth.

One of the best is about the porker that he caught himself up in the Ozarks and brought home to his farm. He couldn't build a pen that would hold the razorback, for it rooted out of everything and roamed at large over the farm.

Bob was blasting stumps in some new ground when a dozen sticks of dynamite turned up missing. He was about to give them up for stolen, when somebody remembered that the razorback had been out that way and must have swallowed them.

They rushed back to the barn just in time to see an annoyed mule plant a vigorous kick in the hog's side. The resulting explosion was terrific.

"You know," Bob says, "for a couple of days we had a mighty sick hog on our hands.

"Last winter I went to see my brother," says Bob. "He joined up with some ritzy hunting and fishing club, and had been writing me about what fine hunting they had out there.

"And do you know what they had? They put me in a little house out in the middle of the lake. The house had an oilstove in it and everything else to make it as comfortable as an old maid's boardinghouse. There was an opening in front to shoot through. I could have taken a nap waiting for the ducks to come in, because when they did the decoys made enough noise to wake even me up. I didn't shoot but one of those ducks. It seemed too much like just plain murder.

"They even had fishing tackle out there in the hut, and I could've caught some nice bream through the hole in the floor while I was waiting for the ducks, but I would have as soon bought 'em in a fish market.

"Stuff like that is what's the matter with hunting today. At least, it's one of the things. The only way to really hunt ducks is to sit half the day on the edge of a lake in a hollow stump, freezing to death, except for a bottle of red corn in your pocket.

"But the biggest trouble with hunting is people getting out in the woods with guns who don't even know which end of them shoots. When you get a driver's license, you are at least supposed to know a little bit about a car, but you don't have to know a blame thing about guns or hunting to get a hunting license. It's getting so that you can't get out in the woods without being shot at by some moron who shoots every time he sees a leaf move.

"I was hunting over on Quiver last season when I looked up over a log right down the muzzle of a brand-new, high-powered rifle. Some sissy britches, all dressed up in store-bought hunting clothes, was holding the thing, and he was shaking like a leaf.

" 'That was lucky,' he said, 'I thought sure you were a deer.'

" 'Well, you're lucky I don't run my antlers through you,' I told him. 'How come your mama let you get so far away from home?'

"I took his rifle and unloaded it, then gave it back and sent him back towards where he said he had come from. And I believe that was one tenderfoot who'll know a little about something the next time he tries to do some hunting. But most of them have to shoot up or kill themselves or somebody else before they learn anything. Maybe it wouldn't be so bad if they just killed themselves, but they're not the kind to be so considerate of their fellow man.

"I've hunted all over the United States and parts of Arkansas, but I never have run across one of these clothing-store dummies who were really hunting anything except a chance to wear their clothes and something to talk about to the boys back in the office who are the same kind of hunters. They're the kind who shoots first, and then look to see whether they were shooting at anything. Hunting is just another way to show that they are real he-men, like showing the hairs on their chest.

"One of these tenderfoot hunters came down from Memphis for a little hunting one winter. He was so green we were able to talk him into going snipe hunting one day, only this was to be a different kind of snipe hunting, in the daytime and with a gun. We took him way back in the woods as far as we could take him without running the risk of his really getting lost. We left him waiting for us to scatter out and drive the snipes back to where he was.

"When he wasn't in by dark that night, we were beginning to be sort of worried and were getting ready to go look for him, when he walked in carrying a possum and smelling exactly like a pole cat.

" 'I didn't get but two snipes,' he said, 'and one of them get to smelling so bad that I had to leave it back where I shot it.'

"Things wouldn't be so bad if all the tenderfeet could be hand-led like that fellow. He's as good a hunter as anybody now.

"The way you have to risk your neck going hunting is mighty bad, but it could be a lot worse down here. They tell me that up North and East menfolks are having to take their wives hunting. That's the hell-firedest thing that ever came along. If it ever gets to be the fashion around here to take the little woman along, there's sure to be one less hunting license sold in this state."

Bob paused to mop his red face. The heat of his argument seemed to have taken hold of his body, too.

"Before I take a woman hunting, or go in the same woods where one is supposed to be hunting," he said, "I'm going to swear off and take up something tamer. Maybe after a few years, the tenderfeet and the women hunters will kill each other out."

16

Swamp Fever

The Indians said the fogs which rose from the Yazoo infected the air with poison which brought death to people long exposed to it. Their first white visitors knew it was more than just superstition, for fevers fell upon them regularly, just as on the Indians. Most of these early visitors accepted the origin of the name Yazoo—River of Death in Choctaw—in the malarial fevers which swept across the Delta.

Actually the white man brought malaria to North America, and the swamp fever of the Delta probably was spread to the area by Indian tribes who made the first contacts with Europeans. The Yazoo had the anopheles mosquito in endless quantity and was able to give the disease a home and a carrier. The first white settlers in the Indian cession lands accepted the risk of the swamp fever when they moved into the Delta, and that risk prevented countless numbers of others from taking the gamble. Several holders of large acreage refused to send valuable slave property into the swamps to clear it out. They hired the clearing of their lands by contractors who used Irish laborers fresh from the old country. It was cheaper to let immigrant Irishmen risk contact with the fever than to lose valuable slaves. Many a good Irish-name family in the Delta today is descended from a hardy laborer who could survive malaria, as well as all the other perils which beset a man fresh from Erin.

Delta pioneers of the period before 1900 recall the time when apparently every man, woman and child in the region shook with chills (ague) every other day. Daily life had to be arranged to accommodate the chills during the "sickly season," which normally lasted from June to October and might be spread throughout the year in bad cases. As a result of malaria, chronic debility became the lot of a good third of the population. Sallow, pale and sickly people regularly subjected to malarial chills could provide little resistance to other diseases. According to legend, Negroes were supposed to develop a natural immunity, but the legend largely grew from the Negro population, where the percentage of illness was not so noticeable to the casual observer. African tribesmen actually had built up a resistance to malaria, but little of it was left in their Delta descendants.

Malaria made itself evident in the folkways of the time. Women were easier victims, and a common method of proposal for the man who did not like to be direct was "Miss Lucy, may I have the honor of buying your coffin?" Often as not the husband had that privilege. There is a plantation graveyard in Sunflower County in which a farmer buried six successive wives before a sorrowing seventh buried him with her predecessors.

In the days when malaria moved unchecked through the Delta, it accomplished the same terrible results that it still achieves in the world as a whole today—killing more human beings than any other disease. Chills and fever were its symtoms. Before men realized it was something else, they called it swamp fever. It was a good name, for malaria thrived in the swamps and any other type of countryside which could serve as a breeding place for the mosquitoes which took it from human to human.

Malarial chills normally came every other day during the height of disease. They began with chattering teeth, crawling "goose flesh" and shivers that wracked the body. Right behind the chill was a burning fever which brought a headache and thirst, ending with drenching sweat as the fever departed. One doctor left this description of a chill: ". . . I felt cold chills playing hide and seek up and down my spine. As the sun's rays became more vertical, the chilly sensations grew in strength. Soon my teeth were chattering. . . . As the God of Day heralded his coming by flaming banners in the east, my fever left me, and was followed by the sweating state. As fast as the sun dried my clothes on the outside the flowing pores of my skin wet them within. . . ."

For nearly a hundred years the Delta's only defense against malaria was accidental. The clearing of land for new plantations, with the accompanying drainage programs to keep it cultivable, also cleared away many of the disease-carrying mosquitoes. The mosquitoes were merely bothersome pests, not disease carriers, in the mind of the average citizen. No one considered a mosquito-elimination program more elaborate than the common practice of burning pine knots in the front yard.

One of the common editions of the countless medical books distributed by patent medicine firms had this to report on malaria in 1898: "*mal-aria* signifies 'bad air.' It is generally understood that malaria poisons are absorbed into the system from the atmosphere. The fact is, there are always liable to be more or less unhealthy conditions in the atmosphere; it is absolutely impossible to prevent malarial germs from entering the system, but it is altogether possible to prevent their doing harm after they get in."

Treatment of malaria had been going on for some time, of course. A Mississippi doctor, Henry Perrine, was one of the first in the world to prescribe quinine, and word of his treatment was brought into the Delta malarial country with the first white settlers. Quinine was too costly and medical findings too difficult to make known to get the quickest possible use for the drug, however. Negroes devised a home remedy not too far removed from quinine. They gave malarial and other fever victims water in which red-oak bark had long been soaked. The high praise this medicine brought indicates that it must have had some of the qualities of cinchona.

Only the eventual acceptance of quinine, and widespread medication, enabled the Delta to hold its own in the battle with malaria. Successful treatment was being prescribed, of course, long before General Gorgas proved the mosquito to be the carrier. The heavy and persistent doses of quinine, plus long exposure, gradually developed a certain resistance to the most serious attacks of the disease in a good part of the Delta populace. The necessity for continual medication made the Delta a rich gold mine to be continually worked by patent medicine manufacturers and salesmen in their period of glory before the passage of the Pure Food and Drug Act.

Signs proclaiming the all-encompassing virtues of Grove's Chill Tonic, 666, and a dozen other proprietary remedies less durable in character were part of the scenery on every ginhouse wall. In the cotton fields the orange and yellow posters with the three sixes were as frequent as the cotton houses. Shipments of chill tonic in actual boatload quantities were often brought up the river, with the salesmen working from the boats themselves. Rich's Tasteless Chill Tonic was sold in the commissaries and small town stores on a "no cure, no pay" basis, in "the neatest package and largest bottle on the market for the money. It is so pleasant to taste, that the *Young, Middle Aged, and Old* all enjoy taking it." Chill tonics were a staple of the Delta diet, almost as much as fat back and molasses.

The catch-all patent medicine remedies had to include claims for the cure of chills and fever if they were to maintain their sales in the swamp country. Smith's Bile Bean was claimed to "cure biliousness, sick headache in four hours, prevent chills, relieve neuralgia, cure fever, a sour stomach, bad breath, and clear the skin." The tonics might cure "weakness of memory, difficulty of recalling names or dates, inaptitude for business or study, lameness, weakness, weakness in the back or loins, weakness of the organs, loss of nervous power and general tone of the system, weak or failing powers, prostration and debility from overwork or mental effort," but it also had to provide relief from chills and fever if it was to become a standard seller in the Delta. Usually the promise was made, either directly, or "If you are taking the large old-fashioned griping pills, try Carter's Little Liver Pills and take some comfort. A man can't stand everything."

One of the much-exploited drugs was "Liquozone," which led off its advertisements with the statement "Liquozone is too important a product for quackery," then promised to cure all diseases that begin with fever, listing in alphabetical order, from asthma to ulcers, some forty-odd ailments which it would cure, including cancer, colds, gallstones, tuberculosis, and the inevitable malaria. Despite its appealing name, Liquozone did not include the high alcoholic content normal in most of the patent tonics. An analysis distributed by the American Medical Association declared it to be nine tenths of one per cent sulphuric acid, three tenths of one per cent sulphurous acid, and the rest plain water.

A few farsighted individuals began to protect themselves and their homes from mosquitoes after the Gorgas discoveries became known, but relatively little was accomplished that was not already foreordained in the interest of personal comfort—protection from the bite of the mosquito, not its consequences. The first real attack on malaria made in the Delta came only after 1920, when a young man from the hills came down to Jackson to become director of the Mississippi Department of Public Health. Felix J. Underwood and the miracles he has accomplished on a threadbare budget are something of a legend in American public health services, but there is no better record than his attack on malaria in the Delta. His first job was to persuade the counties to set up proper public health departments as a means of spreading health education and preventive practices. The people had to be taught that the mosquito bite brought malaria and that the mosquito could be controlled by eliminating his breeding areas. The 1920's were a period when Federal government agencies were a long way from the idea of major health expenditures in Mississippi; Dr. Underwood had to get his pump-priming money from the Rockefeller Foundation.

Dr. Underwood was convinced that most malarial transmissions were made by night-biting mosquitoes. Homes could be screened to keep the mosquito away from sleeping victims. More than just telling about this, the State Board of Health established screen-door factories at strategic points in the Delta. Strong screen doors were made to fit tenant houses and furnished at cost to plantation owners who would agree to screen the cabin windows, which could be done by merely tacking screen wire across the window casings.

During much of the early period of the Delta's history, many of the largest life insurance companies in the country came into the area only for investment purposes. Farm mortgages produced a good income, and eventually financing of farm operations became part of the over-all insurance investment program. Some of these same life insurance companies would not write policies on Delta citizens because of the high malaria mortality and other adverse health conditions. In the late 1920's the State Board of Health submitted the first survey of the accomplishments of the malaria control program, and the insurance companies decided they could take the risk on Deltans. Today all special area rate discriminations have been eliminated.

The depression knocked out Dr. Underwood's screen funds, as well as his co-operating planters, but the depression-born WPA offered him a chance for an even more extensive program. For seven years, beginning in 1935, a malaria control program emphasizing elimination of mosquito breeding places was in operation, with approximately one thousand WPA workers assigned to the project in the Yazoo-Delta area.

WPA ended with World War II, but the war-borne development of DDT as an antimalarial insecticide brought dividends to the Delta. A Federal malaria control program was carried on five years after the war. Dr. Underwood allotted all of Mississippi's share of this program for the mass use of DDT as a residual spray in the interior of substandard homes in the Delta. The Federal program has been ended, but many Delta counties and cities today still carry on a limited spraying program in some fashion, with generally popular results.

The residual spray program, like most of the other malarial control measures, had very important secondary benefits. The spray killed flies and other pests just as it killed mosquitoes. In one county the infant death rate dropped 64 per cent, largely as a result of the practical elimination of dysentery and other intestinal disorders.

Cold figures best tell the story of the antimalarial campaign which the Mississippi State Board of Health has led. In 1920 there were 65,271 reported cases of malaria in seventeen Delta counties, with death resulting in 477 cases. In 1951, in the same counties, with much better reporting facilities, there were only nine cases of malaria, with no deaths!

The Delta feels sure that it has licked malaria, but Dr. Underwood is still on the alert. Malaria is still endemic in the area, and there is always the chance of more aggressive forms of it being brought in by returning troops. The development of rice planting is going to offer opportunities for increased mosquito breeding. Dr. Underwood and his Board of Health will be watching.

The Board of Health has moved on to other jobs in the Delta. The most spectacular postwar job has been the knockout blow given syphilis and gonorrhea in a five-year period. The anti-VD campaign has been pushed on a national scale since World War II, with general success, but it was probably needed more among the Delta's Negro population than anywhere else in the country. Preliminary tests showed the incidence of syphilis to be as high as 30 per cent in some counties.

The general testing program showed that approximately one fourth of the Delta's Negro population and 3 per cent of the white population were infected with treatable syphilis. The anti-VD campaign was aimed at white and black alike, with examinations and treatment available to all on the same basis, but the educational campaign obviously had to be geared to attract the greatest attention among the Negroes, with nineteen infected to each white in a cross section of the population.

Mobile blood-testing units toured every community in the Delta, advertising "Free Blood Tests to Everyone—Tell Your Friends—Bring Your Children—Everyone Can Get a Free Blood Test!" The Negroes were told that "bad blood" was their enemy through an advertising campaign far abler than that of any of the old patent medicine salesmen.

A short film, entitled *Feeling All Right*, was made in the Delta with an all-Negro cast, explaining the causes, effects and proper treatment of syphilis. The natural Delta voices and looks of the actors made the film far more real than a synthetic Hollywood cast. With an actual Hollywood short featuring the boogie-woogie of Cab Calloway as an added come-on, the film was shown in hundreds of churches, schools and theaters over the Delta. Everyone who attended the free show was given a copy of a comic book entitled *Little Willie*, presenting the message of syphilis in more permanent form. The immediate goal was blood tests for everyone at the county health office, or through the mobile testing units, and the message got across.

Radio stations and newspapers joined preachers and educators in the campaign to get blood tested. Within two years over half of the Negroes in the Delta had taken the blood tests. The follow-up treatment was highly effective because the educational campaign had achieved its purpose. The Delta Medical Center was established from a group of old National Youth Administration buildings left over from a war training program. The center was made a rapid treatment clinic for venereal disease, and patients by the thousands were brought in from throughout the area.

The educational campaign had removed any stigma from polite discussion of "bad blood." Those who received the bad-blood report could get a free bus ride to the Greenwood clinic on the banks of Big Sand Creek. Good food and lodging during the six-day treatment made it all something of a nice vacation. The first to return from Greenwood proved good salesmen among others who could qualify, and the major problem during the height of the campaign was to take care of the rush of eligible applicants. Employers and plantation owners helped out by simplifying the time-off problem. The education program on VD had awakened many of them to the economic waste involved. Nearly fifty thousand Delta Negroes went through the treatment clinics before the decline in patients made it necessary to shut down the treatment center at Greenwood and consolidate it with one serving the whole state.

During the same period nearly one hundred thousand gonorrhea cases were being treated by county health departments. By contrast with a record high of nearly two thousand new syphilis cases reported in 1946, only a little more than one hundred were discovered in 1952, even though the effort to locate the cases was as high in the latter year as the period of record outbreaks.

The intensive phase of the campaign has ended, with another great success in statistical terms. Today only 5 per cent of the Negroes in the Delta have treatable syphilis, and less than .5 per cent of the whites, in contrast to the earlier figure of 25 per cent and 3 per cent. The educational and treatment program is continuing along the same general lines, even though the supply of *Little Willie* books has long since been exhausted.

The entire program was accomplished without the necessity of a venereal disease plank in a civil rights platform. There have been no speeches in Congress, either pro or anti. It is illustrative of the kind of positive progress against ignorance, poverty and general apathy which makes no headlines, but accomplishes first things first without benefit of demagogy or histrionics.

17

Last of the Planter-Statesmen

When John Sharp Williams, disgusted at the failure to ratify the Treaty of Versailles and bring the United States into the League of Nations, announced that he "would rather be a hound dog and bay at the moon" than remain a member of the United States Senate and made good his threat of retirement, newspapers over the country commented on the passage of the last of the "planter-statesmen."

"The Sage of the Yazoo" lived inland from the river in Yazoo County, and it is probable that as a young man he knew the Rhine, the Rhone, and the Ruvanna better than the Yazoo, but his career as a Congressional leader far more typified the concept of plantation statesmanship than that of Vardaman, his contemporary in Mississippi, who first moved toward prominence with the impetus of family wealth gained from a Yazoo river plantation.

Like Vardaman, Williams was born outside the state. His Mississippi background was only on the maternal side, where his grandfather, John Sharp, had been chosen to command a company of Mississippi Rifles under Jefferson Davis at Monterrey. Captain Sharp's daughter married in Memphis the son of an old Tennessee political family, Christopher Harris Williams. John Sharp lost his mother during his fifth year, when she died in childbirth. Three years later the boy was an orphan, when Colonel Kit Williams was struck down at Shiloh.

Grandfather Sharp came to Memphis and brought young John Sharp to Mississippi, away from the memory of a visit to his father at Corinth the day before bloody Shiloh began.

In the same county where Albert Morgan was unsuccessfully mounting the picket line of freedom, John Sharp grew up in relative calmness, his relations with Negroes confined largely to the household servants and his playmate Allen. One day Johnny and Allen attempted a butting match in imitation of two rams in the pasture. Allen was the victor on first knock.

Some forty years later, in his campaign for the Senate against Vardaman, the Great White Chief declared that there was nothing a white man could not beat a Negro doing. Williams suggested that a butting match with Allen would prove at least one exception.

Life on a Yazoo plantation was not conducive to a full knowledge of the ways of the world. When young John Sharp was on the first leg of his journey to Charlottesville and the University of Virginia, he entered a busy railroad restaurant, but could find no place to be served. There were some vacant chairs, but as he approached each of them, a lady appeared and he hastily bowed away. After several awkward moments, it developed that the ladies were waitresses preparing to help him take a seat.

At Virginia, John Sharp decided that politics would be his career—perhaps statesmanship was the word in his thinking, for politics was not too respectable a word in the Reconstruction era. Statesmanship might even be a better term, for the young man had become wedded to books and a thirst for knowledge even before he left the plantation. The professional study for those who sought politics was recognized as law, but Williams wanted first the closest proximation to the Grand Tour then available.

He went first to Heidelberg, but a taste of Prussianism which he personally encountered cooled his enthusiasm for Germanic culture. When he refused to yield an icy sidewalk to a Junker cadet, that worthy issued a challenge.

With the choice of weapons, Williams elected pistols instead of the traditional sabers, which were apparently well known to his opponent from the evidence of facial scars.

As the signal to fire was being counted out, the German fired wildly before the word. Williams remained coolly taking aim. The Prussian's second rushed up to Williams's man.

"Does the Freiherr Williams demand his shot?"

"Certainly he does."

The young Junker remained erect as the fire command began anew, and Williams again sighted down the pistol barrel. At the signal, "Fire!", he wheeled suddenly and discharged his pistol into a snowbank.

From Heidelberg he transferred to Dijon, which made a better scene of operations for a study of southern Europe. After a year in France he returned to Charlottesville, to compress into twelve months the study necessary for a Bachelor of Laws degree.

Winning elections in Mississippi in the days of Populism required talents and skills not normally associated with study at Virginia and Heidelberg, but John Sharp was not long in exhibiting them after his shingle was hanging on the bluff above the river in Yazoo City. Any candidate might think that accepting a proffered chew from a plug of tobacco would convince any voter of his acceptance on a democratic level, but the successful candidate knew enough to unabashedly bite off the chew, rather than interpose the slightly high-falutin' use of a pocket knife to slice a sanitary chunk.

The solid background of knowledge, the inquiring mind, the political skill and the tongue sharpened for debate soon attracted national attention in the House of Representatives. His was one of the loudest voices raised against the McKinley imperialism and the Dingley Tariff of 1897, as stated in an address called the "Great American Banana Industry":

> There is in the United States, I suppose, one hundred acres of land where bananas can be grown in the open air, and yet I could, were I the legislating body of this country . . . put a tax of one dollar a piece on bananas . . . and inside of five years I could . . . have created and exploited a vast banana industry. . . . A great many people who formerly ate bananas would not be able to buy any bananas at all, some people would have to buy fewer bananas; but . . . a great many people . . . would eat them because the common people—Dagoes, Jerseymen, and Mississippians—could not.
>
> If I continued that system of taxation in existence for twenty years . . . there would have come . . . a new generation that "knew not Joseph" nor cheap bananas; and the moment sensible people came into power with the idea of revising the banana schedule, these gentlemen who "knew not Joseph" and had gone into the American banana busi-

> ness and, perhaps, formed a banana trust, would come into the Committee room of the National Legislature . . . giving utterance to cries of unutterable woe: "Are you going to strike down the Great American Banana Industry; are you going to reduce the duty from a dollar apiece on bananas to 80 cents? We can't stand it. It will ruin us. Are you going to make the people engaged in banana-raising go to the soup houses? Are you going to discriminate in favor of tropical sunshine against self-respecting American hothouse laborers?"
>
> After fifteen or twenty years "home competition" would have reduced the price of bananas in the American market to, let us say, 40 cents apiece, and then Republican orators and politicians would say privately, in newspapers, and on the stump and within these walls . . . "Lo, and behold! See how a protective tariff has reduced the price of bananas from 90 cents apiece in 1950 to 40 cents apiece in 1965—nearly a 50 per cent decrease in price to the consumer! Protection did it!"
>
> Yes! A reduction from superlative extortion to comparative extortion!
>
> But in all this picture, keep in mind one thing: While protectionism lasted, bananas would never reach three for a nickel, because if they did, that public enemy—tropical sunshine—would be master.

The Williams oratory and wit soon made him a favorite of the press, but this attention did not detract from the respect gained among his Democratic colleagues. In 1903 they named him minority leader, and during the next six years he laid the groundwork for party unity and cohesion that made it possible for Champ Clark to take Woodrow Wilson's New Freedom program through the House of Representatives.

The iniquities of the Republican tariff continued as the

great issue of the time in Congress, thanks in large part to the efforts of Williams to bury the silver-gold standard fight which split the Democrats throughout the age of Bryan.

During the 1904 campaign, "Mr. Dooley" observed: "The consarvative businessman who thinks that if a little money cud be placed in Yazoo City, th' prejudice agin' the Raypublicans, which is on'y skin-deep anyhow, cud be removed, hasn't turned up at headquarters." Despite the efforts at division, the "sound money" Democratic faction in the South was to remain firmly wedded to the progressive economic doctrines which came to fruition under Wilson.

Williams was minority leader during the palmy days of the reign of the Republican Speaker, "Czar" Joe Cannon. His day to day maneuvering of his party in the House was credited with much of the success of the revolt against Czar Cannon, which a young Republican maverick from Nebraska, George Norris, was to lead.

"We have finally gotten to the point where the procedures of this House lie within the secret conscience of the Speaker," the Yazoo Congressman declared on the floor. "There is no duty any more for him to communicate his reasons, his motives, or his rulings to the House."

Vain efforts to secure action on various legislative items were listed by the minority leader, and his plight was parodied in the verse he liked to recite:

When I asked my girl to marry me, she said,
"Go to Father."
She knew that I knew that her father was dead;
She knew that I knew what a life he had led:
She knew that I knew what she meant when she said,
"Go to Father."

Leading the opposition to an autocrat like Cannon gave Williams full opportunity to display his talent for sarcasm, but the daily discipline of the job was galling. The opportunity for advancement to the Senate came in 1907. Even though it involved a contest with the inflammable James K. Vardaman, then rounding out his term as Governor, Williams entered the race.

The direct primary amendment had not yet been adopted, but Mississippi had its equivalent through an agreement which bound members of the legislature to accept the directives of county conventions. The campaign was typical of Mississippi politics, fought with no holds barred, with the one exception that the time of the cry "outside interference" had not yet come.

William Randolph Hearst chose to make the race a national issue, hotly supporting Vardaman, with the national anti-Hearst press generally strongly favoring Williams. The Georgia Populist, Tom Watson, spoke out for Vardaman, and more conservative Southern leaders declared the defeat of Williams would be tragic.

The contest between the two men of the Yazoo typified the divergence between Southern political factions, the continued division lingering from the days of Populism. The division in Mississippi was almost equal. Williams was nominated for the Senate by a majority of 648 votes, out of 118,344 cast.

Although the campaign was in 1907, in conjunction with the general Democratic primary for all state offices, Williams was elected to a term in the Senate which did not begin until 1911. He chose to retire from the House, returning to Yazoo County, "rusticating on the farm, listening to the birds sing, and living the simple life." The scholar of Cedar Grove was behind in his reading, and he chose to catch up in the only way he had to gain leisure.

The Senate under President Taft had a sizable Republican majority, but the insurgent Republicans held the balance of power. Service in the body provided good training for the progressive program of the Wilson administration. A preconvention friend and supporter of Governor Wilson, Williams was a powerful factor in the 1912 campaign, with telling blows against Teddy Roosevelt, who was "so much dissatisfied during the last three years and a half because he ascertained that he could not be both ex-President and President at the same time."

In one speech he enunciated "Roosevelt's Creed":

> I believe in Theodore Roosevelt, maker of noise and strife, and in Ambition, his only Creed (My Lord). He was born of the love of power and suffered under William Taft; was crucified, dead and buried. He descended into Africa. The Third Year he rose again from the jungle and ascended into favor and sitteth on the right hand of his party, whence he shall come to scourge the licked and the dead.
>
> I believe in the Holy Outlook, the Big Stick, the Ananias Club, the forgiveness of political activities, the resurrection of Presidential Ambitions and the Third Term Everlasting. Amen. Amen. Amen.

Although a relatively new member of the Senate aristocracy, Williams's skill as a debater and parliamentarian was used extensively in pushing the Wilson reform program through the Senate. He guided the Underwood tariff reduction bill, with its precedent-shattering new provision for an income tax, to successful passage. His role of leadership made him one of the most influential writers of the Federal Reserve and Clayton Anti-Trust Acts. The anti-trust law fell short of many of the goals of his own anti-trust bill, developed in the days of Republican control.

When the appointment of Louis D. Brandeis as a Justice of the Supreme Court came before the Senate, Williams brushed aside the opposition based on racial prejudice: "I would vote to confirm him because some narrow-minded people might think he had been rejected on that ground," and he "had rather have a radical man upon the Supreme Court Bench who would be sobered by his responsibility, than to have a conservative who would be made more conservative by the same responsibility."

For the alumnus of Heidelberg, the most sobering responsibility of his career came with the war in Europe. He did not hesitate to brand the aggression of Prussian militarism from the start. For more than two years, Williams was the chief champion of preparedness in the Congress, pushing Wilson toward a stronger position on the issue.

In the early days of the fight, it was not the most popular course. Williams's colleague in the Senate was now Vardaman, who chose to make his career in the Congress one of fervent espousal of all forms of isolation.

When the Foreign Relations committee delayed action on a bill to increase the size of the merchant marine through purchase of foreign ships, Williams angrily resigned from the committee with a letter of resignation so bitter, it was ordered stricken from the *Record*. He became a chief spokesman for the creation of a formidable American navy, fearful that the United States would have to match German strength after a victory for the Central Powers in Europe.

When the "little group of willful men" blocked by filibuster action on a bill to allow arming of merchant ships, the champion of oratory in the Senate joined in support of an amendment to the rules to shut off debate by majority vote.

Woodrow Wilson came before the Congress on the night of April 2 with his historic war message, and it was Williams who first noted the magnificence of the passage, "the world must be made safe for democracy." His applause, alone at first, underlined the keynote of the war effort.

Wilson's second administration was the time of World War I and the creation of the League of Nations, but to the elected member of Congress, it was also the period of prohibition and woman's suffrage amendments. The sage of the Yazoo could support neither, despite the strongest personal supplications from the President in favor of the vote for women. The war and the strong demands for prohibition from Mississippi finally changed his vote in favor of the eighteenth amendment.

There was never any personal prohibition for John Sharp Williams, however. His colleagues agreed that he never reached his finest form on the floor until he had imbibed a toddy or two, and he was never bashful in admitting it.

The one Senator who had the temerity to refer to John Sharp's drinking in Senate debate quickly came off second best. After a difference over a resolution which he sponsored, Tom Heflin observed, "Well, whatever else may be said of me, when I come into the Senate chamber, I always come in with full possession of my faculties."

"What difference does that make?" John Sharp retorted.

Mississippi adopted statewide prohibition sometime before the Volstead amendment. The pantry at Cedar Grove never felt this, but, on trips through the state, the Senator did. In Greenville he called on his then colleague, LeRoy Percy, and Senator Percy sent his secretary out for a couple of quarts of bourbon to observe the visit. The young man returned with the whiskey after an absence of an hour, complaining of the long search and the fact that the two quarts had cost $25.

"Ah," said John Sharp, "at last we've found a place where they appreciate the true value of liquor."

In February, 1920, during the first days of prohibition enforcement, he told a friend his personal supply of liquor was down to two and one half quarts and would be gone in another day or two. He didn't know whether to "get some good friend and finish what I have left on hand and each shoot the other, or expatriate ourselves and go to France or Cuba."

It is pleasant to recall that prohibition was never allowed to become an inconvenience for the Senator.

One day his friend Jim Watson, the Indiana Republican, privately remonstrated with him about drinking, as they walked to the Senate Chamber from the Senate Office Building. It was after a Senate speech in which Williams had sharply attacked the Irish faction in the United States then attempting to have the question of Irish independence considered by the Paris Peace Conference.

"One time I made up my mind that I would never take another drink, that I would quit forever," John Sharp answered. "I abstained absolutely for six months, and I tell you the honest truth, Jim, when I say that in all that six months, I never had an original thought."

No man in the Congress was a stronger supporter of the League of Nations, and the great debate over the ratification of the Paris peace treaty was the great cause of his life. Williams was generally the spokesman who answered Henry Cabot Lodge, "the narrow New England sectionalist and narrow Federalist politician."

He told objectors to the League idea that he experienced no difficulty in a joint role as citizen of Yazoo County, the State of Mississippi, and the United States, and thought he would have no trouble in the future adding citizenship in the League of Nations to the list.

The far horizon from the Yazoo beckoned as the only hope for a lasting peace, and the failure in the Senate grated to his marrow.

The resentment boiled up and overflowed in a speech to the Mississippi legislature shortly after the final rejection of the League of Nations in 1920. The debate, he said, had been the "most incoherent gabfest in human history. . . . Men sometimes disparage idealists, but they are coarse grained jackasses who do so, and do it because they are coarse grained . . . the idealists point the way and cheer men's souls."

As for John Sharp Williams, he would "rather be a hound dog and bay at the moon, than to spend one minute in the Senate after the expiration of my term of office."

John Sharp went home to Yazoo County to stay, and the last of the plantation statesmen was gone.

18

Great White Chief

Marion Landing served Yazoo steamboats even before Dancing Rabbit, and after the white settlement of the Carroll and Holmes County hills began, the village that grew up around the landing threatened to outstrip Greenwood as a shipping and trade center. Marion boasted a better road to the hills, and it could draw the trade when the mire of the first Greenwood road closed all wagon traffic.

The man named Marion who had given his name to the landing did not remain a permanent resident, and the village eventually acquired the Biblical name of Sidon, from the plantation along the river which bounded the town to the north.

Sidon plantation, as well as most of the lots in the town and the farms to the south, was owned by the Robinson family, an acquisition dating back to the original purchase from the Choctaw titleholders. In the later 1870's the possession of the estate was in the hands of two brothers, Doug and Jerry Robinson.

Doug Robinson died suddenly in 1882, leaving a widow and small son to inherit half the Sidon estate. Anna Burleson Robinson took her child, Doug, Jr., back to the home of her parents in Winona, thirty miles east of Greenwood.

Before many weeks, she was the rich young widow Robinson, famed as a belle of Winona and sought for introductions by the unattached men of the town. One of these was a young lawyer fresh from his apprenticeship in a Carrollton office, and not long away from a Yalobusha County cotton field. James Kimble Vardaman began his search for fame and fortune in Winona, from where his cousin Hernando DeSoto Money had gone from an editorial office and the mayor's chair to a seat in Congress.

Board and room and office rent in advance and the cost of moving his trunk from Carrollton to Winona had left only fifty cents in the pockets of the young lawyer after his first day in the new town. The first man to enter his new office was not a client, but a solicitor seeking contributions on behalf of a neighbor whose home had recently burned. Without apology for his small donation, Vardaman solemnly signed the petition and turned over the fifty-cent piece.

There were no big cases and few small ones for the new lawyer, and he saw part of the reason in the way the farmers' and working men's money flowed into the nine saloons supported by the town with a population of less than a thousand. There was a gambling room in the rear of each saloon. "Ladies" did not appear on the streets on Saturdays, when farmers came to town and the saloon customers spread out beyond the doors.

A young attorney's practice did not have to be extensive to provide enough of life among the elite of Winona. Foremost among these attractions was the widow Robinson. Anna was within a few months of twenty-nine, and he was only twenty-two, but the differences in ages had little effect upon a swiftly culminated romance. They were married in May, 1883, at the home of the bride's parents. The stormy petrel of Mississippi politics had made his link to the Delta and to the valley of the Yazoo.

There was something besides law to fill his time. The editorship of cousin H. D. Money's paper developed one of the periodic vacancies that had come since that worthy had advanced to Congress, and young Vardaman stepped into the breech.

His first step was to sound a gun for drying up Winona, and the Winona *Advance* was seldom without a prohibition editorial from that day forward. The editorials led to speeches, and young Vardaman, the orator, was soon on the platform with the town's preachers, mounting the tempo of the dry crusade. Success came first when the town's board of aldermen agreed to a referendum on the dry law question and set the date early in 1884. The aldermen ruled that all adult males of the town, Negro as well as white, would vote in the election.

The saloonkeepers met the flurry of oratory and editorials with a mask of indifference as the best means of promoting their cause, but they did bring in an out-of-town Negro orator to speak in an effort to counteract the prohibition sentiments of the colored pastors. The tactics did not work, and prohibition was voted in by a narrow margin. James K. Vardaman, instead of the local preachers, received the major credit for the triumph.

Winona seemed dull after the prohibition fight, and there were attractions a few miles west on the Yazoo. Sidon plantation, property of Mrs. Vardaman, appeared to be yielding poor returns, and the supervisory presence of the owner's husband might change that picture. His widowed mother was making her home in Greenwood with another son, and that growing town offered more to the ambitious young editor and lawyer.

The Vardamans moved first to Sidon, but the operation of the plantation took only a small portion of his time. Most of the work was in Greenwood, arranging business deals and supervising the construction of a lavish, two-story house, designed by Mrs. Vardaman. They moved into the new home in 1889, with James K. already recognized as one of the affluent citizens of the town.

The Leflore County Board of Supervisors employed him as its attorney, an important financial plum that carried with it recognition as a capable attorney. He was employed as editor of the weekly Greenwood *Enterprise*, and won election as the county's member of the House of Representatives in the Mississippi legislature, all three advances in the year of 1890.

The crusader had not forgotten the battle for prohibition in Winona, and the *Enterprise* was not long in entering the fight against the saloons of Greenwood, which numbered approximately one to every seventy-five regular inhabitants of the town. The Vardaman campaign eventually persuaded both Greenwood and Leflore County to enact dry laws, but it took ten years to finish the job, sprinkled with regular violence. The shooting scrape which involved Vardaman himself was to echo through political campaigns for twenty-five years to come.

The generally accepted Vardaman version of the story was as follows:

Chief among the saloon-owner opponents of prohibition in Greenwood was Tom Upshur, proprietor of one of the principal saloons and of several pieces of important business property. Upshur was loud in his opposition to prohibition and particularly bitter in personal remarks about the editorial sparkplug of the dry movement. The threats took on a sinister meaning to Vardaman, when a physician friend warned him that Upshur and a crony, a man named Stoddard, were planning to kill him upon the first opportunity, when they could force a fight. The editor informed a cousin, James D. Money, and the two went about the streets armed during the next few days.

The attack was not long in coming. Upshur and Stoddard confronted him one morning in front of the post office, and when Stoddard heaped a string of curses upon a flow of abuse, Vardaman knocked him from the sidewalk into the gutter. After this blow, Upshur drew his pistol and fired at Vardaman, but the bullet only passed through his coat. Vardaman drew his own gun and fired back, missing wildly. At this moment Money rushed from the post office, firing alternately at Upshur and Stoddard, who raised himself from the gutter and shot Money through the leg. When Money appeared on the scene, Upshur rushed for cover, but not before he and Vardaman had again exchanged wild shots. Both the wounded Money and Vardaman fired at Stoddard, killing him instantly.

The editor was crusading for prohibition, but the politician already had his eye on a further goal, the governorship of Mississippi. In 1894 his colleagues in the House of Representatives made him Speaker, and in 1895 he sought the nomination for governor in the Democratic convention. The young politician from the Yazoo climbed fast, but the ways of older heads with the convention machinery were too much, and Anse McLaurin won the nomination to fight with the Populists. The defeat in the convention was the deciding blow in changing Vardaman over to support of the Populist demand for nominating primaries. Populist ideas were common in the editorials of young Vardaman, as his local political enemies were quick to point out. Vardamanites could express it differently—"As editor, his literary style was faultless; his writing was vigorous, unconventional, and fearless."

He resigned his connection with the *Enterprise* in 1895 to push his campaign for the governorship, but he was back on the job in 1896, founding a new weekly called the *Commonwealth*. The editor of the *Commonwealth* listed five long-range reforms in government as his editorial platform:

1. The initiative and referendum, because of the "primary democratic" principles underlying the measures.

2. An elective state judiciary "more in keeping with the genius of republican institutions."

3. A nominating primary for all state and county offices instead of the old convention method because the "white voters were able and well qualified to choose their own public servants."

4. "Woman participating in governmental matters" because "she is as well equipped to meet the requirements of citizenship as man" and no less "capable than he in determining that which is best for the state."

5. The abolition of judicial injunctions "used by plutocracy to crush and hold in check the robbed and restless toiler."

On more direct issues of immediate concern to Mississippi, the *Commonwealth* was just as vigorously outspoken.

Legislative appropriations were urged for roadbuilding throughout the new rural areas, and strong opposition voiced to the plan for establishing tax exemptions to encourage industrial development of the state. Vardaman did not hesitate to speak out against the practice of leasing convicts to private citizens, even though many of the leaseholders were plantation owners operating in the Yazoo Delta area in which the *Commonwealth* circulated.

He spoke out on national issues as a backer of Bryan's free silver program, and on behalf of the "hundreds of thousands of workers in every corner of the land, whose average yearly income won't reach $200," under conditions "worse than slavery." He backed Bryan's plan for government ownership of railroads and remarked in 1901 that it was "now nip and tuck whether the railroads would own the government or the government would own the railroads."

The *Commonwealth* was a great local booster in the best small town tradition, with semiannual "Greater Greenwood" editions. The Yazoo farm owner saw the opportunities for development of the still unopened territory west of the Yazoo between Greenwood and Belzoni, repeatedly urged the landowners in the area to promote the building of a railroad between Itta Bena and Belzoni. Vardaman called a meeting in Itta Bena in 1898 which was the first step toward the eventual building of the road, and the beginning of the venture that created Humphreys County in 1918.

Real estate development and land speculation were added as a sideline for the editor-lawyer-planter-politician, and he formed a real estate partnership with the business manager of the *Commonwealth*, Henry T. Crosby.

Back in the days of the Winona *Advance*, the Vardaman-edited paper gained the name for printing short excerpts from the writings of classical authors, just as the orator Vardaman was to be known for such quotations. This literary flavor of the *Commonwealth* was so widely known throughout the South that a movement developed in 1897 to establish a Southern literary magazine and make Vardaman editor.

A new job for Vardaman developed in 1898 when he was named commander of a special battalion of "immunes" which volunteered for duty in the Spanish-American War. With yellow fever ravaging the men already in uniform, the army sought to enlist men who had previously suffered from yellow fever in the hope that they could see service with immunity from the disease. Major Vardaman retained his military title until he could replace it with that of Governor, but the military service consisted only of dull training days in a Florida camp. The war was over before the battalion was scheduled for shipment to Cuba.

Of the five political reforms which the *Commonwealth* had demanded, Mississippi has given its official approval to only two, nominating primaries and elective judiciary. It was the editor of the *Commonwealth* who entered the arena for the first state governorship nominating primary of the Democratic party.

The keynote of his campaign had been made clear early in issues of the paper, before his adventure in the army. He said the white race would never share "domination and sovereignty with an inferior race." With him the Negro issue was admittedly "a matter purely of race prejudice, nothing else."

Mississippi had effectively barred Negroes from government participation with her constitution of 1890, and similar white supremacy developments were taking place at the same time all over the South, along with an unusual spurt of placing Jim Crow customs on the statute books as laws. Throughout the South widespread interest in the "Negro problem" developed.

Theodore Roosevelt, already something of a blackguard in the White House because he was a Republican, provided an incident for the writers and political leaders who clamored to keep the Negro in his place, when he entertained Booker T. Washington as his guest in the White House. In Mississippi another incident developed, attracting as much attention on a racial issue as another Roosevelt, Eleanor, was to gain years later. As postmistress of the county seat town of Indianola, Roosevelt appointed a Negro woman, Minnie Cox. A large group of indignant white citizens accordingly refused to patronize the post office at the Sunflower town, sending and receiving their mail from the near-by plantation village of Heathman. The angry Roosevelt ordered the Indianola post office closed until the patrons accepted the postmistress.

Eventually the indignant Indianolans won their point with the resignation of the Negro postmistress, but the incident provoked editors and orators to an early boiling point for years to come. Vardaman published a long and vitriolic editorial brutally castigating Roosevelt and some of the Negroes involved, and papers throughout Mississippi reprinted it.

The extreme point of this abuse was the following paragraph:

> Probably old lady Roosevelt, during the period of gestation, was frightened by a dog, and that fact may account

for the canine qualities of the male pup which are so prominent in Teddy. I would not do an injustice, but I am disposed to apologize to the dog for mentioning it.

The gubernatorial campaign was for 1903, but Vardaman took the stump in the July heat of 1902, denouncing Roosevelt as a "coon-flavored miscegenationist" committing the "monstrous folly of filling the head of the nigger with useless learning." He demanded the repeal of the fourteenth and fifteenth amendments to the Constitution of the United States, but did not explain how he would accomplish this as Governor.

Although a student of his political speeches estimated that six per cent of the wordages consisted of *I*, *you*, *we*, or *our*, Vardaman also liked to refer to himself in the third person, as when he stated:

> A good deal has been said about Major Vardaman teaching mob law. I want to tell you just how far I am in favor of mob law. If I were the sheriff and a Negro fiend fell into my hands, I would run him out of the county. If I were governor and asked for troops to protect him I would send them. But if I were a private citizen I would head the mob to string the brute up, and I haven't much respect for a white man who wouldn't.

Major Vardaman had three opponents in the 1903 campaign, but one withdrew before the balloting, leaving the "conservative" vote to be divided between Frank A. Critz and Edmund F. Noel. The latter, who was Vardaman's neighbor from Holmes County and who was to succeed him as governor, hit bitingly into the editor's penchant for filling his speeches with quotations from popular authors of the day:

> A governor who attends to his business has no time or opportunity to compile speeches from poems and novels. . . . Now, as to the school question, Vardaman talks a lot about it, but don't understand a thing about it. It's not in Edward Markham; not in Thomas Nelson Page, not in any of the books of poetry and fiction, and this accounts for it. . . . A man has a right to change his opinion, as Vardaman says, but he ought not to change his principles like he does his clothes.

Critz was a venerable Confederate veteran with long service in the state legislature, but it was Vardaman who waxed eloquent in his tribute to the Confederate veterans—as the Poplarville *Free Press* expressed it, "old gray-haired veterans wept like children, when, with a heart sincere, and eloquence sublime, he told of his love for these grand old heroes."

The Vardaman-created issue was the Negro, however, and he hammered away continually at this theme.

"You spent one hundred fifty thousand dollars to disfranchise the Negro by the Constitutional Convention of 1890," he told every audience, "and since then you have expended over six million to bring him back into politics by educating him." His defeat, he said, would be an "endorsement of President Roosevelt's criminal policy of social and political equality" and "we would have to kill more niggers in the next twelve months in Mississippi, than we have had to kill in the last twenty years."

Most of the state's daily newspapers opposed Vardaman in the campaign but a good portion were rabidly in his favor.

"A VOTE FOR VARDAMAN IS A VOTE FOR WHITE SUPREMACY . . . WHITE CHILDREN, a vote for the SAFETY OF THE HOME and the PROTECTION

OF OUR WOMEN AND CHILDREN, and a vote for an ABLE, HONORABLE, CHRISTIAN GENTLEMAN," capitalized the McComb *Journal.*

The Charleston *Democratic Herald* reported one of his speeches: "James K. Vardaman has come and gone, and the matchless beauty of his rhetoric, the Gibraltar-like soundness and solidity of his logic and the fire of Robespierean oratory were heard last night by one of the largest gatherings seen in Charleston since the last hanging."

Noel was eliminated in the first primary balloting, and Vardaman won the nomination from Critz in the runoff by a majority of 7,000 out of the nearly 100,000 votes cast.

Having saved Mississippi for white supremacy, Governor Vardaman found that other matters took up most of his time in office, and only the veto of several Negro education bills aroused him to comment on racial issues during the next four years.

Reform of the state penitentiary system, including the abolition of a loophole which got around the constitutional provision against the leasing of convicts; improving the public schools, even those for Negroes; development of the state insane hospital; and prevention of railroad mergers were his accomplishments. He asked for, but did not get, a child labor law, a state bank examiner, a state highway commission, and a state prohibition law.

In 1907 he asked the people to elect him to the vacant United States Senate seat, but another master of campaign oratory, John Sharp Williams, won the nomination by less than a thousand votes. Instead of campaigning on his gubernatorial record, Vardaman lashed out again at the Negro and promised to work unceasingly for repeal of the fifteenth amendment. Ridiculing his opponent's chances of ever accomplishing this, Williams also harped on the early advocacy of government ownership of railroads.

Vardaman lost his second state campaign, but the Vardaman faction had already been installed in Mississippi politics. The long raven-black locks that Vardaman wore down to his shoulders began to turn gray, but this merely added to the glamour of the "Great White Chief," as he was beginning to be called. Dressed in a white suit with a white hat, he would ride from railroad station or hotel to his speaking site in a wagon drawn by a team of white oxen.

After he sold the *Commonwealth* and moved to Jackson with his family in 1904 to take up his duties as governor, James K. Vardaman did not return again to live in Greenwood and the Yazoo country. Most of his campaign oratory was to be reserved in the future for the piney woods and red clay hill country, but the Yazoo counties still voted strongly for Vardaman in campaigns that came.

In one of these campaigns a little-known Vardaman camp follower, State Senator Theodore G. Bilbo, made his first bow in what was to be perpetual limelight by admitting the acceptance of a bribe to vote for the Senate nomination of LeRoy Percy over Vardaman.

When the Great White Chief finally did attain the United States Senate, World War I dominated the national as well as the international scene, and his claim to fame was his membership in the "little group of willful men" who fought the preparations for war, the actual declaration of war, and the American entry into the League of Nations after the struggle was over.

Vardaman's opposition to Woodrow Wilson was enough

to elect young Congressman Pat Harrison to his Senate seat in 1920. After this defeat, there was no place left on the Mississippi scene for James K. Vardaman. Bilbo, wartime governor, had taken over the leadership of the Vardaman faction and was making it a Bilbo faction. After a few years more in the dwindling spotlight in Jackson, Vardaman retired to the home of a daughter in Birmingham, and it was there that death overtook the Great White Chief in the 1930's.

19

Blow for a Landing

Steamboats moving up the river opened up all the Yazoo country and were virtually its only means of communication with the outside world until near the end of the nineteenth century. There are few towns anywhere in the basin which did not begin as steamboat landings, either on the main river system or on one of the innumerable tributaries. Most of the river landings lost out in the race for population after the advent of the railroad and the automobile, but all the population centers which have survived started with a stream.

No purely passenger boats made regular runs on the Yazoo—few have ever operated on any river. Some purely freight boats operated in the fall, taking the cotton crop to market, but most river traffic consisted of passenger-freighters. Occasionally the boats with special cargo continued on into the Mississippi to New Orleans, but Yazoo craft normally stopped at Vicksburg. The exception was the *DeSchmidt*, a classy sidewheeler of the 1880's, which made a round trip between Greenwood and New Orleans every two weeks. The *DeSchmidt* was famed as the first steamer on the lower Mississippi to be equipped with electric lights.

An earlier sidewheeler, the *Wave*, held the record for

travel time from Greenwood to Vicksburg—a twenty-two-hour trip in 1845, carrying a company of soldiers which had been hastily recruited near the end of the Mexican War, anxious to get into the glory of the scrap after most of the fighting had passed. The *Wave* made its record trip to Vicksburg with only three landings for fuel en route, but the soldiers never did get to the war.

Yazoo river boats had a high mortality rate. During flood time, tree trunks and other obstacles proved too much for unwary pilots. All year round the boats were under constant threat of fire from the willow-fired boilers which provided the steam. The river logs cut from the tree banks were a cheap and abundant source of fuel, but the ready supply of the fuel encouraged carelessness in the handling of the boilers on the part of all the ship's crew. There are no accurate records, but veterans of Yazoo steamboating estimate that more than one hundred boats have burned or sunk between Greenwood and Vicksburg.

During the same period when lumbering in the Delta was promoting railroad construction, steamboating was also at its peak. Barges began to be used for the first time. In addition to the Yazoo, navigation aides were provided by the U. S. Engineers on the Yalobusha, Tallahatchie, Coldwater and Sunflower. At the beginning of the timber operation, an effort was made to have the Army Engineers construct a permanent navigation channel between the Coldwater and the Mississippi at Yazoo Pass, the route of the Federal gunboats in 1863. Passage through the Mississippi levee at Moon Lake would be achieved through a lock lift. The insistent demand from farmers in the area for full protection against potential flood dangers occasioned by the navigation construction made the proposed cost so great that the project was never approved.

A three-foot lock was established near Murphy, in Washington County, to help provide navigation on the Sunflower for nearly a hundred miles farther up the river. The lock and attendant dam were abandoned about the time of World War I. A combination of shifts in the Mississippi and the need for better navigation facilities at Vicksburg put that town actually on the Yazoo instead of the Mississippi during this peak shipping period. The Yazoo originally flowed into the big river six or seven miles north of the actual townsite of Vicksburg. When the shifting channel of the Mississippi left only an inlet to serve Vicksburg, the Yazoo was turned down into this old channel. Vicksburg today fronts on the Yazoo, which now joins the Mississippi at the southern edge of the city.

From old Wyatt, once the upper end of navigation on the Tallahatchie but now covered by the water of Sardis Lake, down to the ruins of Fort St. Peter north of Vicksburg, the Yazoo is rarely out of sight of the ghost of an old river landing. None of the others had the spectacular beginning of Point LeFlore, and few have names like Rising Sun, given to a plantation because a planter won title to it in a poker game just as the first rays appeared. (Midnight, a village in Humphreys County which grew up around a railroad station between the Yazoo and Straight Bayou, is named for a plantation won much earlier in the game.)

McNutt, once the seat of Sunflower County on McNutt Lake, has nothing left but a cemetery. The graveyard is supposedly guarded by the ghost of Red Elm, an Indian brave who was the villain in the adventures of the first homesteaders in the region. McNutt got its name from Governor McNutt, who bought a plantation site in the region during the land cessions and often visited it for bear hunts. When the county seat was established, for a county more than twice as big as the present Sunflower, the Governor thought it would serve to perpetuate his name in history. McNutt was on a lake which was navigable most of the year through a connection to the Tallahatchie River. As the seat of the new Delta county, it was visited by lawyers from throughout the state who spread the word about the opportunities available.

In 1870 the Reconstruction legislature put McNutt in the new country of Leflore, seemingly ending its chance for a postwar revival. A few years later the railroad by-passed McNutt, and the end was in sight when the post office was shifted over to the new community of Maryland on the railroad. Today Governor McNutt is remembered only as the chief executive when Mississippi repudiated her public debt. Red Elm's ghost is kept busy occasionally because of the story that planters in the vicinity buried gold under a tree when they learned of the Yankee expedition moving down from the Yazoo Pass. Every few years a tree is dug up or dynamited on the bank of McNutt Lake, but Red Elm has so far managed to preserve the treasure intact.

Maryland, incidentally, eventually became Schlater, in honor of a prominent local resident. Today Schlater, like Grenada, serves as a test for the stranger in the Yazoo. Anyone who pronounces Grenada like the Spanish city, or Schlater as if it were spelled slayter instead of slaughter, is obviously a stranger to the country.

Commercial navigation has been virtually nonexistent on the Yazoo and its tributaries for more than thirty years, but its return is not a complete impossibility. When more modernized barge service becomes available on the Mississippi, new commercial, agricultural and industrial development is likely for profitable customers up the Yazoo, possibly as far as the new heads of navigation at the tributary dams. Truck lines and the Illinois Central Railroad carry the region's freight today. Passengers have to ride the Greyhound bus if they want public transportation, for only the main Eye-Cee line, which bisects the upland country, carries passengers any more. It was one of the Eye-Cee trains which Casey Jones, the brave engineer, rode to his death one night at Vaughn, in Yazoo County.

One of the conductors on this same line, when it was the Mississippi and Tennessee, gave his name to Batesville, the large Panola County town on the Tallahatchie just below Sardis Dam. Railroading has never been a job for weak-kneed men, but in its early days in Mississippi it took real leaders among men to handle the trains, which were likely to encounter innumerable unprecedented situations all as a part of the day's run. Such a conductor was the Rev. James William Bates. No man, either railroad president or Federal official, interfered with his handling of the job.

The railroad officials had to make definite concessions before Brother Bates would take the job, for he was a Methodist minister and cotton farmer already. But when they pointed out how the job would give him increased influence for good in North Mississippi, he took the position—with certain stipulations. There was to be no smoking, no drinking, and no profanity on his train, and it would not run on Sunday.

It was during the Reconstruction period that he first took up railroading, and he was not long running into a passenger to straighten out. The Army Engineers were repairing the Tallahatchie bridge near Batesville. With all freight and luggage loaded, the train was about to pull out of Memphis when a young officer ran up and ordered, with an oath, that he hold up departure while some irons for the Tallahatchie job were being loaded.

"It is just as I say about that," Bates replied. The infuriated army man replied in even more profane language that they had to go. Bates answered again, "It is just as I say." His case helpless, the young officer changed his tune.

"The matter is important, and I will be obliged if you will accommodate me," he asked in a more civil tone. "All right then," said Conductor Bates.

But the irons were heavy, and the officer asked for help in loading them. Bates picked them up and easily tossed them into the train.

"See what a man can do?" he said. "The United States can run over me and take all I've got and I can't help myself, but one of her little sons can't do it. Now you get on the train and sit down, don't open your mouth till you get to the river." The young man did that.

There are several other stories of altercations with passengers that enlivened Brother Bates's conducting career. One is about the time the train stopped to take on water and a long delay developed through some trouble at the water tank. An irate passenger began to express his dislike of the situation in strong language, and the sound of his anger led his language to stronger levels.

Brother Bates cautioned the man against such language, but the reply was an even more profane remark about the conductor of the railroad. Bates was through talking; his answer was a blow to the passenger's jaw that sent him spinning down the twenty-foot roadbed embankment to the muddy ditch below.

"Now have you had enough?" Bates asked, dusting off his hands. "If you haven't there's plenty more where that came from." The passenger elected to remain down on the side of the embankment until the conductor had business elsewhere.

It was only the intemperate and the profane who had reason to fear or dislike Brother Bates, however. He became a traditional figure all up and down the railroad run, and all the people along the line felt free to call upon him to preach, perform weddings, or conduct funerals.

It was a regular occurrence for him to halt the train anywhere along the run, perhaps in some isolated district miles from a station, to get off and officiate at a wedding. Usually the wedding party was near by, or came to the train, but once he had to travel more than a mile in a waiting buggy to greet the couple at the altar.

The irregular stops for conductor Bates were matched by those for passengers with any legitimate reason to halt at any particular point. Picnickers regularly were deposited or picked up at hillside spots that struck their fancy from the car windows.

If Brother Bates's train did not meet any exacting daily schedules, there was one regular ritual that was invariable. Before the run every morning the conductor and his crew would assemble for prayers. Some of the hardened railroaders might have questioned this procedure at first, but it was not long before they all agreed with the butcher boy who said:

"He'll start us off all right, and we'll get there all right."

P
LEFLO
LEFLO

20

White Gold

The district WPA supervisor was in his office late one night checking over records and reports with an official from Washington. An erect little man with white hair and mustache entered the long general office at the opposite end, inserted the hanging key in the nightwatchman's clock, and then walked past the two officials with a nod and a cordial "Good evening."

"Good evening, Colonel," the supervisor looked up from his desk and answered.

"Your night watchman a member of the governor's staff?" the Washington man asked in an attempt at humor.

"No, he was a real colonel of volunteers in the Spanish-American War. And until twenty years ago he was one of the biggest men in this state. He could have sold out any day before the 1920 crash for at least a couple of million."

When he saw that the official was interested in the story the supervisor warmed up to his subject and continued.

"Within a few years after the crash he'd lost everything he ever had, and was living off his friends and relatives when the WPA first came along. When they got up a county historical project here he was asked to be one of the workers, but he turned them down. Said Macaulay was the last decent historian and he wasn't going to make a fool of himself trying to do any better."

Scattered up and down the Yazoo are dozens of other more or less picturesque failures in the grand manner of the colonel, all victims of the 1920 cotton crash. For the cotton South, all the years between the wars were a continuation of that great depression.

Since World War II, cotton has moved to higher levels, but there is no prospect of the dollar cotton of 1919 and of the white gold madness of that era which pervaded the whole Yazoo Delta, when cotton was a more potent king than in the days when Jefferson Davis hoped to use it to dissolve the Union.

Even after a decade of prosperity, the remnants of the wreckage of the dollar cotton dream are still visible along the river. Most of the people who bought uncleared swamplands for a hundred times the price cleared land had brought twenty years before lost their investments during the 1930's, if they hung on that long, and the survivors managed to pull out of the hole of debt only during World War II.

Most lasting monument to the white gold era is Humphreys County, through which the Yazoo passes between Greenwood and Yazoo City. The last county to be established in Mississippi, it was created in 1918 to satisfy the demands of the planters of the region who wanted a medium to establish good roads, drainage, and schools in their districts. Within a few years Humphreys had established the largest per capita bonded indebtedness of any county in the state, and the bonds had to be paid off with dime, instead of dollar, cotton.

Drainage districts, a device whereby farmers banded together to tax themselves voluntarily for special drainage ditches to take the water to the Yazoo and its bayou tributaries, also left their mark of debt. The ditches were rarely successful in completely stopping the water, and their cost continued through the inevitable hard-time taxes.

But while one block of the Yazoo country planters made their investments in new counties and drainage districts during the white gold flood, a very large portion of the planter class was disposing of the new wealth in a spending orgy the like of which the Delta will never see again. Dollars have never been sticky in the Delta, either for planters or tenants.

Vacations in Europe and spending bouts in Memphis and New Orleans still left huge rolls of bills in the cotton man's pockets. When they had the money to buy most anything, why go outside the Delta for amusement? Bring it in!

Guarantees posted by planter alumni brought leading Southern colleges to Yazoo towns for football games played on crude high school fields with bleachers for only a few hundred spectators. The traditional Ole Miss-Mississippi A & M contest, classic of Mississippi football, even came to Greenwood for the year.

Baseball was the real sport, however, and the Delta showed its style with the Delta Independent League, organized in the spring of 1920. It was an outlaw from the start, but that didn't matter to the people who were paying for the baseball, for the Delta League during its one brief year of existence played the fastest brand of baseball outside the majors.

Of the six towns sponsoring clubs, Jackson, the state capital, and Greenville, on the Mississippi, were the only two outside the Yazoo country. Jackson was the only town with a good 10,000 population, and two had less than 5,000, but all the teams paid their players higher salaries than were the average in the highest minors before World War II, and a great many Delta Leaguers were getting more than the Major Leaguers of the day. The stars were drawing around $1,000 a month, fair pay in the days of the Black Sox scandal, and better pay than salaried men drew in Jackson or Greenville, and Clarksdale, Belzoni, Charleston, and Greenwood, the other towns in the league.

The largest group of players came to the Delta by jumping their contracts in the Class A Southern and Texas Leagues. A wealthy cotton factor made it his business to make the Greenwood entry one of the strongest by touring all the Southern colleges and signing up the most promising baseball graduates.

More than a dozen graduates of the Delta loop had seen action in the Majors within the next three years—an extremely good average for a six club league with a twelve player limit. Bill Terry, Hugh Critz, Riggs Stephenson, Luke Sewell, Hank DeBerry, and Jim Edwards were among the stars who cut their baseball eyeteeth in the league that cotton paid for. The pitching must have been very good, or else the ball very dead, for only one player succeeded in hitting a .300 average. The slugger, who hit .307, was Stephenson, fresh from the University of Alabama and about to begin his long career with the Chicago Cubs.

The Delta League was strictly a part of the white gold era, and it had to fade out with the high price of cotton. The following year it was reorganized as the Class D Cotton States League and accepted into organized baseball.

In the heyday year, a brand-new Packard was noticed

outside the ball park in one of the towns, apparently deserted. After it remained untouched at the park for three or four days, a check of the license plates revealed that it was owned by a prominent planter of the district. He had come to town one morning, bought the car, gone to the ball game in the afternoon, and departed without the vehicle, having forgotten all about making the purchase.

A salesman delivered another high-priced car to a farmer at a lonely plantation on the Tallahatchie, bringing along a friend in a like model to drive him back.

"How much is it?" the planter asked.

"Well, it's fifteen hundred dollars, but we can give you plenty of time to pay for it," the salesman answered.

"Hell, if they're that cheap I might as well get another one of 'em," spoke up the planter. "Step around to the commissary and tell the bookkeeper I said give you three thousand dollars."

The salesman and his friend rode borrowed horses back to town.

21

Yoknapatawpha County

The Yoknapatawpha County of the fiction of William Faulkner, as surveyed and mapped by the writer in the continuity of his short stories and novels, lies between the Tallahatchie on the north and the Yoknapatawpha on the south. Jefferson, the county seat, is in the middle. Sifted through his collected works, when they are assembled in historical chronology, is the story of the upper Yazoo tributaries that has been outlined here. Throughout all the Faulkner works is a stream of acute consciousness of the history of the region which changed from wilderness to frontier to battleground in little more than a generation, then through a social and economic revolution and counterrevolution, turned from the main highway into a side road along the path of American history.

It is more than mere coincidence that Faulkner lives in Oxford, in Lafayette County, which is bordered on the north by the Tallahatchie and on the south by the Yocona (pronounced Yockernee). The Yocona was first called the Yockinapatapha, but geographers understandably prefer the modern spelling. Except for the state university, which he always locates elsewhere, Oxford easily becomes Faulkner's Jefferson, and Lafayette is just as much Yoknapatawpha County. With Lafayette County as a base, Faulkner has invented and minutely described an area that is the hill country of the Yazoo sources, which reflects the main themes of the history of the postcolonial frontier South.

Farming is the center of existence for all the people of Yoknapatawpha, for the merchants, mechanics, and professional people of Jefferson live on its proceeds, just as much as the landowners and tenants. The dusty commissary ledgers of one of its plantations record "that slow trickle of molasses and meal and meat, of shoes and straw hats and overalls, of plowlines and collars and heelbolts and clevises, which returned each fall as cotton." It was part of "the continuation of that record which two hundred years had not been enough to complete and another hundred had not been enough to discharge; that chronicle which was a whole land in miniature, which multiplied and compounded was the entire South."

Faulkner has written from an original background of Lafayette County, but Yoknapatawpha is far broader and deeper than the original model. Those of his characters based on historical figures have been borrowed and molded for their brief appearance from throughout Mississippi history. Most of his characters are the makers and mass, not the figures, of history.

As farmers, first, they react to the weather: "the moonless September dusk, the trees along the road not rising soaring as trees should, but squatting like huge fowl . . . the tranquil sunset of October hazy with windless woodsmoke . . . slow drizzle of November rain just above the ice point . . . those windless Mississippi December days which are a sort of Indian summer's Indian summer . . . no movement anywhere save the low constant smoke . . . no sound save the chopping of axes and the lonely whistle of the daily trains" of January and February. "The weather is the one trouble of this country. . . . Everything weather, all, hangs on too long. Like our rivers, our land: opaque, slow violent; shaping and creating the life of man in its implacable and brooding image."

"It was a bright, soft day, a wanton morning filled with that unbelievable soft radiance of May, rife with a promise of noon and of heat, with high fat clouds like gobs of whipped cream floating lightly as reflections in a mirror, their shadows scudding sedately across the road. It had been a lavender spring. The fruit trees, the white ones, had been in small leaf when the blooms matured; they had never attained that brilliant whiteness of last spring, and the dogwood had come into full bloom after the leaf also in green retrograde before crescendo. But lilac and wisteria and redbud, even the shabby heaven-trees, had never been finer, fulgent, with a burning scent blowing for a hundred yards along the vagrant air of April and May. The bougainvillea against the veranda would be as large as basketballs and lightly poised as balloons. . . .

". . . A bird, a shadow, fleet and dark and swift, curved across the moonlight, upward into the pear tree, and began to sing; a mockingbird.

"'First one I've noticed this year,' Freeman said.

" 'You can hear them along Whiteleaf every night,' the first man said. 'I heard one in February. In that snow. Singing in a gum.'

" 'Gum is the first tree to put out,' the third said. 'That was why. It made it feel like singing, fixing to put out that way. That was why it taken a gum.'

" 'Gum first to put out?' Quick said. 'What about willow?'

" 'Willow ain't a tree,' Freeman said. 'It's a weed.' "

As farmers, the dwellers in Yoknapatawpha County love "this land, this South, for which God has done so much, with woods for game and streams for fish and deep rich soil for seed and lush springs to sprout it and long summers to mature it and serene falls to harvest it and short mild winters for man and animals." They live on the edge of the Delta . . . "this land which man has deswamped and denuded and derivered in two generations . . . where white men rent farms and live like niggers and niggers crop on shares and live like animals . . . where cotton is planted and grows man-tall in the very cracks of the sidewalk . . . and usury and mortgage and bankruptcy and measureless wealth, Chinese and African and Aryan and Jew, all breed and spawn together."

As Southerners, the people of Yoknapatawpha attach the deepest significance to blood relationship. Family affection is a theme which can shut out the rest of the world. It is a key to that respect for the past which can inspire or stultify. As boys, they have shared with . . .

> every Southern boy fourteen years old, not once but whenever he wants it, . . . the instance when it's still not two o'clock on that July afternoon in 1863, and the brigades are in position behind the rail fence, the guns are laid and ready in the woods and the furled flags are already loosened to break out and Pickett himself with his long oiled ringlets and his hat in one hand probably and his swords in the other looking up the hill waiting for Longstreet to give the word and it's all in the balance, it hasn't happened yet, it hasn't even begun . . .

The Yoknapatawpha boy daydreams of the moments of glamour in history, but he lives with the everyday reality of history, such as the courthouse and jail at Oxford that have become the courthouse and jail of Jefferson. The prologue that is the past has made the present:

> . . . Cotton: a king: omnipotent and omnipresent: a destiny of which (obvious now) the plow and the axe have been merely the tools; not plow and axe which had effaced the wilderness, but Cotton: petty globules of Motion weight-

less and myriad even in the hand of a child, incapable even of wadding a rifle, let alone of charging it, yet potent enough to sever the very taproots of oak and hickory and gum, leaving the acre-shading tops to wither and vanish in one single season beneath the fierce minted glare; not the rifle nor the plow which drove at last the bear and deer and panther into the last jungle fastnesses of the river bottoms, but Cotton; not the soaring cupola of the courthouse drawing people into the country, but that same white tide sweeping them in: that tender skim covering the winter's brown earth, burgeoning through spring and summer into September's white surf crashing against the flanks of gin and warehouse and ringing like bells on the marble counters of the banks: altering not just the face of the land, but the complexion of the town too . . ." *(Requiem for a Nun)*

When the political philosophy of Yoknapatawpha is expressed:

> We are defending not actually our politics or beliefs or even our way of life, but simply our homogeneity from a federal government to which in simple desperation the rest of this country has had to surrender voluntarily more and more of its personal and private liberty in order to continue to afford the United States. And of course we will continue to defend it. We . . . don't know why it is valuable. We don't need to know. Only a few of us know that only from homogeneity comes anything of a people or for a people of durable and lasting value—the literature, the art, the science, that minimum of government and police which is the meaning of freedom and liberty, and perhaps most valuable of all a national character worth anything in a crisis—that crisis we shall face someday when we meet an enemy with as many men as we have and as much material as we have and —who knows?—who can even brag and boast as we brag and boast . . . *(Intruder in the Dust)*

an unknowing reviewer may dismiss it as "a kind of counter-blast to the anti-lynching bill and civil rights plank in the Democratic platform," but a more competent critic may find it an affirmation of still basic faith in the radical doctrine of America's greatest political philosopher, whose name was chosen for the county seat of Yoknapatawpha. The chronicler of Yoknapatawpha was speaking as a true Jeffersonian in his speech accepting the Nobel Prize:

> I feel that this award was not made to me as a man, but to my work—a life's work in the agony and sweat of the human spirit, not for glory and least of all for profit, but to create out of the materials of the human spirit something which did not exist before. So this award is only mine in trust. It will not be difficult to find a dedication for the money part of it commensurate with the purpose and significance of its origin. But I would like to do the same with the acclaim, too, by using this moment as a pinnacle from which I might be listened to by the young men and women already dedicated to the same anguish and travail, among whom is already that one who will some day stand here where I am standing.
>
> Our tragedy today is a general and universal physical fear so long sustained by now that we can even bear it. There are no longer problems of the spirit. There is only the question: When will I be blown up? Because of this, the young man or woman writing today has forgotten the problems of the human heart in conflict with itself which alone can make good writing, because only that is worth writing about, worth the agony and the sweat.
>
> He must learn them again. He must teach himself that the basest of all things is to be afraid, and, teaching himself that, forget it forever, leaving no room in his workshop for anything but the old verities and truths of the heart, the old universal truths lacking which any story is ephemeral

and doomed—love and honor and pity and pride and compassion and sacrifice. Until he does so, he labors under a curse. He writes not of love but of lust, of defeats in which nobody loses anything of value, of victories without hope, and, worst of all, without pity or compassion. His griefs grieve on no universal bones, leaving no scars. He writes not of the heart but of the glands.

Until he relearns these things, he will write as though he stood among and watched the end of man. I decline to accept the end of man. It is easy enough to say that man is immortal simply because he will endure; that when the last dingdong of doom has clanged and faded from the last worthless rock hanging tideless in the last red and dying evening, that even then there will still be one more sound; that of his puny, inexhaustible voice, still talking. I refuse to accept this. I believe that man will not merely endure; he will prevail. He is immortal, not because he alone among creatures has an inexhaustible voice but because he has a soul, a spirit capable of compassion and sacrifice and endurance. The poet's, the writer's, duty is to write about these things. It is his privilege to help man endure by lifting his heart, by reminding him of the courage and honor and hope and pride and compassion and pity and sacrifice which have been the glory of his past. The poet's voice need not merely be the record of man, it can be one of the props, the pillars to help him endure and prevail.

22

High Water

The rich earth of the Delta is sediment from countless prehistoric floods. The history of civilization in the region has been built around the fight to restrain and control the floods which would ravage instead of enrich the settled land. The fight still goes on. The capacity of destruction inherent in the flood waters is still there, even though control measures have begun to slowly harness the water which falls in the basin at the rate of fifty-five inches per year.

During the first fifty years of settlement in the Delta, high water covered nearly half of the surface of the region some four or five months of the year. Mississippi River flood stages would pour water past the levees and relatively high level riverbanks until joined with overflow water from the Yazoo and its tributaries. During some heavy flood years it was possible to paddle skiffs from the bluff hills, some sixty miles west, to the high ground at the bank of the Mississippi —moving entirely over normally dry land. Sidon, on the east bank of the Yazoo a few miles from the hills, was a favorite starting point for these journeys for returning Confederate veterans in 1865. Other discharged veterans who lived on the Mississippi crossed the Yazoo at Sidon or Greenwood, and walked or rode horseback to McNutt, the Sunflower County seat, before finally leaving dry land for the arduous rowing job.

The vast floods of this type were in good part caused by the Mississippi, and the story of the long fight to keep the Mississippi within its banks is part of the story of another river. The Yazoo flood fight rarely reaches the drama of the Mississippi flood, but it has actually been a harder, if smaller, struggle, and it still has many bitter and frustrating years ahead.

Control of the Yazoo floods was left to chance and isolated local effort for nearly a century. Individual planters cleared their farmsites and established drainage programs to move the water away from their own acres, but usually they merely increased the flood problem for the river itself, by eliminating some of the small natural reservoirs used by the river through the years. After clearance of the land became more intensive, private levees were built to protect individually owned acreage. One private levee inevitably shunts water to the land on the other side of the river, or down the stream a mile or two. In high water times the levees had to be patrolled with armed guards for protection against dynamiters. Shotguns of necessity had to become an integral part of the Yazoo flood-control system, and they did not always work.

Levee boards, organized by state law as governmental subdivisions with tax authority, were the first efforts to coordinate flood control activity in the Delta, but until comparatively recently they have had no major responsibility for any flood fight except that against the Mississippi River itself. The farmers had to organize themselves into local drainage districts, with full taxing authority, as the only means of co-ordinating localized flood-control problems. The first drainage district was not organized until after 1900, and the greatest number were created during the height of the World War I cotton boom. They were not confined to the Delta, but sprung up in the bottom lands of the Coldwater, Tallahatchie, Yocona, and Yalobusha. More than two hundred districts were created, and they spent around twenty-five million dollars in various drainage projects before liquidation or default. A few are still in operation today, but their programs have been co-ordinated with the U. S. Engineers and the Soil Conservation Service.

The drainage districts generally covered the largest contiguous land area where the owners could be persuaded of the common benefits under a joint drainage program. They hired engineers to build drainage canals to take their rainfall runoff to the nearest available river tributary. There was rarely any study made as to the capacity of the creek and bayou tributaries into which the water was dumped. The end result was a patchwork crazyquilt of water passed from one neighbor to another, with generally unsatisfactory results for most of those concerned.

Drainage district taxes were a major cause of dissatisfaction. The extra taxation often meant the difference between survival and default for some of the landowners. The debts had to be refinanced at increasingly higher interest rates, and a great many of the existing districts were saved from defaulting on their bonds only by the Reconstruction Finance Corporation in the early 30's. It was a sound financial transaction for both parties, as well as for the local banks, which could shift their credit resources to more pressing local needs.

The drainage-district failures were primarily because of

complete lack of co-ordination, but the Yazoo basin is a flood-control problem which can defeat far more inspired efforts. Two million, five hundred thousand acres of land are subject to overflow from the Yazoo, with more than a third of this acreage also subject to flood from Mississippi River backwaters coming up through the mouth of the Yazoo. The slope of fall of the river after it reaches the flatland of the Delta averages only three inches per mile. There is not much hill for the water to run down.

Although the excess water is by all technical definitions "flood," Yazoo people generally refer to it as "high water." The hill creeks produce floods which roll as walls of water, sounding off like the rumble of an earthquake. Yazoo water ripples quietly, with monotonous but deadly certainty. The high water always comes with sufficient warning for humans to move out of its path and usually in time to get out livestock and other valuable farm equipment. It will always be "high water," to people along the Yazoo, even when it rises over the rooftops.

High water comes every winter. The extent of its damage depends upon the height of the water and the length of time it remains over land which farmers must get planted before the end of spring. The over-all chief flood cost is the regular delay in getting crops planted—sometimes such a delay as to make it impossible to grow cotton during the year, and at other times holding up the planting long enough to make the crop short. Many a Delta farmer has to make a normal practice of planting his ridges first, with the hope that the wet bottoms will dry in time to get in the same crop.

Yazoo people do not have to rely on dim memories and faded newspaper files to recount the story of the worst flood.

It came in 1932, in time to have its full effect felt in conjunction with the worst of the depression years. For the first fifty years of 1900 there was an average of one major flood every two years, but the 1932 water surpassed even the projected flood forecast by the Engineers in a study completed just the year before. During a ninety-eight day period beginning November 17, 1931, what the weatherman calls "severe storm rainfall" fell in the basin for forty-five days. By February 22, when the rains began to slacken down to normal, considerably more rain had fallen in a three-month period than was ordinarily supposed to fall over an entire year.

The entire middle basin caught the main brunt of the high water, which lasted for weeks. Life had to be gradually adjusted to living in a lake. The wives and children of most of those who had solvent relatives in the hills were dispatched to visit the fortunate dry-land people. Red Cross teams moved into Greenwood, Belzoni, and Yazoo City to furnish emergency aid to tenants who had to move away from both cabins and rations. For some of these, Red Cross rations were generally better than 1932 depression furnish, and the clothes and blankets which were given out were something which might never have come without the flood. For most flood victims, however, it was a double tragedy of both depression and disaster.

At Greenwood a rapidly improvised levee system of brick, concrete, and sandbags, saved the main section of the town from inundation by a matter of inches. Many property owners had already given up and bricked up their stores and office buildings in the hope of holding down the water damage. The anticlimax came when the levees held the flood crest and then were almost broken by the waves from speeding motor boats joy-riding in the flood lake. The boats were a symptom of the town's adjustment to living with the flood. The flooded area householders lucky enough to own them commuted to work by boat, tying the craft to their front porches, or perhaps stepping from them into an upstairs window. Most of the North Greenwood streets had become small rivers, but an elevated boardwalk was built down the center of Grand Boulevard, the town's most exclusive residential thoroughfare, which had become a special channel between the Tallahatchie and the Yazoo. "Flood buggies" (Fords with the car body jacked up four or five feet above the axles) were the only vehicles which moved about.

More than one hundred thousand citizens of the basin were made homeless by the flood, and headline figures like that brought the Coast Guard and newsreel cameramen to the rescue. The newsreel men saw little drama in the Venice-like atmosphere or the water lapping on the main town levee. They took a jaunt in one of the Coast Guard lifeboats out into the flooded plantation area, where the water level was at the cabin roofs. Unfortunately, there were no desperate people clinging to the rooftops—they had all been evacuated a week before by auto and wagon. This did not daunt the newsreel men—they had brought along several Negroes from town, who were placed on roofs and rescued several times (to be sure of good shots) to the glory of the Coast Guard and Yazoo floods.

Greenwood people who saw this were not greatly surprised in the Ohio flood of 1937, when the late Floyd Gibbons, top-ranking radio commentator of the time, made a broadcast purportedly from a diving outfit beneath the flood waters, but actually from the comfort of a Cincinnati radio studio.

Even before an unpaid assistant revealed that Gibbons had been talking into a bucket instead of from a diver's helmet, Greenwood folk were wondering how he could manage to see through the yellow mud of river flood waters.

The Federal government had recognized its responsibility for flood control on the Mississippi in 1873, with the creation of the Mississippi River Commission, although no effective program was authorized until 1928, after the great flood of the previous year. Just a few months before the 1932 Yazoo flood, a flood-control survey of the tributary river was completed and submitted by an Engineer major named John C. H. Lee, an officer destined for considerable fame in Europe a few years later as "Court House" Lee, head of the Service of Supply. Major Lee's report outlined a tentative flood-control program, but the conclusion was that it was not economically justifiable. Yazoo people hoped that their 1932 flood would have at least the virtue of awakening the government to their need, as in the case of the Mississippi flood, but they reckoned without pre-New Deal policies. A new survey made in 1932 produced the same unfavorable recommendation.

Another flood hit the basin in 1933, not quite as bad as the 1932 high water, but playing havoc with the suggestion that 1932 had been an isolated case. Representative Will M. Whittington secured a second supplemental report on the Yazoo. Perhaps it was merely an accident that this report came in July, 1933, and its favorable conclusion may have had nothing to do with changes in Washington, but it was one of the changes which made possible the favorable finding that Federal assistance could be granted "as contemplated by section 203 of the National Industrial Recovery Act."

The actual authorization of the basic Yazoo project came in the Congress in 1936, and two important revisions have been authorized since that time. Floods on the main Yazoo line are to be controlled by a system of four reservoirs in the hills, channel improvements all the way down the line, and levee construction in limited areas where flood danger will still exist. A large-scale levee system is to be established to protect the lower Delta from the direct effect of Mississippi backwater floods. Interior Delta floods will be curbed by progressive upstream improvement of the Sunflower River and its tributaries. Most of the work accomplished since the adoption of the plan has been in construction of the upstream dams, but funds are finally becoming available for other improvements badly needed down the stream. The countless natural small reservoirs that once were part of the swamps and sloughs on every plantation are rapidly being eliminated by the farmers, thanks to guidance from the soil conservation program and a more advanced individual knowledge of the entire problem. The water which is drained off, instead of being allowed to soak into the land, goes immediately into the river, and the lower Yazoo flood problem has been becoming more acute each year as a result. Areas which once were dry enough to cultivate a full crop in four out of five years are now impeded by high water four out of five years, dry enough for a full crop only in abnormally dry periods. The problem grows more acute in the midst of the actual construction program.

The reservoir created by the erection of a dam on the Yalobusha at Grenada is scheduled to be in operation during the winter of 1954, completing the fourth and last of the upland tributary dams. The others are at Arkabutla on the

Coldwater, Sardis on the Tallahatchie, and Enid on the Yocona. The dams are for the primary purpose of putting the upstream rivers in harness, to make the water below Greenwood manageable through levees and channel improvements. In the Delta area east of the dams, considerably more acreage has already been placed in cultivation than that displaced by the reservoir area created by the dams. The Delta acreage is considerably more fertile, and much of the reservoir land is still available for rent as pasturage during the greater part of the year. Both Mississippi and the national economy have sharply benefited by the exchange, and the benefits continue to pile up.

For the people who lived behind the dams, however, the comparative benefits to state and nation brush very lightly on the scales in contrast with sharp uprooting of traditional family and community stakes. The reservoir area for each of the dams naturally included much of the richest farmland in the upland section of the Yazoo basin, for it was in good part river bottomland. Some of the farms to be covered by the water had been in the same families since the first white settlement a century before. Over-all, their average cost per acre to the government had been only $18.25, not a sign of great fertility even in the eroded hills, but there were intangible values on which neither the government engineers nor the people could put a price tag. For seventy-five years the hill folk had been pulling up and going to the Delta, but they usually left some part of the family back at the old home farm. The tie to home had never been erased. The home fires had been regularly rekindled by reunions in the hills. Forced removal has upset this pattern.

The Harmontown community in northwest Lafayette

County, where the greater part of the land was covered by the Sardis lake, was typical of the problems which developed. Harmontown was the center of Beat Three of the county. That portion of the beat not placed under water was completely cut off from Oxford, the county seat. There was no bridge across the lake, and a distance of once thirteen miles was changed to forty by roundabout trails of roads and highways which had to lead through other county seats before they reached Oxford. Farmers still had to get to Oxford to pay taxes and attend to the various legalities connected with the United States Department of Agriculture. They had to keep up the longer trip, too, unless they wanted to abruptly change lifelong buying and marketing habits.

The inconvenience to the remaining inhabitants of the area was not limited to the troubles of the new long route back and forth between Oxford. Perkins High School, a center of community spirit where all their children went to school, had to be abandoned, because there was not enough remaining population. Some old churches could be transplanted out of the path of the water, but others had to be closed when the bulk of their parishioners moved away.

The troubles of the people who stayed at home still seemed light by comparison with some of those who had to move to entirely new areas. With cash payments from the government for the old farm, or portions of it, a few of the displaced farmers were able to buy more satisfactory holdings in the Delta, or other newly opened up low country beneath the dam. Most who tried this were not successful, however, for the land below the dam was already in the hands of private owners who wanted an opportunity to develop it themselves. Most of the land available for purchase was in the same general area as the old neighborhood, which was typically hilly, eroded, and overpriced. The overpricing came from the minor boom to the local land market brought on by the displaced farmers with ready cash. Better hill land might have been found in more distant parts of the state, but few of the purchasers wanted to move far into unfamiliar scenes.

Approximately 350 to four hundred families in the Harmontown area had to make some type of move, as a result of the land purchase program, but less than 15 per cent moved as far as another county. Most of the moves were merely from one part of a farm to a stretch of higher ground above the flood level established by the Engineers. The landowners were paid the value of homes, barns, and other buildings in the reservoir area, and then the buildings were given back with the understanding that they would be torn down or removed. Many were moved intact to the higher ground and continued in use. In Lafayette County fifty-six thousand acres were purchased for the reservoir, but forty thousand acres of this total was leased back to private operators, with former owners having preference in bidding. Because the land is rented with the understanding that it can be flooded at any time required for the operation of the dam, the rental price has averaged less than the total taxes the former owners normally paid on the land. As a whole, former owners who have become renters have fared better under the dam operation than under their previous status. Flooding of the rented land rarely occurs during the crop season, and normal farming operations continue.

County politicians complained loudly about the loss of

revenue from the lands taken from the tax rolls, but a gradually developed system of payments in lieu of taxes has all but eradicated the complaint. Business losses were felt sharply—by the three or four stores in the area through actual movement of families, and by merchants in Oxford shifted outside the normal trade territory of the community across the lake. The business losses have gradually been offset in Oxford by the development of a thriving sporting goods business from local residents and visitors who use Sardis Lake for fishing and boating. Few Oxford people would be willing to go back today to the days before Sardis Lake, for they enjoy both personal and business returns.

The recreational benefits from the flood-control dam have considerably exceeded all early forecasts. More than three hundred thousand people fish in the lake each year, coming from Memphis and all parts of North Mississippi. A state park is being established at the Sardis end of the lake, and the general recreation program broadens each year. The prospects for similar recreational development at Grenada dam have changed the unfavorable local reaction to the new project to one of favorable expectation. It is obvious that the region behind the dams is benefiting from the construction and operation of the reservoirs, even if not on the same scale as the lowland region below.

Despite the obvious benefits, the forcible dislocation of any sizable group of people will never be popular among the people themselves, even when some of them see obvious economic benefits as the result of their shift to accommodate the "dam' dam." Losing the security of personal, lasting relationships in a well-established community is an intangible disaster which will always carry some shock reaction with the people who have to move. Neighborhood patterns of visiting, borrowing, swapping, pleasuring, and sorrowing together can never be disrupted without scars that are hard to heal.

The story of Harmontown is one which has been duplicated wherever there has been large dam construction almost anywhere in the world, but it is a very good illustration of some lessons which still need to be learned if further development of flood-control, reclamation and power projects is not to be halted by the protests of embattled farmers who are terrified into the belief that shackles for American water resources will destroy their way of life. An intelligent program of assistance in relocation for farmers who are displaced, including attention to every aspect of the displacement problem, both economic and social, plus a generally better system of public relations for all government agencies concerned is needed. Every exercise of the right of eminent domain must inevitably involve some type of dislocation. If these dislocations are treated so crudely as to bring about a reaction of public sentiment against conservation construction progress, America can easily become a decadent nation, afraid to exercise great dormant muscles because of the initial soreness which will inevitably come.

Flood control on the main rivers, symbolized by the four reservoirs, will not halt the destructive erosion which has been pauperizing the Yazoo bluff and hill country for more than three quarters of a century. Conservation practices have to be instituted on each farm to halt erosion, and only broader soil-building programs beyond the capacity of individual farmers can reclaim land considered lost. These programs are being established today. They still need better co-ordination and implementation, but results are already becoming evident.

The watershed conservation programs which cover the entire hill portion of the Yazoo basin north of Yazoo City were authorized during World War II and have been in the process of development since funds first became available for the work after the end of the war. The Little Tallahatchie Watershed, covering all the area in the Tallahatchie drainage area from Sardis dam east, was the first authorized, but it was soon followed by the Yazoo Watershed, which takes in all the bluff and upland area of the basin, except the Tallahatchie unit, plus Delta area from the bluffs west to just beyond the Coldwater and Yazoo main channels. Although the two watershed units are technically separate, they are administered jointly. In addition to the normal co-ordination with Soil Conservation Service activities, the work is tied in with the Forest Service operation of the Holly Springs National Forest, which lies wholly within the watershed, consisting of land so badly eroded that it could only be rehabilitated entirely at Federal expense.

The watershed programs, as a national policy, were originally authorized in 1936 in the belief that they could provide effective flood control at the source of the runoffs. The two Yazoo projects, which are among the only eleven actually in operation all over the country, are financed on an almost equal basis by the landowners and the Federal government, with state and local governments adding a minute amount. The program includes soil and water conservation measures which range from crop rotation, winter cover crops, and seeding and planting of trees, to terracing, contour plowing and furrowing, and the erection of small sedimentation filter dams. Some overenthusiastic partisans of the watershed programs have announced that the man-created sponges can soak up any flood which descends from the sky. More realistic students have no such illusions, but they see the upland area programs as concentrated conservation work which will alleviate the flood problem and at the same time offer the one hope of saving vast acreage and possibly reclaiming some of that long since believed to have passed irretrievably on to the sea.

Floods come to the upland watershed in greater number than to the lowland Delta, for the greater runoff of the water fills the small streams with lightning speed. There were 305 floods on the Coldwater during the twelve year period of 1929-1941. Most of them lasted no more than a few hours, but fifteen minutes of water rushing over a June stand of cotton, followed by steaming sunshine, will kill a year's crop on the land. Stream channels become bankful with sand, and bottom-land valleys long under cultivation are returned to nature in the form of willow brakes. The Yazoo watershed programs claim no victories over these floods yet, but farmers who see gullies no longer forming in their fields know that the first checkreins are being put on the water.

Nobody has been able to estimate how much sand and silt is moved from woodland, pastures, and cropland into the stream beds, for most of this sedimentation is thrown up into cones where the creeks first meet the lowlands or the rivers. Delta landowners between the bluff and the river have borne the major burden of this assault. Big Sand Creek, which drains the central portion of erosion-scarred Carroll County, carries about 1,100,000 cubic yards of sand and silt into the

Delta each year, but sometimes only a small part of this vast tonnage gets into the Yazoo at Greenwood. Many acres of sand have been thrown up over once rich farmland. Some disastrous floodings have removed land from cultivation for more than twenty years. The Big Sand takes its silt from a drainage area of 106 square miles. A few miles north, Potacocowa Creek, with about half as much drainage area, averages about half as much sedimentation. A drainage-district levee holds the Big Sand in check most of the time, but the Potacocowa long ago washed away such permanent encumbrances and storms down from the hills to the Yalobusha with more freedom than the Mississippi River had in the days before the levees. The Potacocowa has built a miniature wilderness of sand and willows. In a few spots where there is more silt than sand, some rich cotton land has been created, but in most cases the sand will yield nothing for years yet to come.

South of Greenwood, Abiaca Creek also rushes down from the bluffs in the confines of a drainage ditch before passing on to Tchula Lake. The farmers of the vicinity have long been accustomed to floods from Abiaca and near-by Chicopa, and the state highway department is regularly accustomed to repairing a bridge washout, but the merchants in the village of Cruger rarely have a chance to move their stock above the flash flood waters which seem regularly to attack them. Sedimentation in the stream has grown so much worse in recent years that its normal outlets are progressively choked up, increasing the flooding tendency with each new flood.

Improvement, but no solution, to this flood problem at the bluff line is promised in both the USDA watershed and the U. S. Engineers flood-control programs. The solution, however, may come through local inspiration. The Yazoo people have already seen too many seeming miracles of flood control and conservation to placidly accept the idea that any such problem defies solution. When they refuse to accept anything short of the solution, the agencies operating in the field are going to catch something of the same spirit.

W. C. Neill, a banker who operates at both Carrollton and Greenwood, is typical of the breed who expect results to be achieved. Mr. Neill believes that the individual farm retention dams authorized under the watershed program, which cost no more than four or five thousand dollars each, can control the waters of a hill creek, if used in combination with the normal conservation practices. Thanks to his educational efforts, one small tributary of the Big Sand is being used as an experiment. If this works, he hopes to get the same treatment for the entire Big Sand. Mr. Neill's bank believes that the farmland around Greenwood is part of its business assets and is not afraid to spend money to teach sound conservation practices in its use. The Big Sand effort is one example, but general newspaper advertisements like this are also typical:

> WHAT IS A "W" DITCH?
>
> . . . a "W" Ditch is a method of drainage which takes advantage of proper row arrangement and the natural contour of a field under cultivation.
>
> The above illustration of a "W" Ditch is on Luther Wade's Star of the West Plantation. Before it was installed the area in the foreground (app. 40 acres) was non-productive. The row arrangement was just the opposite of what it is now, causing run-off of rain to collect in a large area.
>
> The re-arrangement of the rows and the employment

of the "W" Ditch has caused more water to remain in the rows and the surplus to be easily carried away.

Utilizing a "W" Ditch in this particular incident has made what was once non-productive land even more productive than the area in the background of the picture.

The Yazoo River at Greenwood carries a load of silt which averages three million cubic yards a year. There is little increase in the total in the remainder of the river, which moves over such a flat terrain at a sluggish pace that it deposits as much as it picks up along the way. Only during long dry spells, with the river at the lowest level, does the Yazoo lose the muddy yellow color that is the landmark of erosion. For more than eleven months of the year it fits the classic description: "too thick to drink; too thin to plow."

Greenwood is the center of the Yazoo flood-control and conservation problems, and perhaps that is why Leflore County has been the focal point in the development of an active educational campaign for soil conservation in the basin, which has included adoption of a statewide "Land Use Emphasis Week" program in which business groups take the most active part. Part of the campaign is no more than the normal lip service given any Chamber of Commerce community booster plan, but another part of it is the practical education of the men who finance farming. When these men who set the pace of agricultural development at the local level are willing to give financial assistance to help promote individual conservation practices, the Yazoo has lost the curse of cotton slavery.

Runnymede plantation, between Itta Bena and Greenwood, includes a five-hundred-acre gumbo tract along the route over which slaves "hopped" cotton bales from Itta Bena to Fort Pemberton in 1863. The various operators of Runnymede, down through the years, had invariably planted cotton and corn on the land, even though their plowhands complained it was "stiff enough to break a plowpoint." They usually lost money on the operation.

The Runnymede gumbo plot lies along Highway 82 in full view of passing motorists. In 1950, the soil conservation committee of the Greenwood Chamber of Commerce, working with the Leflore County Soil Conservation District, persuaded C. C. Rushing, the farm manager, to let them establish the five hundred acres as a soil conservation "picture window." The plows were taken out of the gumbo, and pasture grasses substituted. By 1953 it was possible to feed more than one hundred head of cattle on the land, and the operation was in the black for the first time.

Thanks to practical demonstrations like that at Runnymede, the Greenwood salesmen for soil conservation are not only convinced that they are improving the financial returns for farming operations in the area, but that they are also saving Yazoo land for new generations to use.

In the justifying authorization of the Yazoo Watershed program, the Department of Agriculture estimated annual benefits of $2.28 per acre for each $1 of cost for the watershed. The flood- and sediment-control benefits were estimated at $1.57 to $1, with the private on-site benefits expected to average $2.24 for each $1 of cost contributed by individual farmers. Using 1940 figures, the survey revealed a gross income of $19,283,000 for the 17,023 farms in the watershed. Cash operating expenses and the value of home-used products cut this gross in half. The 31,036 families who lived on the farms gained a net cash income of $289 per family. "Having very limited cash resources, the people of this area generally lack the advantages of adequate medical attention, simple sanitary facilities, balanced diets, and essential social privileges and facilities," the survey added. Obviously the watershed program will yield dividends far beyond immediate cash returns for each of the acres it holds back from crumbling into the waters of the Yazoo.

The river first brought the ancient mound builders to the Yazoo basin, and it opened up the area to white settlement. The combination of man-made erosion and floods took the economic life out of the upland country, but the presently established program for control of this destruction of the soil may actually bring it to a greater production of wealth than ever before. The gullies bottled up and leveled off with a bulldozer will not be suitable for a return to cotton production, but they can grow pine trees, and grasses rich enough for a pasture operation. The timber and the cattle will bring better long-range yields to the farmer than would have ever come from continued production of cotton. Terracing and crop rotation will save acres still in row crops from going the way of the gullied land.

In the Delta country the relief from Yazoo high water will reclaim for production vast acreage which was yielded back to the river not long after it was first cleared up, as a result of inevitable floods. An improved drainage system over the whole land drained by the Yazoo will make individual soil conservation projects more practical on various individual farms, increasing both the yield and the life of the soil. Water is going to be drained, but it is also going to be collected for supplemental irrigation.

The over-all flood-control-conservation program is the

true gospel to individual farmers, because it means the difference between the life and death of their land, and to Chamber of Commerce groups, because it means the long-range life and death of their trade communities, but it is symbolic of the over-all conservation problem just as important to the nation as a whole. Each year the population of the United States increases by several million. The total land available for cultivation is gradually being reduced, and the percentage of the population engaged in farming is falling at a rapid rate. The present fertility of the soil not only must be preserved, but in many cases it will have to be restored, if America is to meet its future responsibilities.

The loosely co-ordinated flood-control and soil-conservation programs in operation in the Yazoo basin are typical of what must succeed throughout rural America. There is room for improvement in every aspect of the programs, both public and private, but to desert them would be disastrous.

23

Mechanized Revolution

The depression of the 1930's ran roughshod over the Yazoo basin. The crash came in 1930, but it had been building since the 1920 debacle. This time there was no partial recovery within the next year. World economic conditions brought the depression, but the Delta could not recover while cotton and the cotton agricultural economy was sick. The long recuperation has produced economic and social revolution in a little less than twenty years. The Delta is still the last stronghold of the plantation system, but today the plantation system is widely different from the ante bellum feudal baronies, or even the outmoded sharecropper system that lasted for seventy-five years after the War Between the States. Crops are still made on shares today, but under a vastly changed procedure from the day when the tyrant of unavailable and expensive credit took its toll from the landlord, tenant and sharecropper alike.

The yoke of the archaic credit system began to be lifted at the same time the first steps were taken to stabilize the price of cotton above the poverty level. The two steps were both part of a New Deal farm program, both tied to the even broader and less identifiable policy of making capital and credit easier to obtain all over the South. Combined with a long-delayed advance in the industrial revolution—new mechanization of cotton production for the first time since the invention of the cotton gin—cotton farming as a way of life has drastically changed for the better in the Delta. Everyone concerned has shared in the improvement. Basically, the improvements stem from the fact that there is more money for everyone, from the biggest planter to the most obscure cotton picker.

The long experimentations of the national farm program, once it was accepted as Federal responsibility, is a story to tell somewhere other than here. It is important to the Yazoo story, however, because it removed a great part of the burden from a self-defeating credit system. The first improvements came hand in hand. With price-stabilization measures to give the cotton farmer a better chance to break even and end the system of piling up debts, new avenues of agricultural credit were opened up. The agricultural credit agencies enabled farmers to organize their own production associations and credit co-operatives to finance crop production, using as original capital funds loaned by the government. The Reconstruction Finance Corporation was an example of credit agencies outside agriculture which eased the burden of rural banks by taking over credit responsibilities which were devouring resources needed for the agricultural community. Other production loans handled directly by the Department of Agriculture have eliminated some of the more risky credit operations and thus held down the cost of credit for the farmer who is able to use the normal banking channels.

Banks in the plantation country have been among the

greatest beneficiaries. Price supports which bring stability to the cotton market take some of the gamble out of the advance of money to produce a cotton crop. The local banks had begun to move back into the credit field long before this time, but not until stability came to the cotton market could they finance the annual production of their farm communities without the always-imminent threat of disaster and collapse. The various credit agencies, both private and governmental, have managed to work in the field with co-operation instead of excessive competition, with respect for each other's methods. Most of the Production Credit Associations in the Yazoo basin have paid back the original capital advanced by the government and are today entirely farmer-owned and operated, all within a period of less than twenty years.

The old-style plantation economy which had developed in the Delta was beginning to come apart at the seams under the hammer blows of the depression when the first rescue efforts were made by the government. Bankrupt planters, struggling to keep their lands out of the hands of the tax receiver, could no longer finance the traditional winter "furnish" for sharecroppers. Thousands of sharecroppers and tenants were put at the mercy of the Red Cross, or whatever local charity happened to be available before the days of government-financed relief agencies, although many a farmer, proud of the tradition of paternalistic care for tenants, lost his land by continuing to offer it as security for winter furnish which could never be repaid from six-cent cotton. After the relief program began, hungry tenants flocked to the towns in the winter, raising new fears of permanently displaced labor.

Delta sharecroppers, who had starved unnoticed from

the time when the tenant-credit system was first forced on the region as a direct result of the Reconstruction efforts of earlier-day reformists, did not gain national attention until the Federal government was already moving to correct some of the basic troubles. A group of well-intentioned outsiders, headed by religious leaders like Sherwood Eddy and Reinhold Niebuhr, established a co-operative cotton farm in Bolivar County. A few years later they bought Providence Plantation, east of the Yazoo in Holmes County.

The co-operative farmers made the mistake of trying to stretch their capital by buying land beneath normal Delta standards of fertility. Combined with inexperienced management and variable labor, the burden was too much. When the co-operative members found they were receiving less return for their labor than tenants on neighboring plantations, both experiments were resolved in quiet failures.

The first results of the Agricultural Adjustment Administration acreage-reduction program for cotton also brought cases of labor displacement, but most of these were soon adjusted. Provisions were included in the law to protect the tenure of tenants and sharecroppers. The fear of wholesale labor displacement was still in the air, however, when John and Mack Rust began the first publicized experiments with a practical mechanical cotton picker. The industrial revolution was beginning to combine with the economic revolution to produce a complete face lifting of the last cotton plantation stronghold.

The first successful demonstration of the Rust picker took place at the Delta Experiment Station in 1933. After he watched the machine pick as much cotton in an hour as a man could pick in a week, Station Director W. E. Ayres called it "the missing link in the mechanical production of cotton," but professional Jeremiahs as well as worried citizens began to cry out in fear of change. The Fraternal Order of Eagles resolved on "the heavy menace hanging over the Negroes of the South." The *New Masses* saw further proof of the self-destruction of the capitalistic system, with "Starvation for the masses . . . croppers and laborers forced off the land . . . humanity stranded by capitalism." It was the day of the Technicrats and technological unemployment. A few politicians suggested the machine be outlawed, and one newspaper favored dumping it into Deer Creek.

The early fears of the eviction of thousands of farm laborers from their only means of livelihood by the new machine were real to many Deltans. The conscientious Rust brothers announced plans to restrict production of their machines and to plow back part of their earnings into a foundation which would work to alleviate some of the hardships among sharecroppers and tenants. Many planters entertained the same fears. The displaced sharecropper had a brief moment of glory as a *cause célèbre* in the metropolitan press, but the problem never materialized because of other economic realities. The Rust picker, although it eventually became part of the basic design for several other models, did not go into mass production. Technical defects which had to be ironed out were one reason, but the lack of a market was another. Even though he was beginning to get re-established, the average cotton planter of the thirties did not have the cash to invest in practical experimentation with the new device. Before these difficulties were overcome, wartime labor shortages ended any possibility of mass unemployment among the sharecroppers, no matter what the mechanization developments might be.

The fears about farm-worker displacement might never have developed had more attention been paid to the history of another mechanization development in the Delta—the farm tractor. The tractor first came into the cotton field without fanfare back in the 1920's, but it had made no real headway

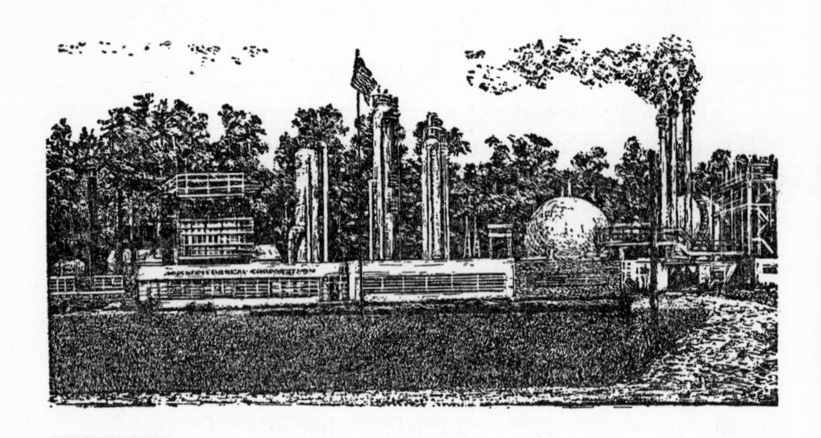

by the time the cotton picker first appeared. Conservatism about switching to new production methods was one reason, but the basic one was again the lack of capital to make the switch from mule to horse power. The Delta had had just enough experience with large scale tractor farming to be ready to switch to it full scale when acute wartime labor shortages left no alternatives. During World War II the only check on mule displacement on Delta cotton farms was the limited production of tractors. Planters who once had to watch their tenants to prevent corn being taken in excess now had to watch out for gasoline, until Diesel oil, butane, and other fuels not usable in an auto came along.

Mechanization in the Delta has been advancing since the end of World War II at a pace restricted primarily by the unavailability of machines. The dire predictions of homeless, evicted sharecroppers and resulting social upheaval have been nothing more than predictions. In contrast to the fearful prophecies, there is still a war-born labor shortage in the area —sometimes an acute shortage as far as skilled labor is concerned. During the decade 1940-1950, the Delta lost some 15 per cent of its Negro population. The demand for war workers and general industrial expansion all over the country gave impetus to the migration, but the Delta farm migrant, in the main, has merely moved to a Delta town. The town Negro has moved on, perhaps to Detroit or Chicago, but in most cases to another southern city like Memphis, to account for the net loss for the area.

The migration would have had a devastating effect upon cotton production in the area without the aid of the partial mechanization which has been going on in the same period. In most crop years there has been a shortage of laborers for tenant and sharecropping operations, and for day labor like chopping and picking cotton, but the greatest shortage has been in workers capable of handling the new machinery that now goes hand in hand with farming in the Delta.

"Tractors are worse than mules if they're broken down in the shed or in the field, and if you have to keep a man constantly on the road to town for spare and repair parts," is the way one pioneer tractor farmer explains the present situation.

"My major problem is getting drivers and mechanics who know how to take care of their equipment, getting the greatest amount of working days with the least expense for repairs. A tractor can't go into a wet field as fast as a mule can. If your plows and cultivators have to be pulled by a tractor, you have to get the most out of every good day."

Today the tractor does the plowing in the Delta, but the human "hoe hand" still has to do the main job of thinning out and weeding the plants, while the human cotton picker is a long way from being displaced. Mechanical devices have shown themselves capable of accomplishing both these jobs, however, and it is only a matter of time before plantation mechanization will have run the full cycle.

In 1946 only about 1 per cent of the Delta's cotton crop was picked by machine. In 1952 the percentage had risen to 14, and it will continue to mount as more pickers become available, and the labor supply for hand cotton picking continues to dwindle. Improvement in cleaning equipment in the cotton gins, plus refinements in the machine pickers themselves, is beginning to make it possible for mechanically harvested cotton to grade as high in quality as hand-picked cotton.

Machines for cultivation and weed control—in other words a machine to replace the man with the hoe—have been harder to find. A combination of mechanical, chemical, and flame devices is now being used and is eventually expected to solve the last problem remaining as a barrier to full mechanization. At present one experimental system is to apply weed-killing chemicals before the cotton plant emerges from the ground, follow this with post-emergence herbicides and oils, and then kill any weeds and grass which do manage to begin to grow with a flame-thrower and plows. In most cases spells of rain and muddy fields interrupt this or other mechanical processes long enough for the grass and weeds to grow strong enough to resist anything but a hoe wielded by a human hand. Until the cotton chopping operation is completely mechanized, it will not be feasible to completely mechanize the picking operation. The same labor which chops the cotton must be given a chance to pick it.

Farmers are supposed to be notoriously conservative about adopting any new production method, no matter how highly advertised its advantages may be, but Delta planters seem to prove the exception to the rule. One reason for this is the long and successful history of the Delta Branch of the Mississippi Agricultural Experiment Station on the banks of Deer Creek at Stoneville. The Delta Station, an example of full co-ordination and co-operation between state and Federal agencies, is recognized as the world's greatest cotton research center. Almost every improvement in cotton production and processing for the past quarter century has originated or been influenced by the work being done through the station. Working in co-ordination with the extension service and other Federal and state agricultural agencies, it has not only provided the successful research, but has taken the lead in getting the information to the cotton farmer in practical form, without delay. The best example of this came in 1947, when a radically new type of fertilizer was first tested, and put into mass production and use, all within the space of a few months.

Various types of nitrogen fertilizers have been part of cotton production in the Yazoo basin for more than half a century, because even in the most fertile soils farmers have felt the extra cost more than offset by the added production. Midwestern agricultural areas did not begin to use nitrogen on a large scale until after World War II. When their demand was added to the growing scramble for ammonium nitrate, by 1947 there simply was not enough to begin to go around.

For some years the parent Mississippi Experiment Station at Mississippi State College, working in close cooperation with the Tennessee Valley Authority's fertilizer division, had been carrying on limited experiments with types of anhydrous, or liquid, ammonia. In addition to the development of the liquid fertilizer itself, machines for its application were being designed and built at Starkville and Stoneville. Even after the 1947 crop was being planted, the demand for nitrogen brought a mobilization spurred on by the Delta Station and the Delta Council. Fertilizer research experts from the Department of Agriculture, TVA, and various private manufacturers were brought in for consultation. Group meetings were held over the Delta to explain anhydrous ammonia to the farmers and to demonstrate its use. Farmers took the word of Dr. W. B. Andrews and F. E. Edwards of the Experiment Station, and eagerly ordered it in quantity. Chemical plants were fortunately able to quickly switch into anhydrous production. As a result, more than one hundred thousand acres of Delta land were fertilized that year which otherwise would have gone untouched. The increased yield for the year was estimated at $4,500,000.

It is no accident that today the largest industrial plant on the Yazoo is the Mississippi Chemical Company at Yazoo City, built on a subscription basis by Mississippi farmers to relieve their fertilizer shortage. (Individual farmers, with the help of the RFC, put up the entire capital for this multimillion dollar enterprise, an interesting commentary on the progress of farm credit in Mississippi.) Today anhydrous ammonia has become a major item in the nation's total fertilizer production.

Mechanization of cotton involves more than the basic elements of plowing, chopping, and picking, and Stoneville has supplied a lot of the answers here. Thanks to advice about the increased necessity of insect control measures, power-driven stalk shredders are now used extensively, just as soon as the last cotton is picked. It is cheaper to destroy insects and their hibernation places in the old stalks than to buy new poisons to fight them in the spring. The new process of defoliation has been introduced to improve the quality of the plant for picking and to reduce late insect hazards. Chemicals for defoliation are usually sprayed by air, just as is a large percentage of the insect poisons used throughout the growing season.

Crop dusting, both for insect poisons and defoliants, has become a major industry. Tramp pilots do a good part of the work, but there is such a year-round demand for dusting operations that it has become a standard local business, usually in the hands of young men who learned how to fly planes through the courtesy of the United States Air Force. At the height of the dusting season, the hedge-hopping biplanes used for the job seem to be as thick over the Delta land as bees over a patch of clover. The scent of chemicals is in the air night and day. The same smells in the days of chemical warfare training in World War II would have brought clangs on the gas alarm and widespread donning of gas masks.

Insecticide manufacturers, like fertilizer and farm implement manufacturers, participate in research at Stoneville with special grants. Government funds are stretched a long way.

The Delta Station at Stoneville has contributed more than ideas and advice to the Delta. Even before business and law firms learned the system of using the government as an employee-training ground, the Stoneville research laboratories had begun to scatter their personnel over the Delta. Today they can be found as plantation operators and managers, seed breeders, fertilizer manufacturers and implement dealers all over the Delta. Delta seed breeders have set the pace for the entire cotton industry. Breeders like George Walker and the Delta and Pine Land Company have brought standards of quality to the field which are felt anywhere in the world where cotton is grown. The Delta grows an average of slightly less than 10 per cent of the American cotton crop, but it breeds the seed for two thirds of the crop.

Another important area institution on the creek bank at Stoneville is a private organization, the Delta Council. It was first organized to spearhead a good-roads movement in Mississippi when the entire state was in the mud in 1935. The date coincided with the revolution in cotton, however, and the Council quickly shifted to its present mission—which is basically that of providing leadership beyond the sphere of a government agency such as the Experiment Station. Financed both by public membership and local governmental subdivisions, the Council has some of the job of a regional Chamber of Commerce, but its role in educating and co-ordinating the economic leadership of the Delta has been much broader than that. One of its recent presidents, W.M. Garrard, Jr., set this as the goal:

> Full and effective utilization of resources, both natural and human, will come only as the Delta really appraises its production shortages and gears itself to building a new prosperity using as tools the soils, forests, fields, and people of Mississippi. Seen in the immediate future as the results of a more complete utilization of natural and human resources are higher standards of living, better educational opportunities, improved health, and greater freedom for economic development.

The Delta Council has established a tradition of an annual meeting with featured speakers scheduled for the stimulation of their message, with diversity instead of homogeneity of views expected. Dean Acheson released the Marshall Plan trial balloon at the 1947 meeting. Other speakers have included such varied names as Henry Wallace, Harry Byrd, Ezra Taft Benson, Benjamin Cohn, James F. Byrnes and William Faulkner.

Plantation mechanization has broken the back of the cotton monopoly, after the Union army, bankruptcy, and the boll weevil had all failed. Lifted from bondage to the old credit system, the farmer has been able to practice intelligent diversification. Cotton is almost certain to remain the dominant crop, and the Delta will continue to produce more than a million-bale average, but each year the plantings grow closer to the goals of the Soil Conservation Service specialists who minutely map the soils of each county and classify them according to the best type of crops for a sustained yield basis. Dairy and beef cattle pastures are being established on farms where once the landlord refused to let his tenants keep a cow, for fear of losing cotton acreage. Even though an occasional cowboy boot is beginning to appear in south Delta towns as the mark of Texas cattlemen who are buying land where they can graze a cow on one acre instead of the fifty required on the traditional range, most of the Delta cattlemen are cotton farmers and the sons of cotton farmers. Spinach for truck crops is now raised on plantations where sharecroppers once had to plant cotton right up to the cabin door.

The major signs of diversification are the oat and soybean bins and elevators scattered throughout the region. More than a few odd eccentrics make beans their cash crops, while others balance them with cotton. Normally beans yield in a wet year when cotton is cut back, and vice versa. Thanks to production entirely within the Delta, Mississippi has become one of the five major rice-producing states of the nation within the past five years. The tenacious quality of holding moisture of buckshot gumbo land, which bankrupted many a cotton farmer and cotton banker, has proved to be a major asset for the rice producer. But the irrigation plants the rice farmers have established must cause many an old Delta flood fighter to whirl in his grave. The Delta was carved out of a swampland wilderness by people pushing back the overabundant supply of water, and now farmers are pumping onto their land instead of off it, even though the annual rainfall is just as high as it was during the years of the great floods!

The irrigation practices, which include the use of surface as well as ground water, have attracted the attention of the dairymen and even cotton farmers. Limited experiments and research indicate that the Delta cotton planter can profitably adopt some of the irrigation procedure of California and the Southwest, just as he can learn from their drainage systems. The water problem is beginning to run its full course on the farm.

The impact of mechanization is not confined to the farm, of course. Not many years ago the major implement stocks needed by merchants for the cotton trade were plowpoints, hoes, and duck for cotton sacks. Seeds were usually saved from the gin. Today the implement business, sales and service, is the biggest in the Delta, with the farm truck side of the automobile business thrown in. There are several active, small-scale implement manufacturers. All Delta towns are small, but the big ones and medium ones are growing, while the small ones are falling behind in the race. The farm service centers expand, while the trade centers get farther apart. Merchants dependent upon the daily pay trade of the cotton chopper and cotton picker are finding the going tougher and tougher, as farm labor becomes more scarce, more skilled, better paid, and more selective in its shopping habits. The towns are all seeking industrial payrolls as the value of well paid labor becomes apparent. The day when half of the Negro population of the town lived on an annual eighteen weeks of regular employment in cotton chopping and picking is past, and town economies are healthier for it.

The much-abused G.I. vocational training program went a long way toward reducing the shortage of skilled farm labor and mechanics in the Delta, but the shortage has continued as part of the over-all tight labor supply. Part of the long-range solution is better vocational education in the public schools. The Delta Council took the lead in selling the state legislature on the necessity of establishing a new Negro college specializing in the training of vocational teachers, and the Mississippi Vocational College at Itta Bena is the result. Humanitarian motives have meshed with enlightened self-interest, and the Delta took the lead in the long-delayed awakening to the necessity of equal school facilities for Negroes in Mississippi. Farmers trying to teach illiterate hoe hands how to operate expensive machinery awakened to the necessity of Negro education before the prodding of the United States Supreme Court aroused some of their neighbors.

A casual traveler over the Delta today might conclude that the Negro students have the best of the division of school buildings and facilities, for every county is beginning to boast of several modern plants for Negroes advanced beyond the average white schools. The division is, of course, still far from equal, but the awakening to Negro educational needs is changing the face of the Delta.

Educational skills are part of the missing ingredients for the successful completion of the mechanization pattern. Before the mule gave way to horsepower, it took an average of 160 man-hours of labor to produce one acre of cotton. Today the average is down to fifty, and as low as twenty on some of the more advanced farms. A goal of fifteen hours is not unreasonable. Attainment of the goal will keep cotton in a continuing competitive position with synthetic fibers, but its most important reality for the people of the Delta will be a higher return for the land and labor which will have gained the productive efficiency.

Mechanization has had its greatest impetus on the large plantations, but it has not been a process confined to the large operation. The tractor has been perhaps the greatest boon of all to the family farmer, for it has enabled him to cultivate an acreage unbounded by the limits of a two-mule team. It takes some of the worst drudgery out of farm labor. It will never be economical for the forty-acre farmer to own a cotton picker individually, but these and other expensive items of equipment are beginning to become available for him. If the present course is followed, small farms will remain rooted in the Delta next to the big plantation, stronger and more economically productive than ever before.

The one-tractor farmer who has replaced the two-mule farmer is a much stronger economic entity than the old-style family-farm cotton producer in the South. Small independent operators are more secure in the Delta today than they ever were before. After considerable floundering during an early period of lax administration in the first days of the Farm Security Administration, hundreds of former sharecroppers and tenants are becoming independent farm owners and solid, substantial citizens through the assistance of the program supervised by the Farmers Home Administration. The FHA rides herd on its clients in much the same manner as a landlord with his tenants, but this supervision, as the farmer meets new responsibilities of independence, has been a key to recent successes in the operation. The State of Mississippi has followed suit with a similar program of farm ownership loans for veterans, operating with success by both economic and social scales.

The old plantation system has left the Delta, but it is a long way from being a new "factory in the field" system of the type now widespread in the Southwest. The United States Employment Service may help furnish cotton choppers and cotton pickers in periods of labor shortage, but cotton farming is still basically a struggle with the elements to produce the fiber and a gamble with the economy to gain returns for the product. There is probably a higher percentage of active owner-management than at any time in Delta history.

Mechanization came to Delta cotton as part of the revolution that has destroyed or minimized most of the undesirable features of the old plantation system which took a strangle hold on the country after the War Between the States. Only the richness of Delta soil enabled the system to survive as long as it did. That richness today is helping to smooth the transition into mechanized cotton farming in conjunction with a new system of diversified general agricultural production. Human labor has new dignity. The old pattern of exploitation and exportation is breaking up, and the Delta is happy to see it go.

ACKNOWLEDGMENTS AND BIBLIOGRAPHY

The Yazoo is basically the product of a lifetime of listening to stories about the river and the Delta country to which it has given its name. Very little published material deals primarily with the Yazoo, but there are side glances in most of the history of Mississippi and the Deep South.

It would be impossible to list all of those who have contributed in some fashion to the writing of *The Yazoo*, but acknowledgment should be given to a great many. Heading the list should be Hodding Carter of Greenville, Mississippi, who lives on the Mississippi, instead of the Yazoo. As the author of *The Lower Mississippi*, he first encouraged Rinehart & Company, and its editors, to consider my application to write a volume on the Yazoo. This was back in 1947. Various delays, primarily because of my political activity and public duties, resulted in the manuscript's not being delivered for nearly six years.

The late Herschell Brickell, a native of Yazoo City, was especially helpful in giving me side lights about the naval warfare on the Yazoo, in which he had first become interested as a boy inspecting the site of the Confederate Navy Yard.

Others who gave me specific assistance of great value include Mrs. Sallie Humphreys Gwin and her daughter, Mrs. Mildred Gwin Andrews, granddaughter and great-granddaughter of Mildred Maury Humphreys, the heroine of the chapter "The Woman's War"; Dr. James W. Silver, chairman of the Department of History, University of Mississippi; Dr. Felix Underwood, Director, Mississippi State Board of Health; Colonel George F. Dixon, U. S. Corps of Engineers; George A. Morris, Vicksburg District, U. S. Engineers; Miss Charlotte Capers, Mississippi State Department of Archives and History; Dr. Frank H. Smith; Read P. Dunn, Jr.; and Rex Magee.

I had expert assistance in copyreading and typing from two members of my secretarial staff, Audrey Glenn and Meg Holmes, and from my wife, Helen McPhaul Smith.

The following original papers, magazine articles, and books were used as specific references:

The Journal of Mississippi History (Many articles from this publication have been helpful. Special mention should be made of articles by Dr. Dawson A. Phelps, Edwin A. Miles, and Miss Willie D. Hadsell.), Mississippi Historical Society, Jackson, Mississippi.

ADAMS, SAMUEL H., *The Great American Fraud*, P. F. Collier and Son, 1905.

BETTERSWORTH, JOHN K., *Confederate Mississippi*, Louisiana State University Press, 1943.

BISHOP, ABRAHAM, *Georgia Speculation Unveiled*, Hartford, Connecticut, 1798.

CHAPPELL, A. H., *Miscellanies of Georgia*, Columbus, Georgia, 1874.

CLARK, THOMAS D., *Pills, Petticoats and Plows*, Bobbs-Merrill, Indianapolis, 1944.

COWLEY, MALCOLM (Editor), *The Portable Faulkner*, The Viking Press, New York, 1946.

CRANDALL, WARREN D., and NEWELL, ISAAC D.,

History of the Ram Fleet and the Mississippi Marine Brigade, St. Louis, 1907.
DICKSON, HARRIS A., *An Old-Fashioned Senator*, Frederick A. Stokes, Philadelphia, 1925.
FEDERAL WRITERS PROJECT, *Mississippi, a Guide to the Magnolia State*, Hastings House, New York, 1938.
FORD, JAMES A., "Mound Builders of the Mississippi," *Scientific American*, March, 1952.
GARNER, JAMES W., *Reconstruction in Mississippi*, Macmillan, New York, 1901.
GOLDBERGER, JOSEPH and SYDENSTRICKER, EDGAR, *Pellagra in the Mississippi Flood Area*, U. S. Public Health Report, Reprint No. 1187, 1927.
GRANT, U. S., *Personal Memoirs of U. S. Grant*, World Publishing Company, Cleveland, 1952.
HANDY, W. C., (Editor), *A Treasury of the Blues*, Charles Boni, New York, 1949.
HARRISON, ROBERT W., *Flood Control in the Mississippi Alluvial Valley*, Delta Council, Stoneville, Mississippi, 1952.
HASKINS, C. H., *The Yazoo Land Companies*, Knickerbocker Press, New York, 1891.
HIGHSAW, ROBERT BAKER, *The Delta Looks Forward*, Delta Council, Stoneville, Mississippi, 1949.
House of Representatives Document 792, "Report on Survey of Little Tallahatchie River Watershed," 77th Congress.
House of Representatives Document 564, "Report on Survey of Yazoo River Watershed in Mississippi," 78th Congress.
HUDSON, ARTHUR PALMER, *Humor of the Old Deep South*, Macmillan, New York, 1936.
KIRWAN, A. D., *Revolt of the Rednecks*, University of Kentucky Press, Lexington, 1951.
LEWIS, LLOYD, *Sherman: Fighting Prophet*, Harcourt, Brace & Company, New York, 1932.

McILWAINE, SHIELDS, *Memphis Down in Dixie*, E. P. Dutton, New York, 1948.

MONTGOMERY, FRANK A., *Recollections of a Mississippian in Peace and War*, The Robert Clarke Company, Cincinnati, 1901.

MORGAN, ALBERT T., *Yazoo—on the Picket Line of Freedom in the South*, Washington, 1884.

MULVIHILL, M. J., SR., *Vicksburg and Warren County, Mississippi*, The Mayor and Aldermen of the City of Vicksburg and the Board of Supervisors of Warren County, Mississippi, 1931.

NICHOLS, RALPH R., and KING, MORTON B., JR., *Social Effects of Government Land Purchase*, Mississippi State College Agricultural Experiment Station, State College, Miss., Bulletin 390, June, 1943.

OSBORN, GEORGE COLEMAN, *John Sharpe Williams, Planter-Statesman of the Deep South*, Louisiana State University Press, Baton Rouge, La., 1943.

SCHLESINGER, ARTHUR M., JR., *The Age of Jackson*, Little, Brown & Company, Boston, 1945.

SHANNON, FRED A., *The Farmer's Last Frontier*, Farrar and Rinehart, New York, 1945.

STONE, ALFRED H., *The Negro in the Yazoo-Mississippi Delta*, 1901.

WEAVER, HERBERT, *Mississippi Farmers, 1850-1860*, Vanderbilt University Press, Nashville, 1945.

WHARTON, VERNON L., *The Negro in Mississippi, 1865-1890*, University of North Carolina Press, Chapel Hill, 1947.

WHITE, REV. GEORGE, *Yazoo Fraud*, Marietta, Ga., 1852.

YOUNG, STARK, *The Pavilion*, Charles Scribner's Sons, New York, 1951.

INDEX